AROUND THE WORLD

MY MOSTLY SOLO CIRCUMNAVIGATION IN A 35 FOOT SAILBOAT

In Six Years

HENRY HOLT

Suite 300 - 990 Fort St
Victoria, BC, Canada, V8V 3K2
www.friesenpress.com

Copyright © 2015 by Henry Holt
First Edition — 2015

All rights reserved.

No part of this publication may be reproduced in any form, or by any means, electronic or mechanical, including photocopying, recording, or any information browsing, storage, or retrieval system, without permission in writing from the publisher.

ISBN
978-1-4602-5016-7 (Hardcover)
978-1-4602-5017-4 (Paperback)
978-1-4602-5018-1 (eBook)

1. *Sports & Recreation, Sailing*

Distributed to the trade by The Ingram Book Company

Contents

Preface vii

Part I: From the Bahamas to Thailand 1

My Sailing History 3
The Adventure Begins in Georgetown, Bahamas - February 2002 7
Rum Cay 10
Cuba 13
Jamaica 16
The Panama Canal 19
Ecuador 28
36th Day - June 22, 2002 - 4,200 Miles - Arrival in Tahiti 46
July 15, 2002 - Raiatea 50
Bora Bora 52
The Cook Islands - Named after Captain James Cook 62
Niue 67
A Lost Day in My Life - Crossing the International Dateline 70
Tonga 71
Fiji 83
Soso Village 87
New Caledonia 92
Sixth Day - Hit by a Rogue Wave 97
Australia 99
Darwin 115
On to Indonesia 117
Komodo Dragons 120
Bali 124
Singapore 127
Jakarta 128
Thailand 132

Part II: From Thailand, Back to the Bahamas, and Some Closing Stories 135

Tsunami - December 26, 2004 137
Maldives 143
Avoiding Pirates 150
Djibouti 152
Into the Red Sea - February 14, 2006 154
Eritrea 156
Sudan 160
Egypt 165
The Mediterranean Sea 173
Turkey 174
Greece 185
Messina, Italy 195
Spain - Majorca 203
Hit by the Levanter Gale 205
Gibraltar 211
Canary Islands 216
Crossing the Atlantic 222
Back to the Caribbean 225
Patricia Arrives 227
Saint Vincent 229
Bequia 231
Puerto Rico 238
Dominican Republic 239
The Bahamas Again 241
Rum Cay Again - End of the Circumnavigation - May 21, 2008 ... 243
Our Wedding 247

    Murphy's Laws 250

    Preparing for Offshore and Blue Water 251

    Nautical Terms and Some of my Own 265

The photo of *Chyka* on the cover was taken south of Martinique in 1999 by Cyndie Koning. I wrote often about her in this book.

Preface

As I wrote this story I was determined to adhere to the facts without exaggeration. The events were usually powerful enough, ranging from astonishingly beautiful scenes, challenging situations, to sincere dear friendships, and even love. There were frequent concerns as to what might happen and times of great danger. So there was no need for dramatization, which in any case I would have considered dishonest.

The total distance I traveled, only during the circumnavigation, was about 34,000 normal statute miles. Because sailboats so often must sail off the planned course, depending on wind direction, the total distance over water was more.

As is the case with all ships and nautical charts, distances sailed in this book are told in nautical miles, which are 15 percent greater than statute miles. Boat and wind speeds are in knots, which are nautical miles per hour and so again, 15 percent more than miles per hour.

I often told of the wind conditions. To keep it simple I abbreviated them. Examples are:

'E 15-20' means an east wind blowing between 15 and 20 knots; 'NW-25' is a northwest wind of 25 knots.

A VHF (very high frequency) is a marine radio used to communicate with other boats or shore stations. I had one built into the 'nav' station (nav is short for navigation), and another in the cockpit. I had a hand-held unit as a backup and to take along when going ashore or to another boat.

Please remember, you can find definitions of the nautical terms I used at the end of the book.

I am grateful for the important help I had along the way from my weather reporters: Cyndie Koning, my daughter Sandra, and my eventual wife, Patricia. By satellite phone they gave me six day forecasts when I was at sea or in remote places where I could not access the Internet.

In the early stages of writing this book, daughter Karen had many good ideas of how to improve it.

Patricia worked with me through the many revisions, editing and suggesting improvements.

The people at my publisher, FriesenPress, have been impressively helpful, guiding me along the way of organizing, writing, and making revisions.

Henry Holt
2015

Part I

From the Bahamas to Thailand

February 2002 to December 2004

Years from now you will be more disappointed by the things you didn't do than by the ones you did do. So throw off the bow lines. Sail away from the safe harbor. Catch the trade winds in your sails.

Explore. Dream. Discover.

— Attributed to Mark Twain

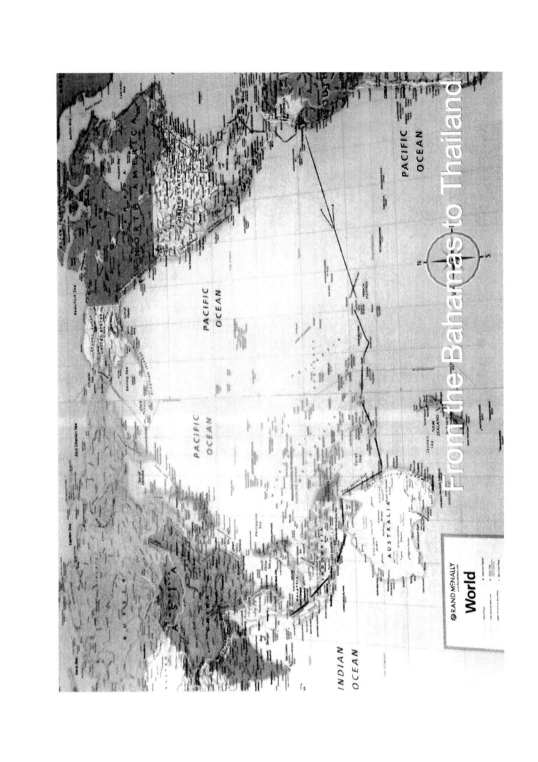

My Sailing History

Nantucket Island, 24 miles south of Cape Cod, is about as quaint and salty as a place can be. Its harbor is full of sailboats and other boat traffic. From family vacations there since I was a boy and working in a hotel on the island, I learned to love it and its history of sending whaling ships into the Pacific on voyages of two or three years for whale oil. There was then no other liquid fuel; it was before petroleum was discovered. Whale oil made the island rich.

I was inspired by books. The story of *Moby-Dick* by Herman Melville begins on Nantucket Island. The thought of adventure sailing in the Pacific grew more intriguing with my reading of such books as *Lord Jim* by Josef Conrad, *Two Years Before the Mast* by Richard Henry Dana, and *Sailing Alone Around the World* by Joshua Slocum, the first person to do so in 1895 to 1898.

One time on Nantucket my first wife, Sonja, our daughters, and I stayed at a cottage that had a sailing dinghy. I took it out into the harbor to see what would happen. The water was calm and the wind light, but I had no idea what I was doing. After awhile drifting around I ended up on the beach far north of our cottage.

The next day in town I bought a little book on how to sail. After learning a few fundamentals, I was able to practice them. During vacations in beachfront locales, we often rented small sailboats by the hour.

When we lived in Milwaukee on Lake Michigan, I joined the Milwaukee Community Sailing Center. Over years I enjoyed taking courses on how to sail centerboard and then the larger keel sailboats. After working my way up to getting rated for heavy air (a wind speed of 15-20 knots) on all of their boats, I became an instructor.

One evening I was training four women. One of them said, "You know, my husband and I want to sail around the world. Anyone can do it." I thought she was pathetically naïve. But then in time I read books and cruising magazine articles about people who were sailing over oceans and around the world and realized she may have been right.

Over years I took all six of the week long live-aboard cruising courses by American Sailing Association. I took the Offshore Sailing School course. With Sonja and our girls I chartered sailboats in the Bahamas. And I crewed for others.

One time in particular I had an extreme lesson on how to *not* do it. It was on a 43 foot sailboat owned by a man called Lou. The plan was to go out from Beaufort, NC and south direct to Miami. With us were a sailing friend of mine from Milwaukee and a friend of Lou's who was big in sailboat racing. They all had many years of experience coastal cruising and racing. But none of them had ever even sailed offshore nor, of course, any blue water sailing, which means out of sight of land.

We met at the Beaufort airport. Lou drove us to the boat. In a half hour, without even giving us time to learn our way around the boat, we departed in waning twilight out into the Atlantic Ocean and on our way to Miami. After we were past the coastal charts area, I asked Lou, "Who is doing the navigation and where are the ocean charts?" He said, "We don't need them. We have GPS!" I was stunned. *No charts!*

Then I thought, *Wait a minute, I get it - bad joke. How stupid of me to fall for it. Ha-ha.* But it was not a joke. We actually were sailing in the ocean with no charts of where we were and where we were going!

Using projections on paper from his coastal charts, I extended them with pencil out to cover where we would be in the Atlantic Ocean all the way down to Miami. On them I showed what I knew of the course of the northbound Gulf Stream, and from then on I tracked our positions as we sailed along.

When after two days our speed over ground diminished to about two knots I showed Lou that we were in the Gulf Stream and needed to go about 70 miles toward shore to get out of it.

The cable steering system broke twice. The first time it happened, I asked Lou to bring up his emergency steering tiller that every sailboat has. It attaches directly to the top of the rudder shaft. He showed it to me, but then remembered, he had lost the connection nut to it.

Being good at fixing things I was able to tell Lou how to repair the cable system. Two days later, after the second time fixing it Lou and I came back on deck to find the other crew had lost control of the genoa sail. Its starboard side sheet (a line to the aft corner of the sail to control its angle to the wind) was flailing around violently. The cockpit was enclosed, so we were protected. But Lou started to go out on deck saying he would grab the sheet. I shouted, "Lou, don't go out there." He did so anyway, and in two seconds the sheet whipped him and injured his right eye. He crawled back into the cockpit holding a hand over his eye and collapsed onto the cockpit seat cushions, unable to see anything out of the injured eye.

I used my miniature travel first aid kit to clean up and bandage his eye. Of course, his boat had no first aid kit.

We were some forty miles off Jacksonville, Florida. On VHF I called the Coast Guard. They had me talk to a doctor. He told me the problem was serious, but immediate treatment was not necessary, and that we should sail to the marina in Jacksonville.

We entered Jacksonville harbor in the very early morning. The aircraft carrier *J. F. Kennedy* was then departing. We gladly obeyed their polite requests on VHF radio as to how we should keep out of their way.

From the marina, medics took Lou to a hospital. The lens of his eye had been dislocated. He flew home to have an operation.

Choosing a Boat

In 1994 Sonja and I moved to Germany for my last assignment with The Torrington Company. With friends I attended the annual Duesseldorf boat show, the largest in the world. There I became quite interested in perhaps buying an Island Packet.

After retiring, I continued to read about cruising sailboats. I visited several boat builders. My choice was Island Packet. I judged theirs to be the most seaworthy ocean cruising sailboats of all. My only hesitation was that their boats did not have stern swim platforms, which are aft of the cockpit with a ladder that lowers into the water for swimming and stepping into the dinghy. I had learned to love them when sailing in the Bahamas.

With wonderfully good fortune, Island Packet just then announced the first of a new series of sailboats having swim platforms. The first one of them was to be the Island Packet 350.

Having a length of 35 feet, it was the perfect size for a single-hander who wants safety, comfort, and room on board for others. So at age 63, I bought my first and only sailboat.

The boat came to me by way of an Island Packet dealer in nearby Chicago. It was January, when no one there wants to buy a boat, so I got her at an attractive price. In addition, they said that if I would let them show her at the Chicago Strictly Sail Boat Show, they would reduce the price for her even more. I agreed. What else was I to do with her in winter?

I named her *Chyka* (pronounced CHIGH *sounds like eye* - ka), which means 'seagull' in Russian. When I was young, I learned the word while attending a year long course in Russian at the Army Language School.

After a year equipping and getting used to sailing *Chyka*, I was ready. Sonja had enjoyed our chartering sailboats, but she did not want to join me for long distance cruising. We agreed she would join me on *Chyka* from time to time along the way, and she did.

In July 1998 I sailed from Milwaukee, intending always to someday return with *Chyka*, which sadly never happened. You can read why I did not at the end of this book.

With my daughter, Karen, I sailed the Great Lakes, the Erie Canal, to New York, along the coast of New England, and out to Nantucket. The next spring I sailed down the East Coast, mostly on the Intracoastal Waterway, to the Bahamas and into the Caribbean, where I cruised, almost always solo, for three years prior to the start of the circumnavigation.

The Adventure Begins in Georgetown, Bahamas - February 2002

Sonja and I sailed from Nassau through the Exuma Islands to Georgetown. She and I had previously cruised in these islands; now we had a few days to again enjoy Georgetown before my Canadian crew was to arrive.

This trip with Sonja was our last attempt to save our marriage. Over the years we had many good times together. We tried everything, but serious difficulties persisted. We later divorced. Most fortunately, we respect each other and are friends.

This is one of my favorite places in the world. One can anchor near to the little town or off one of the lovely beaches a mile across the harbor on Stocking Island. In either case it is an easy dinghy ride into town for groceries, a few bars, restaurants, a bank, the colorful, old (and only) hotel there, The Peace and Plenty, and a pretty white church perched on the hill overlooking the town and its harbor.

Georgetown is the Bahamas' cruising boat Mecca. By the early months of any year some 200 to 300 sailboats have sailed down the Exuma chain of islands to stay for weeks or months. There are organized events, volleyball, lectures, cruising classes, and lots of beach parties.

Many cruisers arrive intending to continue south to the Caribbean. In Georgetown they learn about and face the reality of it; sailing further through the remote Bahama Out Islands and on into the Caribbean is difficult. The winds are strong and on the nose. The Equatorial Current is against you, and frequent cold fronts come off Florida bringing bad weather.

So most of them reluctantly say, "Oh well, perhaps next year," and go back north. That is why Georgetown is known as 'Chicken Harbor'.

I do not fault them. Sailing further south from here is not an easy job. I have done it twice. Cruising does not have to be difficult, only if you choose to risk making it so. If you do, you have to be careful.

Here, almost all cruising sailboats anchor. One time before, I docked at the Georgetown Marina. Incredibly, its facilities were filthy and dysfunctional. It could be a gold mine for any marina operator who would invest in improvements and care for the place. *Chyka* has been in Georgetown four times, twice going south and twice going north. Each time returning there, I expected someone must have done something about it. The last time I was there was in 2008. It was the same.

My Canadian Crew

During most of 1999 and 2000 I had cruised in the Caribbean along with the Canadian boat *Breakaway*, Barry Grove, Cyndie, and their two kids, Zak and Molly. We all became close friends.

The Western Caribbean is notorious for strong winds and rough seas. This is particularly true of the passage from Jamaica to Panama. I was glad to have Barry and his two sailing friends, Jack and Pat (not the Patricia I later married) Armitage, join me for the passage to Panama. Jack and Pat were enthusiastic racing sailors. Racers are in the habit of doing anything to increase speed. During the trip they became impatient with my cruising mode of reefing the sails down in high winds to increase comfort and safety.

After the Canadians arrived, there were five of us on board until Sonja returned home three days later. For a boat having a length of 35 feet, *Chyka* had a lot of interior space. Accommodating five on board for a few days was not a problem.

The crew had brought way too much luggage for living on a boat. But they also generously brought a huge bag of food. Among the supplies were two enormous jars of peanut butter, which never goes bad. Three years later I came to the bottom of the second jar.

After Sonja returned to Milwaukee, we had a safety meeting. I had a list of topics to cover, e.g. location of safety gear and fire extinguishers, how to operate the inflatable life raft (not to be confused with the inflatable dinghy), the man overboard procedures we would use depending on the situation, the operation of the EPIRB (Emergency Position Indicating Radio Beacon), the GPS, scheduling watches, and so on.

We left Georgetown March 1, 2002. It was a rough 40 mile close reach sail to Conception Island. Not yet having their sea legs, the Canadians were seasick until we approached the quiet but tricky beach anchorage.

I had sailed to this place twice before. Coming into the lee side of the island all became calm. Jack was at the helm following my instructions. We were looking at the depth gage and reading the colors of the water. Barry was watching from the bow. We made it safely through the coral heads and anchored well near the beach.

My friends took *Li'l Chyka*, my inflatable dinghy, to snorkel the nearby coral reef. I had explored it two times before and stayed alone on board to rest.

Rum Cay

(In the Bahamas, 'cay' is pronounced *key*.)

This tiny island is actually where my six year circumnavigation was started and completed.

In late 1492 Columbus landed on Rum Cay, being the second island he discovered at the end of his first Atlantic crossing to the New World.

With a declining population, recently estimated to be about 50, this little island is alone and remote. One gets to Rum Cay only by private plane, on a private boat such as *Chyka*, or on the island boat that arrives once every ten days to deliver supplies and maybe one or two passengers.

Sailboats usually anchor in the bay near the town. From your boat it is minutes by dinghy to a 60 foot high coral wall extending from the bottom up almost to the surface of the water. It is a spectacular snorkeling and scuba diving site. I have never been more amazed at the wonders of a coral reef and the brightly colored reef fish living in it.

From where you tie up your dinghy to the town dock, Kaye's Bar is in view under the trees. Some cruisers, having had many years of exploring these islands, say that for them Kaye's is the best bar in the Bahamas. Of the many tropical bar restaurants I have known, it is the most unusual, modest, cozy, and friendly of them all. The floor of the actual bar area - not the dining area - was sand making it a beach bar. On the bar was a collection of metal puzzles to take apart, which have amused idle bar flies like me for many years.

Kaye's Bar - It is said to be the best bar in the Bahamas.

The bar was then and still is owned by Delores Wilson, Kaye's mother, who made dinner for us. In the journal Delores keeps there, we read what Sonja had written in it three years before. On the beach road in front of Kaye's Bar Sonja had bought shells from the little boy, Shali, whom Delores had adopted.

Kaye runs The Last Chance, the island's only grocery store. It is the size of an average living room. Well named, it is the last chance to provision for cruisers going from Rum Cay south into the Caribbean.

Great Inagua

We had a rough overnight sail south to Great Inagua, the third largest island in the Bahamas. Pat was sick the whole way. Finally at 10:00 PM of the second day we eased up close to the beach in total darkness, watching the depth gage and radar, and dropped the anchor. We stayed two nights to rest.

Pat told me later she considered flying home from there due to seasickness. The poor girl should have. Despite all we could do, she was sick most of the way to Panama.

Cuba

Departing at 6:30 AM we were surprised that the only other boat anchored there was still quiet. They had told us the night before they would sail with us to Cuba. It was *Jolly Friends*, whose captain was named Vernon. The name of that boat was a misnomer. I will soon tell you why.

It was an easy fast broad reach to Cuba. Vernon's boat eventually caught up with us. We heard him on the VHF radio talking to an approaching freighter who would not answer him. We often call freighters to clarify how we should cross. They cannot maneuver as quickly as we small boats can. Therefore, we ask them for instructions. But often they do not answer, which then means we just have to stay out of their way. Vernon became angry and said he would report them to the coast guard. But whose coast guard? A good laugh.

At noon the next day we entered the picturesque harbor of Santiago de Cuba, the original capitol of Cuba. The entrance is between high hills. On top of one of them sits the imposing old El Morro fort. We motored under it and past side inlets until we arrived at the marina. By radio we were told to anchor off until cleared by the Ministry of Health.

I had warned the crew that clearing into Cuba is known to take a lot of time and patience. This is due to the Spanish culture of bureaucracy made worse by years of communism.

A man and a woman both in uniform rowed out to us and came on board. They asked questions in a friendly way. Each had a cigarette (their own) and a beer (ours). They found us bug-free and told us to dock at the marina pier. There the fun began.

Officials came on board from the departments of Customs, Immigration, Agriculture, Transportation, and maybe a couple more. At one time there were six of them sitting with me in the main cabin carefully filling out and energetically stamping away on all colors of forms.

Fortunately, I had learned Spanglish, primitive Spanish, when I was in the Dominican Republic and Puerto Rico. These people spoke no English. You can get away with murdering their language and they will understand you and be happy. A butchered phrase like "Me go Havana yesterday," is for them perfectly comprehensible. Just don't try it with your French in Paris.

Cuban beer is better than most American beers. But my new amigos were glad to sample beers otherwise not available to them that we had in the refrigerator. One man eyed my bottle of Scotch. I asked if he would like to have some: "Yes, please!" And then it was beer for some and Scotch for others. They were interested in talking about the United States. We discussed politics openly and honestly.

I was not worried about USA laws. Americans were allowed to go to Cuba but were not allowed to spend any money there. So stupid! But for me that was not a problem. The Canadians paid for everything there for us. And I made up for it with them later.

Vernon, who had sailed here with us, was docked nearby. As crew he had a young couple, a delightful pretty girl and her boyfriend, who was perhaps the most immediately disagreeable person I have ever met. He was arrogant, insolent to everyone, and rude to his girlfriend.

We all went to nearby Santiago de Cuba, a city right out of Southern Spain with grand old buildings and, of course, a cathedral on the plaza. We had pleasant beers at the terrace bar of the Casa Grande Hotel overlooking the plaza and the surrounding hills.

The Canadians were one time in town while I was busy on the boat. Pat wrote in her journal:

> The people are open and curious about us, as we are of them... The local markets turned out to be very meager by our standards. There is some begging, but very little. On the other hand the Cubans will ask for things like vitamins for their kids, spare clothes and fishing line. But they will insist on repaying with a service or some food stuff. The lady who did our laundry invited us into their small home. We managed to visit with mostly hand gestures and broken

Spanish on our part. I had brought small gifts, toothpaste, hand cream, shampoo, lipstick and a Canadian flag. They reciprocated with eight fresh eggs.

In the evening Vernon asked me to come over to his boat for a talk. He was having problems with his crew. The reason they were late leaving Great Inagua was that the lovers would not get up for departure. When Vernon asked them to get moving, the boyfriend yelled through the door of their cabin that they were on vacation, not slaves, and they would get up whenever they wanted!

I told Vernon my opinion: get rid of them, she being pleasant, but he an ugly customer, who I was sure could be dangerous on board. I asked Vernon if he was confident to single-hand. He seemed unsure. So then I said he should wait to find new crew, trustworthy and willing to cooperate. The next morning both our boats departed. Vernon had decided to keep the lovers. I hoped it was just to get his boat to Jamaica where he could then get rid of them.

Jamaica

It was an easy overnight sail to Montego Bay, Jamaica. Winds were light and downwind. Gourmet Chef Capitaine Henri made dinner. The crew complimented me on the "awesome salad" and the "totally awesome pasta dish." I had for years impressed cruising friends with my pasta dishes.

Pat and I were on our watches together. She wrote:

> Henry and I have been practicing star identification… Sailing at night is a beautiful experience, and with the Autohelm, GPS, and radar it really amounts to a watch with hourly plots on the chart as a check on navigation.

In the morning dolphins rode our bow wave. After arriving at the Montego Bay Yacht Club, we had Scotch on board *Chyka* followed by dinner at the terrace restaurant. Then a sound sleep for all.

On the morning of our departure Jack contributed something important. He had noticed that *Chyka's* mast was curved off to one side about half way up. I had regularly adjusted the rigging to the recommended tension requirements, but I had never checked for this. Jack instructed us how to correct it. Racers are fastidious about tuning their boats' rigging.

A Five Day Passage to Panama

Friday, March 15, we left Montego Bay in good weather, rounded the west end of Jamaica, and there found winds E 30-38. (This is Force 8, also called a 'fresh gale'.) The waves were rolling us badly. Pat was very worried. We double-reefed the mainsail and the genoa. In the lee of Jamaica the winds became light. We saw whales and dolphins.

That night Pat became seriously seasick. I had given her Bonine tablets before we left, and she had taken her other medications, a patch and an acupressure band, none of which helped her.

On Saturday we were swamped twice by high waves. From one of them green water (not broken up into spray) gushed into the center hatch and through the dodger window, which was wide open. (The dodger is a canvas hood with plastic windows and supported by an aluminum tube frame. It protects the forward part of the cockpit.)

Poor Pat lay on the cockpit seat cushions under a blanket. Then we moved her to the aft cabin bunk where she lay there holding a bucket. The first rule when seasickness starts is to stay on deck, perhaps even at the helm from where you are aware of the horizon. When it gets serious the best is lying down in the aft cabin, the place with the least boat motion, with closed eyes. This reduces the cause of seasickness, conflicting signals of what we see and the equilibrium sensors in our ears.

Sunday night we had winds E 28-30, which is Force 7, a moderate gale. We were swamped again and slammed violently. The waves were 8 to 10 feet high. At 1:00 AM I asked that everyone, when on deck including in the cockpit, wears a safety harness tethered to a strong point. They gladly complied. Even with *Chyka's* special equipment for such an emergency, and a lot of training I had, a man overboard recovery in such conditions at night would be almost impossible.

On Monday, a wave broke clear over the entire deck. The crew was increasingly stressed.

That night with a strong following wind we had sailed too far off course and needed to go back toward the course line. To do this we either had to go upwind and tack (changing the mainsail from one side to the other going upwind) or jibe (changing the mainsail to the other side while going downwind). I said we would do it with a controlled jibe, something they did not know about and distrusted. I had been trained for it and had done it alone many times in heavy weather. It went smoothly.

Panama

On the morning of Tuesday March 19 we approached the coast of Panama. While entering the harbor of Colon we had a German freighter alongside also heading to the entrance. Barry was at the helm. I asked him to drop back and go astern of the freighter. He did not want to. But after some discussion as to how to determine if a boat is on a collision course, we graciously allowed the Germans to go ahead of us. How kind we were!

We arrived at the Panama Canal Yacht Club. There was no place for *Chyka*, so we tied up alongside a Baltic 75. Pat, being a welding engineer, advised the skipper about a mast weld repair. I treated my crew to Champagne, beer, Scotch, and then after a nap, crew appreciation dinner at the yacht club. I slept ten hours.

After beers and lunch at the club my friends took a cab to tour the Canal Zone and afterwards to the airport for their return to Canada.

I was grateful to my crew for having come so far to help me sail such a difficult passage. Pat was sick most of the way but did not complain. And surprisingly her notes to her Canadian friends about the trip make it sound as if it had been fine. Well, there were times she was alert and happy during our days together. And it is also my experience that we often look back on an adventure as less harsh than it seemed during the event.

Preparing for the Panama Canal was complicated. I found an agent, Pete Stevens, to organize it all. He arranged for the permits, payment of fees, and the required four line handlers to be with me on board as *Chyka* went through the locks.

Phyllis on *Eros*, organized the delivery by truck of a load of booze from the tax free area of town for all of us doing the transit of the canal. For me it was a case of Scotch and four cases of Heineken. I wished later I had ordered three times as much. So did others. The Pacific is wide. I met Phyllis and her husband, Terry, three times later in the Pacific. Each time it was, "Phyllis, we need you to organize another booze run."

The Panama Canal

The French, under the direction of Ferdinand de Lesseps, who had so successfully organized the construction of the Suez Canal, made a huge effort to create a canal between the two oceans across Panama from 1880 to 2003 when the company doing the job went bankrupt.

And their intention to dig the canal at sea level was flawed by the fact that the difference between Atlantic and Pacific tidal levels would have turned their canal into a fast flowing river most hours of the day.

De Lesseps had been warned about this problem but chose to ignore it, counting on some solution to be found later. This is particularly strange considering that plans for the Suez Canal had been originally shelved due to the mistaken calculation that the Mediterranean and the Red Sea were at different levels.

No one then knew the cause of yellow fever or malaria, both of which during the French years there killed about 22,000 workers. They did not know that both diseases are transmitted by mosquitoes. Their hospitals had dishes of water under the bed feet to keep ants from coming into the beds. In those dishes the mosquitoes bred. No one knew why it was that malaria was more common in the hospitals than anywhere else in the area.

When the French gave up, America became interested in constructing the canal. The project, which was then done from 1904 to 1914 was spearheaded by Teddy Roosevelt.

In 1908 a Cuban Doctor, Carlos Finlay, confirmed what a few doctors had suspected for many years, that malaria and yellow fever were spread by mosquitoes. The eradication of mosquitoes in the Panama Canal Zone became a top priority. Swamps were filled, all locations of stagnant water were drained or oil was spread on them. People who found a mosquito in a building were required to report it so that the building could be fumigated.

The American plan was to lift ships up 85 feet by means of three locks at each end of the canal so that the ships would then motor across Panama to the other end and there be lowered back down with three more locks. In addition to solving the problem of the different sea levels at the ends, it saved having to excavate a further 85 feet deeper into the ground most of the way across Panama.

Most of the 102 steam shovels used to dig the canal were made by the forerunner of Bucyrus-Erie of South Milwaukee, Wisconsin. I was a sales engineer calling on Bucyrus-Erie. They proudly displayed framed pictures of Teddy Roosevelt sitting in a white suit on a Bucyrus steam shovel working in the Canal Zone.

Into the Panama Canal

At four o'clock in the morning of March 27, 2002 my four Panamanian line handlers came quietly on board *Chyka*. Their job was to control the two bow and two stern lines from *Chyka* to others above who guided us through the locks. All cabin lights were on. I explained to them in Spanglish everything they needed to know about *Chyka*.

We motored out into the pitch dark of the bay to a designated lighted buoy, tied up to it, and waited. At 5:30 AM a launch approached and pulled alongside. Ruben, the pilot assigned to us, stepped on board. He and the line handlers stayed on board for the day.

Ruben instructed me what to do in excellent English. He often spoke on a special radio frequency with the canal people and other pilots on ships along the way. And he told me so much about Panama and the operations of the canal.

At first come the Gatun Locks. They are three steps of parallel lock chambers raising ships the 85 feet up to Gatun Lake. (All the locks of the Panama Canal are 110 feet wide and 1,000 feet long.)

Chyka was rafted up (tied together) with two other sailboats, one boat doing the motoring for us. We entered each of the three chambers behind a cargo ship. After the last lock we separated and went under power the 28 miles across Gatun Lake and through the Gaillard Cut, the canal's enormous excavation through a rock mountain.

The Norwegian Dream

Coming the other way, the only cruise ship we saw looked familiar. It was the *Norwegian Dream* on which Sonja and I had transited this canal exactly one year earlier to the day. From its observation deck we had watched the wonders of the canal going by, the excavations, and Gatun Lake. Being an engineer I was fascinated watching how the 'mules', small electric locomotives, smoothly guided our ship through the locks. In so many ways the construction of this canal is an awe-inspiring engineering feat finished 88 years before my transit of it on *Chyka*.

The year before, as the *Norwegian Dream* passed through the Pedro Miguel Locks, we had a close view of a small marina off to the south in the woods with a few sailboats. I thought if ever I would sail the Panama Canal, I might like to stop there. And now I did.

***Chyka* at the Pedro Miguel Boat Club, Panama**

Pedro Miguel Boat Club

After being lowered 28 feet at the Pedro Miguel Locks, I turned immediately left and went into the place. There five people waited to help me dock. Ruben and the line handlers returned to Colon.

This is another remote place I loved. I thought it could be right out of a Josef Conrad novel, perhaps *Lord Jim*. The club's two story colonial building was almost hidden by red and purple flowering trees and bushes. The upper story was a long room with a high wooden ceiling. The walls were only lattice screens through which one could see the canal locks. There was a lounge, a library area with plush chairs for reading, a common kitchen, and an office. Often during the day I heard a faint hum and would look up from my chair in the library, or from *Chyka*, to see a ship gliding nearly silently through the nearer of the two locks only 200 feet away.

Katherine was the Club Manager, a full beauty, so kind, the daughter of an American Canal Zone family, and perfectly fluent in Spanish. She let me use her computer to do email. She drove me to Panama City to shop, to visit her home, and go for lunch.

Most of the boats here stay for a long time. Everyone knew everyone else. Richard on *Crocodile Rock* could repair anything on a boat. Coreen on *About Time* gave me a haircut. "No payment, please," she insisted, but I gave her my usual and always well appreciated gift for cruisers, a can of cashews.

There was a delay to schedule the transit of *Chyka* through the remaining two Miraflores Locks. Nobody then had any idea how many days it might take. I didn't care. I loved the place. I worked on the boat. In the library I read *John Adams* by David McCullough.

Late one night a man knocked on *Chyka*. He had been in the lounge and answered the phone. Pete Stevens, my canal agent, asked him to tell me I should be ready to go early in the morning.

With a canal pilot, Alex, together with a trainee pilot and four line handlers on board, we departed. First we had to winch *Chyka* with land lines over a mud flat and into the open waters of Miraflores Lake.

We motored several miles to the Miraflores Locks and waited about an hour at anchor for instructions. Then Alex was informed we should proceed to be locked through *alone*. He was astonished. It was very unusual. I never learned why it happened. I do know that scheduling ships through these locks is complicated.

Just little *Chyka*! Think of it! For any vessel, regardless of size, to go through a Panama lock, whether a freighter or *Chyka*, requires 26 million gallons of water! As we entered each of those gigantic locks I thought *Chyka* deserved her name. From above she must have looked like a seagull floating on a lake.

Then out we went under the Bridge of the Americas, part of the Pan-American Highway, and into Pacific waters. After leaving my canal crew off at the Balboa Yacht Club, I moored *Chyka*.

The next day I met Pete Stevens at what they called a yacht club. It was an outdoor bar under a roof. Pete went around with a grin telling everyone, my sailboat went through the Miraflores Locks alone!

Enrique, the local boaters' favorite cab driver, took me to Balboa for final provisioning for the Pacific.

May 8, 2002 - Into the Pacific

With shipping lanes from the Pacific converging on Panama, I knew I would get little sleep that night, so I slept late in the morning. I moved *Chyka* to the dock to load final supplies of water and diesel fuel.

Unfortunately, the water I took on contained a lot of sand. It settled to the bottom of the water tank and for years caused me serious water pump problems.

I motored out past several islands and into the Gulf of Panama. The wind picked up, so I could turn off Big Rudy, my wonderful 37 HP Yanmar inboard diesel engine, named after Professor Rudolf Diesel, and hoist sails. (Li'l Rudy was my Mariner/Mercury 3½ HP outboard engine for the dinghy.)

Pelicans are fascinating birds. They seem so sad and stupid sitting on something. But in the air they soar wonderfully. Here they glided smoothly in long lines two feet off the water evenly spaced. There was one line with what I counted as 77 of them. Probably they do it that way to cover the maximum area of water to find fish.

In the evening the wind increased to 22 knots. I reefed sails. I had not been at sea for a long time and felt a little seasick. I knew it would pass in a day or two.

Darkness fell quickly as it does in the tropics. I saw several ships. There was a lightning storm to the east. The shoreline of the Gulf of Panama was closing in on me to the west, so during the night I slept in naps of only 15 minutes and frequently scanned with radar out 25 miles.

I had radar installed because of New England fog that one time caused me trouble. There is no fog in the tropics, but soon I found the wonderful advantages of having radar daytime and nighttime anywhere. Even in clear daylight you can spot ships and low shoreline 25 miles away instead of only a few miles visually. It was always surprising to me that so few other cruising sailboats had radar.

At dawn I rounded Punta Mala and entered the wide-open Pacific with its longer more gentle swells. From here it was 800 miles to the Galapagos Islands. I planned to stop there for fuel and water before going on to the Marquesas Islands and Tahiti.

After a day of pleasant sailing the wind died and I had to motor. I was far enough away from shipping lanes that I could sleep taking longer naps.

The only land between Panama and the Galapagos Islands is Malpelo Island 270 miles off the coast of Colombia. It is a strange island rising like a mesa straight out of the water 980 feet high and about one mile long. It is owned by Colombia. I came too close to the lee side of it and so into its wind shadow. The wind died completely.

After getting past Malpelo Island the wind increased and turned to the southwest, so exactly against me. The northbound Humboldt Current (also called the Peru Current) together with the wind dead ahead prevented me from making progress south even with the engine on!

For two days the situation remained the same. I could see it might stay this way for days or weeks. I could not make progress south. Even if I could have, I would never have had enough fuel. If I went west I would have ended up in the doldrums, an area with no wind, perhaps for weeks. And I did not want to retreat the 300 miles to Panama and risk then repeating it all over.

I decided my best option was to head east across the Humboldt Current 120 miles to South America. Then sailing south close to the coast, the Humboldt would be of no trouble.

The problem with this plan was that I had no coastal charts of South America, because I had never expected to go there. All I had of South America was in a small world atlas. I decided to do it anyway.

I remembered that when the *Norwegian Dream* stopped at Manta, Ecuador, the year before, we had seen sailboats there in its harbor. Now, after crossing the Humboldt and approaching the coast, it would be about 160 miles from there down the coast to Manta.

How fortunate it was now and for the entire voyage, that Sandy and the rest of my family had insisted I buy the Iridium satellite phone. With it I called Sonja for help. She called Bluewater Books and Charts, I being certainly one of their best customers. They gave her the coordinates of the entrance of Manta Harbor, which she passed on to me via the phone.

This night was the first of several when a tern flew along in the glow of my starboard bow green navigation light fluttering and gliding in and out of sight for hours. It seemed like a white spirit showing me the way.

May 13 - South America in View

I had my famous 'Omelet McHenry' for breakfast. It was excellent, but next time, I would mix the cheese in with the eggs; otherwise it burns semi-permanently to the pan.

11:15 AM – Land Ho! Punta Galera was 14 miles away. I approached the coast and headed south staying about two miles offshore, that being as close to the shore as I dared without charts and still keep out of the northbound current. It was a rainy afternoon.

At 10:00 PM just ahead of me an open fishing boat, not showing navigation or any other lights, suddenly flashed a bright white light to warn me off. It happened soon again. To go on I would have had to stay at the helm full time and I was tired.

In order to take a long nap I hove-to (past tense of heave-to). I did this many times during my journey. To heave-to is like parking a sailboat under control at sea with the bow pointing mostly into the wind and waves. You bring the jib (the smaller of the forward sails) to the windward side, haul in the main, and lash the wheel hard over to the downwind side. The main then keeps the boat heading upwind while the jib prevents the boat from tacking. Then with the anchor light on you go below and sleep as long as you want. (The anchor light is the bright white lamp at the top of the mast to show any other boats approaching that you are there.)

May 14 - Crossing the Equator

With a soft gray overcast dawn, a light wind and a calm sea, viewing the mountains ten miles away, I crossed the equator at 6:01 AM.

Sailing along a coast is far more difficult than in the open ocean. One must be on watch for other boats, reefs, and rocks.

Manta was too far away to go the whole way in daylight. I was bone-tired. I was watching with binoculars for a possible place to anchor. Midmorning, I eased *Chyka* carefully into an inviting bay north of what I later learned was Cabo (Cape) Pasado. I used my depth sounder and experience in reading the colors of shallow waters. I found a spot, motored around it to test for hazards, and dropped anchor. There was protection of green hills on three sides and only a slight ocean roll. Along the shore were pretty beaches, no houses, and no people. *Chyka* was the only boat. The only thing I heard was the surf gently breaking on the beach.

Wonderful, until a huge swarm of dragon flies invaded the cockpit. *So, that's why I am the only one around here!* But in 30 seconds, they found nothing of interest and left.

Lying on cockpit cushions I watched the frigate birds circling overhead. These large, high soaring birds are common also in the Caribbean. They don't fly too far offshore, because they cannot land on water, nor can they do so on flat land. Their legs are too short to gain flight from those places. Only from steep shore hills or from trees can they jump off and down to gain flight.

I would have liked to stay a week to rest, swim, read, and sleep. I did all those, but only in that one lovely afternoon and evening.

Departure was at 6:30 AM. The day before, when coming into this bay, I had seen surf breaking over a reef far out from the point. Now I gave the whole area a more than generous wide berth, which means in sailors' lingo to keep far away from it.

Ecuador

It was 43 miles to Manta, Ecuador. The coordinates Sonja had given me led exactly to the entrance buoy. Sonja had told me I was to call Harbor Control or the Yacht Club on VHF. I tried them both many times. Later I learned no one uses VHF radio around here. They are supposed to, but they don't.

Sonja had also told me, "The Yacht Club is eight cables south of the breakwater." She had asked, "What is a cable?" The person at Bluewater did not know. Who would? These sailing directions were written in the nineteenth century. I looked in my books and found that a cable in those days was a standard length of manufactured chain equal to one tenth of a nautical mile.

At the south end of the harbor near what was supposed to be a yacht club I found six anchored sailboats. There I also anchored. Later I learned the others had all came here for the same reason I did, or that they needed some repair.

Patience with Bureaucrats

I had to clear in, meaning to get permission to enter a country from their officials. I walked to the Capitana del Puerto, the Police, and Immigration, all in different parts of the city. As in Cuba and other places one must be understanding, patient, forgiving, accepting of their ways, and all that. The following from my journal is really without exaggeration:

> *Across the counter sits the clerk in an immaculate, pressed, white uniform patiently asking questions of this Americana, who speaks really bad Spanish. He pokes glacially at a 1940's*

typewriter until after 30 minutes of work he bursts into fast conversation with his boss and then tells me, 'Sorry, this is the wrong form,' and we start over.

With those ancient typewriters they all type three copies of everything using the old days' carbon paper. He hits the keys slowly, one - after - the - other -, using his index fingers. After only a few letters, he leans forward to peer at the results obtained so far.

Learning how to deal with clearing in and out of countries, I would say the Caribbean Islands are high school; Cuba is college; Ecuador is graduate school.

During the 16th and 17th centuries Spain brought gold and silver from western South America north to Panama and across it to the Caribbean for shipment from there to Spain. Such a valuable, easily stolen commodity required careful tracking. There were lots of papers, and they filled them up with records of who had what, who gave what to whom, and when.

I was lucky to meet Xavier. He was managing the development of a sport fishing club just next to the dock where one ties up the dinghy to go ashore. He spoke excellent English. We had lunch at Picanteria el Marino, a seafood restaurant on the beach where everyone knew him.

I needed to better prepare for light or dead wind conditions in the Pacific. Xavier took me to a place where I bought four more plastic jerry cans, fuel containers usually holding five gallons. With these I increased my fuel capacity from sixty to eighty gallons.

May 17 - A Most Fortunate Discovery

While rigging the radar reflector my eye was caught by an ugly sight. (A radar reflector is a round assembly of aluminum plates about one foot in diameter. When hoisted aloft, it shows ships far away where you are.) The mainsail tack loop had broken through. (The tack loop attaches the forward corner of the sail bottom to the mast.) This defect in a heavy wind could have caused total loss of the sail.

Estraya, the local sailmaker came on board. He said he could fix it. How quickly? *"Un momento.* Ah, maybe three, ah, maybe four (I was expecting him to say days) hours"! It cost me five dollars plus one dollar cab fair to bring the sail back. He was so happy with my generous tip.

I had ordered a fifty gallon drum of diesel fuel. I siphoned it into jerry cans. With three trips *Li'l Chyka* brought it all out to *Big Chyka*. Thirty gallons went into the main tank and the rest stayed in the jerry cans.

Li'l Chyka also carried out 25 gallons of high quality drinking water at $1.50 per gallon. I kept it separate from the boat's main water supply. The water I had loaded in Balboa was the worst, and I wanted water I could rely on.

In the evening after provisioning with Xavier at a supermarket, I did email at the nearby Internet café. At the next computer was a man who spoke good English. I mentioned that I had a sailboat here. He said he had earlier seen a sail spread out in front of the town sailmaker, and that they told him the sail belonged to a man who planned to sail alone to Tahiti!

May 18, 2002 - Departure to Tahiti - Nonstop 4,200 Miles

4,200 nautical miles are equal to 4,800 normal statute miles. This is the same distance you would drive from New York City to San Francisco and then back again to Minneapolis.

Leaving the other boats, we all shouted best wishes to each other. From there I looked north and saw a maze of fishing boats rafted together with lines stretching way out in all directions.

I proceeded as slowly as I could and still maintain steerage. Twice I had to quickly shift into reverse to back out of some mess of lines where I saw no way through. Finally at about 10:00 AM I broke out of all that and went past the cruise ship dock where the *Norwegian Dream* had been.

After an afternoon sailing southwest along the coast as close to it as I dared, I felt the northbound Humboldt Current. I angled into it and the southwest wind, maintaining a slow actual course over the ground of due west. The plan was to continue this way until I crossed the Humboldt Current, then head southwest to where I would pick up the trade winds.

At 7:30 PM in total darkness several men in an open fishing boat ahead of me suddenly turned on lights. They shouted and gesticulated violently that I should turn away to the north. Of course, I did so. They must have had fishing nets rigged behind them.

Third Day - May 20 - 249 Miles from Ecuador

The mile numbers I will tell you from now on will be at local noon time.

I was not used to the unusual ocean swells coming to me from the high southern latitudes. I put a cup of coffee down for just a second. A wave hit and tipped the cup over. The coffee went into the dry goods bin, to the locker below it, then under the stove. I swabbed and washed. The coffee had sugar in it, and all crawling things love sugar.

A school of dolphins surrounded *Chyka*.

4th Day - May 21 - 374 Miles Out - Crossing the Humboldt Again

This morning flying fish were skimming the waves all around. Something like 20 of them ended up on deck where they would soon die. If I had not been rather busy with the boat I could have gone forward to gather some and fry them for breakfast. I had often enjoyed flying fish at the Spice Island Marine restaurant in Grenada. They are delicious.

Crossing the Humboldt is similar to crossing the Gulf Stream from Florida to the Bahamas. But there, the Gulf Stream is only 90 miles wide and takes an overnight. Crossing the Humboldt is 400 miles and takes four days. Both currents run up to three knots. Sailboats move five or six knots through the water. You need to crab enough into the current to maintain progress directly across it. Therefore, actual progress is slow until the crossing is done.

Because I was not hardened to the rolling, my abdominal muscles were strained. It took two more days until I was in condition for this.

Meeting Cyndie in Tahiti

I had long before agreed to meet Cyndie, Barry's wife, in Tahiti on June 24 on her way back to Canada from Australia, where she was to present a paper. At the time, it seemed that it gave me plenty of time to get there. But with the delay at the canal and the 300 mile detour to Ecuador, it became problematic.

It is interesting how the deadline affected the voyage. The first change was to drop plans to visit the Galapagos and the Marquesas Islands on the way.

More significantly, I needed to stay alert, sail *Chyka* safely but efficiently, and to develop the best possible navigating strategies for the prevailing and anticipated conditions of wind, sea state, and current. By concentrating and staying on top of it all, I learned more and made faster progress than if I had lounged along any old way.

Modern sailboats do better not going directly downwind, because then the mainsail blocks the wind to the foresails. You can sail wing and wing (having the genoa and the mainsail out in opposite directions), but that takes constant hand steering, unless you have wind vane self-steering, which for me had too many disadvantages.

I found that I made the best progress downwind by going off about 30 degrees. The autopilot could then easily be in charge until I was ten to thirty miles from the plotted course. Then after jibing I would gradually go back across the course line to the other side, and so on. The distance sailed was then greater, but with all sails full, the actual speed to destination was better, and sailing was much smoother. This I did most of the way further to Tahiti and often in the Atlantic.

5th Day - May 22 - The Green Flash

My God, I saw it! Just as the last of the sun dropped under the horizon there was the flash. All these years I had wondered if it was a myth perpetrated by mean-spirited people for their amusement getting gullible others to imagine they too may have seen it. ("Oh, ah, right, I saw something, maybe, I guess so, well, OK, guess I saw it." Ha-ha!) But I did see it!

Green flashes sometimes occur for one or two seconds just above the sun as the last of it disappears under the horizon. It is caused by the atmosphere then separating the colors of the sun's light.

It is said that seeing the green flash is facilitated by the liberal application of rum. This is not true; I was drinking Scotch. I saw the green flash brilliantly three more times before arriving at Tahiti and sometimes beyond.

There was always time to watch the birds. Here, near the Galapagos Islands were masked boobies. Like pelicans they are the kind of goofy looking birds you notice at the zoo, but when they fly you have to be impressed. They soar and soar and then suddenly dive for their dinner.

Late in the day I saw for the first time storm petrels. They and the shearwaters are the only ocean birds one finds more than three hundred miles offshore. Both of them were with me most of the way across the Pacific.

When 100 miles from the Galapagos Islands I passed a huge sea turtle. *Could it survive so far out?*

Yes it could! I later learned sea turtles cross oceans between foraging grounds in search of jelleyfish.

On the 8th day I wrote, "This is the greatest sailing in the world. Where is everyone?" The day started with a sea so calm that the sunrise clouds were reflected in the sea as if in a mirror. Then with enough breeze to cause fish scales on the water *Chyka* moved along gently under sail almost straight upright.

A day later there was a moderate southeast wind. *Chyka* was moving well with reefed sails. But it was somewhat lumpy due to large swells from the Roaring Forties some 2,000 miles to the south. These long, smooth waves I carefully calculated as being 10 to 15 feet high.

I was not used to this degree of motion. When I was on deck a gallon of my expensive drinking water fell over, blew off the cap and emptied itself into the galley side locker, and down it went into the pots and pans. Later the brass oil lamp tipped over spilling oil making an awful mess and destroying one of the piles of candy bars the Canadians had given me.

My two huge bricks of mozzarella cheese purchased in Panama City had turned watery rotten. I threw them overboard. Probably all soft cheeses go bad quickly. I should have bought cheddar.

International law specifies what kind of trash may be thrown overboard and at which distances from shore. Far offshore one may jettison everything except plastic and oil. Tin cans can go over. Glass bottles I filled enough with seawater so they would sink. Arriving in Tahiti after 35 days at sea I had only two small bags of trash to bring ashore, almost all plastic.

The subject of what may be thrown overboard and where reminds me of the following:

An Encounter with the U.S. Coast Guard - Three Years Before

My first time off the West Coast of Puerto Rico the U.S. Coast Guard stopped me for a routine inspection. They asked me to keep on course but sail slowly. A huge inflatable launch was lowered from their cutter and came to *Chyka*. It carried five men with wide smiles and large guns. They came alongside and tied up. Two of them came on board.

The officer in charge had a two page check list of the required safety equipment, all of which I had to show them. Anything missing or out of date, e.g. fire extinguishers and flares, was a violation. I was not worried. I had equipped *Chyka* carefully.

It was the last question that caught me. "Where is your special decal saying that the discharge of oil overboard is illegal anywhere?"

I said, "I am sorry. I would not do that, but I don't have such a decal. I did not know it was required."

The officer said to his aid, "George, have a look in the engine compartment for it."

George replied, "Sir, Mr. Holt and I have already gone through the engine compartment for the other things. It is not there."

"George, please have another look around the engine area, but this time only for the decal, and do so carefully."

Finally, *My God!* Of all places! There it was, on the inside of the engine front cover where no normal person would ever look.

As they were leaving *Chyka* I asked the officer, "How did you know the decal was there?"

He replied, "When I stepped on board your boat and looked around a minute, I said to myself, *We are never going to find a single violation*. I have been doing this job for many years. I don't like being wrong and I seldom am." It was a very nice compliment.

11th Day - May 28 - 1,114 Miles - You Had No TV?! What Did you DO?

I wrote in my journal, "Good day to tell you, because everything is fine and under control. The sails are full and steady. The GPS is working with the autopilot to guide *Chyka* along at a smooth 5.5 knots." And then I wrote:

> *Today I cleaned and oiled some of the interior teak, planned a possible emergency installation of my backup autopilot, and remounted the florescent lamp in the main cabin.*
>
> *There are the daily tasks, washing myself and the dishes, cooking, listening to news on short wave, checking electricity, and looking out often, knowing I will see nothing but the beautiful sea and soaring birds. Navigation now in mid-ocean takes little time. There is never a problem getting the safety critical jobs done, e.g. engine check, sail trim, systems monitoring.*

Every day I study French for one hour, which is a pain. I watch the clock like a bored school boy in class. I spoke it fairly well in Belgium, but I need to review and improve it for French Polynesia. I am reading about Tahiti and my potential Pacific destinations. There is astronomy to study, and Boris, my chess computer, keeps calling me.

There were many good books on board to read. Marinas worldwide usually have cruisers' libraries in or near the laundromat, where you can take, donate, or exchange books.

12th Day - 1,254 Miles - A Dreadful Sound

At 3:00 AM a loud, ugly hissing sound had me out of my bunk as would have a fire alarm. I rushed up to the cockpit.

I could see no cause for the hissing, but I had no time to worry about it.

The wind had increased to 27 knots. Large waves from the south were slamming *Chyka* and washing into the cockpit.

Chyka was in trouble. I needed to double-reef both the main and genoa sails, which in such a wind and sea state is difficult, especially when going directly from full sails. I had always reefed early as the wind increases. But now being so far offshore I was sleeping two hours at a time. And during those two hours the wind had gone from light to strong.

From then on I always sailed with at least a single-reef in the main. Having two foresails, I usually had no need for the extra area of a full main anyway. And going from single to double-reef is so much easier in any conditions than from full to single or double-reef.

After getting *Chyka* under control, I started my search with a flashlight for the cause of the noise in the cockpit. There in a corner of the cockpit was my StormySeas inflatable safety harness ready in case I needed to go forward on deck. It was inflated, which can be done by mouth, or it will inflate automatically when in the water. The rough seas coming aboard had soaked it causing it to inflate with the impressive hissing noise. So there was no sea monster! Back to bed.

I had already known that I had no use for the inflatable feature of my safety harness. Falling overboard when underway offshore alone is hopeless. I only used the harness to attach myself to the jacklines, strong cloth straps that I always rigged on both port and starboard decks before going far offshore. Clipping onto a jackline you can go along the deck always being attached to the boat.

13th Day - May 30 - 1,408 Miles - The Great Circle Route to Tahiti

Force Six conditions (Wind 22 to 27 knots), large waves, going fast. I was trying to make up for prior lost time, but it was rough. It was now an effort to even sit or lie down unless held in by pillows to fight the rolling.

I could not make my famous 'Eggs McHenry' (not the same as 'Omelet McHenry') for breakfast. I had two eggs remaining. One tested bad by floating in water. The other was good, but then again, bump - *slam!* The egg rolled away and broke on the floor.

I was becoming concerned about my being so far off course on the sea chart. *Chyka* all this time was being guided by the GPS programmed to take me to a waypoint approaching Tahiti. (A waypoint is the latitude and longitude of a location on a route or of a destination.) For a week I had noticed *Chyka* was heading increasingly south of the route I had plotted to Tahiti. It appeared I would end up somewhere in the Antarctic. *What's happening?* I decided to wait another week or more. Something told me that the GPS was smarter than me, and to be patient.

And so it was. After a few days the track began to parallel the chart course. And then after a week more, *Chyka* gradually started to come back to the course.

The GPS was guiding *Chyka* on the great circle route to Tahiti. On the globe it is the direct and shortest route, but on a flat chart, depending on direction and latitude, it often appears to be a longer curved line. That is why when you fly from Chicago to London, your airplane will come close to the southern tip of Greenland, whereas on a flat map it appears to be 600 miles south of Greenland.

14th Day - May 31 - 1,589 Miles
- Fresh Water and Electricity

With the solar panel and the trolling generator I made enough electricity to keep the batteries up without running Big Rudy. (The trolling generator is mounted on the stern rail and is powered by a propeller at the end of a long line trailing behind.) But I did run the engine once every three days under no load to provide hot water for my showers and dish washing.

   I washed my face and underarms and shaved every day. I showered once every three days. I didn't perspire much anyway, because the temperature was always pleasantly in the seventies.

   I had plenty of water to get to Tahiti. I didn't need and never used the rain catcher I had worked on. I had made it wanting to avoid the expense and trouble of having a watermaker (converting salt water to fresh). They gobble up electricity and require a lot of maintenance. Being mostly alone I never had to worry about having enough water.

15th Day - June 1 - 1,708 Miles
- 1,200 Miles from the Nearest Land

I was about as far from any land as you can possibly be in the world. This is a direct quote from my journal:

> *I sometimes think it is amazing I am doing this. Now it is very late at night. Outside it is ugly, blowing, and raining. The nearest land of any kind is Easter Island 1,200 miles away. Yet, here I sit writing this in comfort and safety in this cozy well-lit cabin feeling secure and happy.*

   Just look at a globe with the middle of the Pacific Ocean facing you and read this quote from the *South Pacific Handbook* by David Stanley:

> *The Pacific, greatest of oceans, has an area exceeding that of all dry land on the planet... Covering more than a third of the planet's surface, as much as the Atlantic, Indian,*

and Arctic Oceans combined, it is the largest geographical feature in the world. It's awesome 165,000,000 square kilometers (63,000,000 square miles) have an average depth of about 4,000 meters (13,120 feet).

You could drop the entire dry land mass of our planet into the Pacific and still have room for another continent the size of Asia.

For two weeks I had not seen, nor heard on VHF any other vessel. Just when I thought this had become my private ocean and that it should be renamed 'The Holt Ocean', the VHF radio came alive. The sailboat, *Andrea K*, heading to the Marquesas Islands, was speaking to a northbound container ship. From them I learned that a sister ship *Columbia* would pass through my area the next day. I needed to pay attention to that.

The wind was too light and I couldn't keep the genoa full. I thought of the square rigged ships of history and how their sails were so much better for downwind sailing in these trade winds than our modern sailboats.

My first Pacific squall came suddenly in the late afternoon. It was a scramble to head up wind and reef the sails way down. It passed. I was tired of fighting all this; it's either too little or too much wind. I put *Chyka* on a broad reach, closed up the boat, and went below to forget the whole thing.

21st Day - June 7 - 2,496 Miles - Potential Serious Problem

When I woke up at 6:00 AM it was 77 degrees and 78% humidity. It's the tropics. So I opened wide the main cabin hatch, looked up through it, and saw a real problem. The mainsail outhaul line had frayed badly against the boom opening and would soon part. I considered several options to fix it, settled on one, planned the procedure, prepared what I needed, and did it.

Unlike racing sailors, ocean cruising sailors react to a problem carefully, taking time to plan. Cruising gurus say, "Just avoid making the problem worse." This true story illustrates the difference between racers and cruisers:

Ernst Aebi, his brother, and crew departed Bordeaux for Ireland on their large recently refitted sloop. Unfortunately, they had not conducted proper sea trials.

(Ernst is the father of Tania Aebi, the youngest person to solo circumnavigate. At age 18 to 21, she did it in a 26 foot sailboat. Read, if you can, her wonderful, honestly written book, *Maiden Voyage*.)

Far out and at night in heavy weather Ernst and crew tacked for the first time. The new boom being too long caught on the backstay and could not go over. The ship upset to a knockdown (when the boat is blown over on its side to where the mast hits the water.)

Ernst, being a double A type, sprang into action. He rushed to the helm shouting a stream of orders to everyone. His brother grabbed him by the neck and calmly asked, "Ernst, could we please have a glass of wine, maybe a sandwich, and discuss what we should do?"

I told you I washed and shaved every day. I don't like the feel of a stubble. After all, I was the Captain of this whole ship! And what was the Captain's uniform? Well, let's start at the top.

I wore a hat when on deck. Next, underwear. And that's it. And sometimes only the hat. No one out here seemed to mind and it was getting hot.

On June 9 I called Sonja. At $1.50 per minute she only wanted to know if I was alive and nothing more. But I rattled on a few minutes loosing track of how many. Everyone knows I talk too much. Well, I am in good company. John Adams disliked only one thing about himself, his talking too much.

Getting up from bed every two hours was not so bad. I had a quick look into the dark all around, checked sails, instruments, and radar all in one minute. And I was asleep again the next minute.

24th Day - June 10 - 2,852 Miles - Voice of America

Every day I listened to news on Voice of America shortwave. They do a good job of balancing points of view. For every person interviewed there is another with a different opinion. An understandable exception is that they end the news with an editorial, written by the Department of State, explaining the opinion of the U.S. Government on some issue.

On June 12 squalls at first had me scrambling to head upwind, the best direction to sail in a squall. The first ones didn't amount to very much, so then with reefed sails I didn't bother to change course for them. But I was ready to do so in a few seconds.

The wind was persistently close to aft. I was sailing as far as 50 miles off course before jibing and heading back to the course line. Today looking at the data from the past days I discovered a pattern in wind shifts that could help. At sundown the wind tended to shift clockwise and at dawn counterclockwise. I saw I could use this to better choose when I should jibe so as to sail closer to the course and make faster progress.

27th Day - June 13 - 3,174 Miles - Planets and Stars

After a pastel sunset I watched Mars set, while above it was Venus close to a quarter moon. At the same elevation to the south was Sirius, brightest of all stars, and next to it was Canopus, the second brightest star. (It is seen in southern latitudes.)

Reddish Mars had set. I would not see him much more this year. But blue white Venus was high above and would be with me evenings for months to come before returning to being a morning planet.

After the sun and the moon, planet Venus is the brightest object in the sky. The Arabs called her goddess of the heavens. To the Romans she was the goddess of love, beauty, grace, and fertility.

To see the five brightest objects in the sky, other than the sun, all together from any point on earth I think must be unusual.

Longitude

For many centuries, way before Columbus, sailors could calculate their latitude (where you are north and south) anywhere on the seas. But they had no way to find their longitude (location west and east.) Ships were being lost for not knowing well enough where they were.

In 1768 England's Royal Society, the National Academy of Sciences, sent Captain James Cook and two astronomers to Tahiti to observe from there the rare transit of Venus across the sun. Their measurements together with those of another team sent to the north of Norway to observe the same event at the same time, enabled their scientists to calculate the distance from Earth to Venus, and from that followed the distances to the other planets. The result was that the Royal Society could then establish a means for sailors to calculate their longitude anytime they could view the stars.

In honor of the Royal Society, Cook named this group of islands the Society Islands. Although long since solidly part of France, not England, they are still called the Society Islands.

There is magic in sunsets. They are a kaleidoscope of glorious, slowly modulating colors. Each view of them is a gift to you. No one has ever before seen exactly what you see, and no one ever will again. Here they were spectacular.

I had a good sound system on *Chyka*, two speakers in the main cabin and two in the cockpit. I often played CDs, but not at sunset. Then with a sundowner or two I wanted to hear the whisper of the wind and the quiet rushing sounds *Chyka* made gliding through the water.

I was approaching the Tuamotu Archipelago of atolls. In this book I often mention Pacific Ocean reefs, motus, lagoons, and atolls.

After a volcano erupts and forms an island, coral grows along its shore forming a fringe reef. Over millions of years the volcano sinks back into the earth leaving a lagoon between it and the reef, then called a barrier reef, which continues to grow. Eventually the entire island sinks back deeply into the ocean floor leaving a ring of coral islands, called an atoll, surrounding an empty lagoon. Some of its islands develop vegetation including trees. These islands are called motus. Some of them have beautiful beaches, small communities, and even hotels.

30th Day - June 16 - 3,519 Miles - A Mistake

I needed to cross the Tuamotu Archipelago between its atolls to get out again into the open Pacific and on to Tahiti. I surely would have anchored in one or two of these atolls, if I had not been so anxious to get to Tahiti.

The first atoll was Pukapuka. It sits by itself 120 miles east of the archipelago. I decided to pass to the north of it. In the morning the wind was east-northeast, so I put *Chyka* on starboard tack (the wind being from the starboard side) to stay north of the atoll and keep going fast. I had predicted that about the time I passed Pukapuka in late afternoon the wind would shift direction clockwise and so help me after a jibe to put *Chyka* on a good port tack (when the wind is coming from the port side). This wind shift pattern had been the trend for many days as I wrote in my journal four days before. But now it did not happen that way.

That this was a mistake became evident by 1:00 AM. Instead of turning clockwise the wind continued backing counterclockwise to the northwest trapping me 55 miles north of the course line. Now I had to waste 12 hours to claw my way back to the course making little actual progress to Tahiti. If I had then been on the course line, I could have been riding this northwest wind. At noon my miles made good to Tahiti for the past 24 hours was only 94 miles, the worst of the trip. I thought, *More mistakes like this and I will never get to Tahiti in time.*

34th Day - June 20 - 3,953 Miles - A Tough Dangerous Day

I was approaching the Fakarava Passage to cross through this archipelago. Ahead was a lot of lightning activity. I prepared *Chyka* for squalls.

The highest points on these motus are their palm trees. One does not see them on radar until sometimes only six miles away and visually when only three miles off of them, and then only in clear daylight.

For the next two hours I patiently sailed in light air at 3.5 knots or less. There were dark rain clouds all around. I did not want to be here at night, so I turned on Big Rudy. I was motor-sailing directly into a strong frontal system. Soon I took down all sails.

Just as I entered the passage with motus Kauehi on my left and Aratika on my right, it hit with a sudden 20 knot wind ahead. Then rain, hard rain, the kind that blinds you when driving even with windshield wipers going high speed. I thought it could not last long. It lasted three hours. There were steep waves from ahead and ocean swells from behind. The wind picked up a lot of water from the waves and sprayed *Chyka* constantly.

The atolls were on both sides, but I could see nothing, not even the surface of the water. I stayed below the whole time at the nav station watching my position on the GPS, the chart, and looking at the depth gage. Occasionally I went up to the helm to make a course correction on the autopilot.

Motoring at high engine RPMs I could only maintain a speed of one half to two knots.

I was worried. I had not heard or read anything about such weather fronts in this area, so I had no idea how long it would last. I was completely dependent on engine and GPS. If I had gone into shallow waters, it would have been impossible to drop anchor quickly enough to avoid a grounding.

But at 1:00 PM it quieted down to ten knots of wind ahead and *Chyka's* speed increased well.

Lesson Learned

First of all, I should not have attempted the passage with possibly bad weather. Secondly, when it hit I should have turned back immediately and out again to the safer open ocean.

In case Big Rudy would have to take me the rest of the 250 miles, I siphoned 25 gallons of diesel fuel from my ondeck jerry cans into the main fuel tank. It then contained 37 gallons, enough to motor if need be 370 miles in normal conditions, more than enough.

At 5:00 PM I could see palm trees on the islands both to port and starboard. These were the atolls Toau and Fakarava. As a calm red sunset changed to dusk, another sailboat crossed my bow, the first vessel I had seen since Ecuador. It was heading into Fakarava atoll. Darkness was only 20 minutes away, so I hoped the person knew what he was doing. I sailed out of the passage and rejoined the Pacific.

The next day was calm, pleasant motorsailing. The sunset was one to dream about, bright changing colors from all directions so that you don't know where to look. By 8:00 PM the wind picked up a little from the south. With all sails out and Big Rudy purring slowly to assist, I motorsailed along at six knots. It appeared I might get to Tahiti the next day.

36th Day - June 22, 2002 - 4,200 Miles - Arrival in Tahiti

The night sky was clear with a full moon. I continued motorsailing.

At 6:30 AM, out of the dawn mist appeared the mountains of Tahiti - 7,000 feet high, way over the clouds, and forty miles away.

I rounded Venus Point where Captain Cook built his observatory to study the transit of Venus. Then I sailed down the West Coast of Tahiti to the harbor of Papeete, the capitol of French Polynesia. I 'Med moored' *Chyka* (anchor off the bow and stern lines to the dock, common in the Mediterranean).

When I stepped ashore I thought I could feel the dock sway a little under my feet. I assumed for a second it was a modern floating dock. (They rise and fall with the tides conveniently taking all attached boats with them.) This unsteady sensation when on land often happens after being a long time at sea. The dock was actually a concrete sea wall.

What a luxury it was to walk around in *Chyka* standing straight up and not having to always hang onto something. How strange it was to look out the companionway and see people walking along the dock close-by!

Even with serious mistakes, I made it, and two days before Cyndie was to arrive! I considered it a good job.

I needed to shop, clean *Chyka*, do laundry, and the scheduled engine maintenance. At Immigration there was Phyllis, who had organized the booze run for us in Panama.

Papeete harbor was active with canoes, from singles to sixes, proof I was in Polynesia, where canoeing is their history, culture, and recreation.

I looked forward to sleeping as long as I wanted.

Cyndie Arrived at Night

I was way too early at the airport to meet her. I brought her back to *Chyka*. We talked until 3:00 AM.

The next day, Tuesday, we shopped and did email at an Internet cafe. Cyndie walked around Papeete, while I arranged a tour of the island for us the next day and bought gasoline for Li'l Rudy. After drinks on *Chyka* she put on a pretty red dress and we had dinner at one of the food trucks that are part of the colorful night market along the harbor front. The atmosphere there was festive; the food, French and Italian, was excellent.

On Wednesday the guide I had found gave us a tour of Tahiti, the Lagoonarium, Ferns Grotto, Paul Gauguin Museum, and the spectacular waterfalls at the north side of the island.

Cyndie was, and still is, happy about this event. (Remember, *Chyka* was Med moored stern to the dock, so we just stepped off *Chyka* onto shore.) As we were having drinks in the cockpit a couple walked by. The man was humming a song I recognized. I said something to him about it and we talked. They said their boat was *Active Light;* Cyndie recognized the name. For years she had received reports about their cruising from a friend of a friend of hers.

Moorea

Twelve miles west of Tahiti is the island called Moorea with 6,000 foot volcanic mountains hugely in view from *Chyka* or from anywhere on the West Coast of Tahiti.

After fueling at Marina Taina we motorsailed over to Moorea. Sailing along the north coast of it we looked down into Cook's Bay, which was 'Captain Cook's favorite anchorage in the entire Pacific'. As I continued my crossing of the Pacific Ocean, I visited three other bays that also were, 'Captain Cook's favorite anchorage'!

We anchored inside the barrier reef of the entrance to Opunohu Bay. From *Chyka* there was a spectacular view into the bay and the high steep mountains so close behind it. We swam, had leftovers from the night before, enjoyed the sunset, and looked at the pictures in my album of our cruising days in the Caribbean.

We stayed there at anchor for most of three days. The weather was perfect. *Li'l Chyka* took us to the bottom of the bay to find that the acclaimed tropical garden there was closed. Cyndie walked the beach back along the bay. I returned to *Chyka* and later picked her up from shore with *Li'l Chyka*. We again swam off *Chyka* and snorkeled on the reef. Cyndie made her famous Caribbean scratch pizza. We enjoyed sunsets, and talked each evening until late.

June 29 - A Humpback Whale

After a morning swim to the beach we raised anchor. Cyndie's flight home was to depart very early the next morning from Tahiti. Rounding the northeast point of Moorea, a humpback whale surfaced and swam very close and alongside us. I don't know how you could have a more impressive whale sighting. Humpbacks are among the largest whales, being between 40 and 52 feet long. This one made *Chyka* look very small.

We anchored in the lagoon off Marina Taina of Tahiti and rested. In the evening we had drinks and pizza by candle light. Just before midnight we dinghied ashore with Cyndie's baggage. It was pitch black dark. Cyndie held the flashlight. We came close to hitting an unlit buoy. Cyndie yelled, "HENRY!" just in time. Our taxi was waiting to take us to the airport.

June 30, 2002 - Cyndie Departed

It was in the wee hours of the morning at the airport. We had something to eat. It was a sad good-bye. In my journal I wrote, "I will treasure those five days I had with Cyndie, and I will miss her." I was back on *Chyka* by 3:00 AM. As before, and ever since then, we have been dear friends.

In the morning when I woke I decided I would do absolutely nothing for the day, not even plan anything.

At noon there were many outrigger canoes going by, the usual singles up to sixes, men's and women's. They change their paddles from side to side frequently and paddle always quickly. That night I slept 14 hours.

I stayed there at anchor eight days, going ashore to do shopping, buying charts, repairing a sail, refilling a propane tank, and doing laundry. On Le Truc, the truck bus that takes you into town, I met Debbie on *Different Worlds*. I was later often with her and her husband, Al, as you will read.

Being directly on my way west I returned to Moorea. Because the wind was so light, it was a motorsail back to Opunohu Bay and anchor exactly where I had done so with Cyndie. Again, I noticed how the green mountains beyond the bay ascend seemingly vertically.

I stayed there five days. In that lovely quiet spot I did many long neglected small boat jobs and one big one, which was to replace the propeller shaft zincs. They prevent electrolysis corrosion, and they must be replaced when they wear out. It's a difficult underwater job. A chess buddy in Milwaukee, Phil Kremsreiter, had given me diving weights, without which I could not have done it.

July 15, 2002 - Raiatea

My next destination was Raiatea, the largest of the nine Leeward Islands of French Polynesia. It is about 130 miles west of Moorea.

I picked up the anchor at 8:30 AM and sailed into calm clear weather motorsailing along so smoothly. It seemed too easy. Was this like what Josef Conrad wrote about in *Lord Jim*, being smugly content that all was perfectly fine, until his ship suddenly hit something causing utter disaster?

At sunset there was another green flash! And that was followed soon by the clear high silhouette of the mountains of Raiatea still 64 miles away. They were gray with an orange background from the setting sun. The night became dark with cloud cover. With no moon or starlight I sailed in total blackness. I thought dawn scheduled for 6:30 would never come.

When it did, the morning sky cleared as I approached Raiatea. I rounded the north end of it, entered Apouiti Marina, and Med moored to a dock. The manager of the marina, Jean Michelle, met me. Also waiting for me was Jean Claude Bocher, a reporter from the newspaper *La Depeche de Tahiti* (The Tahiti Express.) He wrote an article about my journey with a photo of me at the helm.

This marina is a Moorings base. I had chartered with The Moorings in the Caribbean before *Chyka*. The marina restaurant, La Voile D'or (The Golden Sail), was a frequent treat for me. It had rather better cuisine than what was served on board *Chyka*.

I was glad to again see Phyllis (booze run lady in Panama) and Terry on *Eros*. They were tied up at the seawall.

I could see Bora Bora, another of the Leeward Islands and the most famous of them, rising up over the horizon some 25 miles away. I decided to sail there for a brief visit to explore a little, knowing I would sail there later in the year to do a better job of it.

Bora Bora

Due to light winds it was a motorsail arriving there in the afternoon. The view of it from offshore was spectacular. Its peaks rise sharply through and above the clouds that seem to always surround them. There was no problem entering through the reef into the lagoon of Bora Bora.

I wanted to practice deep anchoring for when I knew I would need it later in the trip. Just off the town I anchored in 82 feet of water putting out all of my 165 feet of chain and with a 60 foot extension of nylon rope.

There I had before me the beautiful scene of Mt. Pahia rising steeply up 2,000 feet behind the town.

Back on Raiatea I moved *Chyka* to the Chantier Naval boat yard. They hauled *Chyka* out for bottom maintenance and kept her on land awhile.

Jean Claude, the newspaper reporter for the *Tahiti Express*, came on board with his father-in-law. They invited me to dinner at Jean Claude's home.

It was located high up overlooking trees below and the Pacific Ocean beyond. The living area was mostly open to the terrace from where we enjoyed the scene at sunset. Soon after, we watched Venus set.

There were also Jean Claude's charming wife, Pascale, their young son, Stanley, and Pascale's parents. I gave them two bottles of good Bordeaux wine and my usual gift of a can of cashews.

We discussed our stories, world history and languages. My French was by then much improved and adequate. Interesting people. Jean Claude had met Pascale in Brazil after he had lived years in Africa. From Brazil the two of them came here in their sailboat.

I had two weeks until my friend, Ron, was to arrive. I took *Chyka* on a short trip to the other side of Raiatea but spent most of the time docked at the Chantier Naval marina doing boat jobs. One job was to varnish the outside teak on *Chyka*. You are not supposed to do it in direct sunlight. And you are not supposed to do it after it has rained; and also you must not do it before it will rain. So when should you do it? In the tropics rain comes and goes at any time.

In the Caribbean I complained about it to a French Canadian fellow sailor. He told me, "But Henry, if you do it at night no one will see!"

As it often happened in the Caribbean, after a few minutes varnishing under a clear blue sky, I felt droplets of rain, looked up, and saw that a small dark cloud had suddenly appeared from over the mountain carrying rain. Frustrating.

Ron Peterson

Ron arrived September 29, 2002. Beginning in 1964 we had both worked for the same company. Twice he was my boss. We were always friends. After we both retired he cruised with me on *Chyka* in New England, along the East Coast, and in the Caribbean.

We rented a car to tour Raiatea Island including a vanilla farm and one of the largest *maraes* in Polynesia. (A marae is a religious ceremonial, open air temple made of stone by the Polynesians of long ago.)

This marae is located near Faaroa Bay to where I had sailed in July. From here the Polynesians sent their boats out in all directions founding settlements in so many places over the vast Pacific including Hawaii around 500 AD and New Zealand about 1250 AD. Their explorations of the Pacific went as far as 2,500 miles away.

How Did the Polynesians Ever Do It?

This much we know: They did it with catamaran canoes up to 90 feet long having platform decks and shelters to carry as many as 100 people with animals, food, and water. Their boats were propelled by sails, or paddles, or both, depending on the wind.

How they navigated in this vast ocean so long ago is not well understood. We do know they had an incredible knowledge of the stars and the directions to them as they rise and set. Also, there was a lot about the reading of waves coming from areas of far off islands. After the discovery of an island, routine travel to it was often established.

Why would people of Raiatea more than 1,500 years ago volunteer to go off into the enormous Pacific with no idea of where they were going? Well, very long before, no one knows exactly when, the Polynesians had migrated from Southeast Asia, island to island across the Pacific to this place. Ocean exploration was in their culture. I suspect there was a generous reward for a crew that would come back with evidence of a new island,.

About 900 years after the Polynesians sailed from Raiatea and settled Hawaii, Columbus crossed the Atlantic, about the same distance, with his vastly more seaworthy ships. At least he thought he knew where he was going. The Polynesians may have known legends of far off islands that gave them hope. I wonder how many of their boats went out and returned with nothing, and probably many of them, not at all.

Taha'a is the island just north of Raiatea. Before crossing over to it we docked in town to buy food. While shopping, Ron said we needed basil. He liked to cook and we just had to have basil. I didn't know how to say the word in French, so I went back to the boat to look it up. Then knowing how to say it, the store didn't have any. But eventually we found a store that did.

Seven Days Exploring Bora Bora

We moored in Hurepiti Bay of Taha'a Island and had dinner ashore. In the morning we sailed to Bora Bora, a pleasant six hour sail and anchored off Matira Point in the lagoon. Ron made chopped up tomatoes mixed with basil, of course. I added my pasta with olive oil, which I always used instead of butter. Excellent. So it was worth our searching for basil.

After Bloody Marys at the legendary bar of the same name, we took a tour of the island in a jeep over incredibly rough mountain roads. We saw the seven inch (bore diameter) cannons the U.S. installed within months after the start of World War II high up overlooking the entrance to the lagoon to discourage the Japanese from invading. They wisely never tried to do so. These canons were manufactured in 1908, very old, but they would have been enormously effective.

We took an excursion boat to swim with sharks and rays. They were lured there by food from the driver. The water was crystal clear. The sharks were sand sharks and so of no threat.

We motored *Chyka* most of the way around Bora Bora through the lagoon picking our way carefully through shallows and coral heads to anchor off Motu Pitiaau off the southeast coast. We were alone. Right before us was the magnificent trademark picture of Bora Bora rising steeply from the lagoon through dark green forests, then further above becoming jagged rock mountains up to 2,300 feet. As usual when at anchor, we swam off the boat.

Each evening we enjoyed cocktail hour, the sunsets, and conversation. Ron and I liked Scotch. Every time he visited me on *Chyka* he generously brought a bottle of one of those excellent and very expensive single malts.

Patricia and I also like Scotch, but we drink the cheapest. All authentic Scotch is at least very good, being controlled by Scotland to be aged three years or more in oak barrels.

My conversations with Ron were interesting. We commented on the day's activities, consulted my books on points of interest, and planned the next day and beyond.

We discussed how we would have reorganized The Torrington Company for which we both had worked. We came up with great ideas to fix, at last, so many problems. Unfortunately, we were a little too late, having both long before retired.

And we discussed politics and religion. Well, we talked politics some but not much. Talking politics with Ron had always been difficult. His attitude about it was that all government was bad and there was no hope.

Religion, on the other hand was a good subject for us. It was fun, because Ron was very Christian and I am an agnostic, but one that is interested in the stories of Christ's teachings, and of Paul's.

In 1998 as I was about to set sail from Milwaukee, a neighbor, Chuck Glen, gave me a Bible, saying that every ship needs one. It is a marvelous Bible. It has an index to all of the issues, the subjects, and all those who appear in the Old and New Testaments. Ron and I used it well and often. Patricia and I consult it sometimes to see what Jesus or someone said about something.

Ron and I started with Matthew and considered the meanings of what happened, and what Jesus really meant when he said this and that. I would read one verse, then we would discuss it for a long time. In all of three weeks we never got past Matthew 5!

We dinghied from *Chyka* to the coral reef south of the motu, known for its excellent snorkeling. Brilliantly colored butterfly fish came to us in large numbers touching our masks and hands.

Two days later we were again moored in Hurepiti Bay of Taha'a. A couple, long time cruisers, came over to us for beers and nuts. The lady and her parents knew Don Street, the legendary first one to write a cruising guide of the Caribbean. I had met Don three times in the Caribbean and later in Annapolis at the annual boat show there.

In the morning a man in a small outboard boat with his two little girls came by and sold us croissants. He left us information about his restaurant on a motu off the other side of Taha'a.

Huahine

From an overnight anchor off Tahoru Islet we sailed six hours to Huahine Island east of Raiatea and anchored off the main town, Fare. Ron made his excellent cheese, fried peppers, and salami sandwiches.

The next day a guide took us on a tour that included three maraes, a place where we fed eels, and a pearl farm. After beers in this pretty town, we motored two hours to anchor in 80 feet of water in Baurayne Bay. It is beautiful, large, completely quiet, and surrounded by steep, green hills with rock faces. *Chyka* was the only boat there.

We motorsailed to the small town of Avea, anchored, and swam with fins to the shore, snorkeling on the way to see if the Pension Maurari was serving meals. It was. In the evening *Li'l Chyka* took us there for an excellent dinner.

Next was again, the anchorage off Fare. The town was busy with preparations for the following day's annual six-man canoe race to Raiatea and then Bora Bora. The race takes three days.

Early in the morning, police came by to ask us to leave because of the race. We moved to the South Pass and waited with many power boats and a few charter sail boats to observe the start.

Suddenly they came and past by us in a rush, about seventy six-man canoes with power boats following them. It was a wonder of energy and colorful confusion. We boaters, observing it all, just tried to stay out of the way. After the canoes were ahead, we were clear to sail out and back to Raiatea.

**Six Man Outrigger Racing Canoe - They are
seen often in the South Pacific**

It was then a pleasant beam reach sail. We passed some canoe stragglers and one canoe swamped. It's a wonder more did not do the same, because the sea was choppy - bad for such small boats, but of course, it was nothing for *Chyka*.

Having crossed back to Raiatea we anchored well in Faaroa Bay, where I told you I had been with *Chyka* before and later with Ron on our tour of the island.

October 17, 2002

In the morning *Li'l Chyka* took Ron and me up the Faaroa River starting at the end of the bay. It is more a stream than a river being so narrow we had to brush the branches away from us as we slowly made our way along through a variety of plants, trees, and flowers. And above them all were often dramatic views of the highest mountains of Raiatea.

The man who with his daughters eight days before had come by in Hurepiti Bay to sell us breakfast croissants was Giuliano Tognetti. Looking at the information he had given us, we decided to sail to his remote motu.

A pleasant, scenic, fast four hour downwind sail brought us up the east coasts of Raiatea and Taha'a and to Giuliano's motu island. Approaching, we talked to him on VHF radio Channel 68. He gave us unclear instructions how to approach and anchor. We proceeded carefully. Suddenly the depth decreased from deep to 4.8 feet! *Chyka* draws 4.5 feet (meaning the keel goes to a depth of 4.5 feet.) We retreated and anchored in 40 feet of water. (The depths near reef islands change quickly.) It became dinner time.

We dinghied in carefully. It was shallow and the outboard suddenly bounced off coral rocks. We did not know there was a marked channel into his place. Then we saw Giuliano standing on the beach. By using hand signals he guided us in.

After we docked, there was some time before dinner. We walked all around his lovely tiny motu island and returned to Giuliano's as it became dark. There was his small restaurant and kitchen all under trees near the beach. He did it alone tonight because his wife and kids were away. It became dark. After drinks we ordered mahi-mahi. The only other customers were John and Linda from Australia who were chartering. Our dinners could not have been better.

As we were leaving to return to *Chyka*, Giuliano shined a spotlight to show us the safe channel out to open water by reflectors on markers. From there we saw *Chyka's* anchor light, the only light in the wide darkness.

We returned to our starting point, Apooiti Marina in Raiatea. Jean Claude and Pascale joined us on *Chyka* for drinks and then dinner at Voile D'Or.

Ron Departs - October 20, 2002

It was Sunday morning. Ron being religious, we attended a service at the nearby protestant church. I was so glad we did. We were early and were greeted by what seemed like most of the women of the congregation. The women were beautifully dressed and wore wide hats. The men wore flowery shirts and long pants. The interior was bright and colorful. We loved the service, mostly because of the frequent singing by two groups singing a cappella in close harmony.

After a final lunch for us at Voile D'Or, we took a taxi to the airport. As is common in airports of Polynesia, there was Polynesian music, this time a singing duo with a guitar and an eight string ukulele.

Patricia also knew Ron for as long as I did. Her first husband was also with us in The Torrington Company.

She and I visited Ron a number of times after I completed the circumnavigation. The first time was at his home in Norfolk CT for an overnight. He told us then he had been diagnosed to have Alzheimer's.

We could not believe it, but it was so. We visited Ron a few times in his assisted living home near Detroit. Our last visit with him was in September 2011. As we had done before, we all had lunch at a local restaurant. His memory was in serious decline.

In December 2012 his son, Matt, told me Ron still had some memory. I sent Matt what I had already written of Ron's sailing with me in the Pacific. Matt read it to Ron. He told me Ron remembered with pleasure some of it.

Ron died in February 2013.

To Avoid Tropical Storms

The season for South Pacific cyclones is November 1 to April 30, somewhat the opposite of when hurricanes occur north of the equator, June 1 to November 30.

The distances from island to island in the Pacific are so great that when sailing from one to the next, there usually would not be time enough to find refuge anywhere from an oncoming cyclone. Anyway, I have almost always stayed out of the storm latitudes during tropical storm seasons, or I put *Chyka* on land. And that is what I now did.

On November 8, 2002 I returned to Milwaukee. For five months I enjoyed being with my family and helping them all however I could.

I flew back to Raiatea arriving April 8, 2003. Yes, there were still many days of the cyclone season before I could sail on, but they were well spent. *Chyka* got a fresh bottom paint (special antifouling paint to protect the hull from the growth of sea organisms). And there was the kind of maintenance that is only easily done when a boat is out of the water.

The Oldest Single-hander in the South Pacific

Then at the marina were two other single-handers, Torben Wanscher, a Dane, and Jack Oldenburg, a Swede. I mention both of them many times throughout this book.

Before Jack showed up, I had the honor of being known as the oldest single-hander in the South Pacific. Unfortunately, Jack was two years older than me. So I was demoted.

Phyllis and Terry on *Eros* were there with a new crew person, Ryan, who later proved to be of critical help to them, as I will tell you. We all went to town twice with others for dinner and once on board *Eros*.

Jean Claude, Pascale, their young Stanley, and I had our last dinner together at Voile d'Or. We talked so long that Stanley went to their car to sleep. They are such dear and interesting people. I knew I would miss them. We later corresponded a few times. But with few exceptions, time and distance sever the bonds, though not the memories.

I gave extra books and charts of these islands to Rob and Dee Dubin on *Ventana*, an Island Packet 40. They were more experienced cruisers than me and had done professional promotion videos for Island Packet.

Rob came on board one day for a visit. Looking around, he commented on how I had rigged my preventer, which keeps the boom from slamming too hard to the other side during an accidental jibe. (This happens when going downwind. The wind gets in front of the main and quickly flips it and the boom across the boat, possibly causing injury to a crew member, damage to the rigging, or even a dismasting.) Rob explained that the way I had rigged the preventer could cause the destruction of the boom in heavy weather. What he said made complete sense to me. Soon I corrected it.

The Cook Islands - Named after Captain James Cook

I moored *Chyka* in the lagoon just outside the boatyard to be ready for an early departure the next day to Rarotonga, the largest of the Cook Islands. Al and Deb on their sailboat *Different Worlds* came by saying they would do the same.

It was a 540 mile five day trip. Late the first night Al and Deb passed me close to port. Their larger boat was sailing one knot faster than *Chyka*. Each day it became rougher. There were breaking waves and spindrift, spray blown off cresting waves during a gale.

Sailing during the day of arrival was easy. I entered the harbor of Avarua on Rarotonga, and anchored next to Al and Deb. As I did so, the third boat there, *Free Spirit* from California, shouted over I should come over for beers in 30 minutes. I did, and so did Al and Deb. Later Al cooked for us fish *au gratin*. They had caught the fish on the way here. On their boat Deb did the cruisers' radio net, weather, navigation, and the computer. Al did the cooking.

Rarotonga

I stayed here in this little harbor sixteen days. It took me several days to install the new backup autopilot ST 4000. For years I had worried about what would happen if the prime ST 6000 would fail.

Hand steering single-handed over such long distances would be exhausting and in heavy weather difficult. During all those years I carefully serviced the ST 6000. But it did finally fail four years after the circumnavigation. Then the backup autopilot ST 4000 was there to take over.

Avarua is a charming town. But its harbor is a small difficult place. The wind blew black volcanic sand over and into our boats. Late one morning our boats at anchor were told to leave the harbor so a freighter could arrive, dock, and turn around to depart.

Unfortunately, just at that time my regular wheel steering system was disassembled due to the ST 4000 installation. A tug came to drag *Chyka* out of the harbor. Al was on board to help me. The tug left us out there in rough water. Having no steering at all, we could not sail or motor. Fortunately, I knew how to deep anchor. We did so in 90 feet of water. That gave me time to reassemble the wheel steering system. We then could return to the harbor and anchor. Next was dinner ashore at Trader Jakes with Al, Deb, Tom and Linda.

Another Challenging Day

It started at 7:00 AM with another broadcast from Harbor Control. We had to again leave the harbor to make room for another arriving freighter.

Eros arrived with Phyllis, Terry, and their new crew, young Ryan. Their passage to here from Raiatea was much rougher than mine: They lost their autopilot, Phyllis was very sick, and Terry fell, injuring his leg.

Ryan was new to cruising, but confident. He was such a great help to them. The fact that they got beat up, and this being their second circumnavigation, shows that the passage from Raiatea to this place can be a challenge.

Terry steered around the harbor trying to find room. I radioed they could tie up alongside *Chyka* a few hours: Another freighter was to arrive. But instead, for some reason they went out and stayed at sea. We could see them out there pounding the steep waves until at last the freighter came in and later departed.

Then with the harbor finally clear, *Eros* came in to Med moor at the town dock. Terry was too dependent on his bow thruster, which now did not work. Al and I went over in our dinghies to help.

While Al controlled the stern, my job was to push *Eros* at the bow to starboard. I was nosing *Li'l Chyka* hard into Eros with Li'l Rudy running at high RPMs. At that time I had no idea how slippery it can be between the rubber of an inflatable dinghy when wet and a fiberglass hull. Suddenly the nose of *Li'l Chyka* slid off sideways from the hull of *Eros* with my outboard still at nearly full throttle. I was dumped into the water. *Li'l Chyka* went off about to destroy whatever she could. I was just able to grab a trailing line and overturn her. I swam over, killed the engine, and so stopped the chaos.

A Most Fortunate Party on *Chyka*

Several days later there was a party on *Chyka* for all cruisers in the harbor. There were five couples including Phyllis and Terry with Ryan, also Al and Deb. We had snacks and drinks until 11:00 PM.

The reason this was so fortunate a party is this: Tom, who was there with his wife, Ann, on *Linda* from New Zealand, asked about my staysail boom, which he thought was unusual. Its unique design had important advantages. Before it got too dark I invited him to tour the foredeck with me to look at it.

As we inspected the staysail arrangement, Tom looked to the bow and noticed something important. My forestay, which keeps the mast from falling back, was close to being disconnected. The pin of the bottom shackle had partially backed out. At sea, the mast could have fallen backwards destroying the rigging. The next morning Tom helped me correct the problem.

As if to convince me I needed to move on, I had to reanchor, not once but twice more, to make room for ships coming in.

I realized that I should have sailed further north through these islands to avoid Rarotonga. That is the way Jack and Torben were sailing. When sailing the northern routes through the Cook Islands, one stops to anchor in pretty bays of remote islands. But then I would have missed the wonder of Beverage Reef, my next place. So it often is!

It was early Tuesday. I was trying to get ready to depart. Again at 7:00 AM I had to reanchor for another arriving ship.

Now get this! If I had not been a seasoned veteran of border bureaucracy I would have been a case. The Harbor Master had no more departure tax receipts. He had to first fill one out before I could get clearances to leave. So I had to walk to town to get the receipt and pay for it. I walked back to the Harbor Master.

Having the tax receipt completed, I went again into town to get a clearance for departure from Immigration, and then to another odd place in town to Customs for their clearance. So all that killed Tuesday. At last on Wednesday I was able to depart.

Beverage Reef

Al, Deb, and I had planned to meet at Beverage Reef on the way to Niue. It is a submerged coral atoll. We happened to learn about it from an unofficial posting on the port bulletin board. It was a sketch with coordinates for the entrance. Strangely, it is not on any charts, not in the cruising guides, and it sits absolutely remote in the ocean completely below the surface of the water. It is 450 miles away from Rarotonga. The closest land to it is Niue 130 miles further west. How did any mariners ever find it, other than by suddenly running aground there to their probable destruction? Fishing boats still occasionally get caught on the reef.

Al and Deb departed before I did. It took four days of rough seas weather sailing to get there. On the third day I heard on the shortwave cruisers' network Deb, Cathy, and Phyllis talking. They were worried, because they had not heard anything from me, and that they would wait one more day before doing something about it. I was too far away from any boats to transmit on VHF. I could receive shortwave, but could not transmit on it. I called Phyllis on my satellite phone to tell her I was OK.

I had only the sketch map of the reef and the GPS position of its only entrance, which is on the west side of its lagoon. As I approached, there was nothing to see but the ocean. I radioed Al and Deb. Deb said they were fine, well anchored in the east end of the lagoon about two miles across from the entrance. She gave me their position.

It was Sunday June 1, 2003. I timed my arrival to the entrance for 10:00 AM. Then the sun would be high enough that I would be able to see the bottom and the underwater reef as I entered. I used all my knowledge of reading water colors and the depth sounder to slowly fish my way into the lagoon. If I had gone hard aground, there would have been no help, except possibly a little from Al and Deb. It was then a slow careful motoring over to anchor next to *Different Worlds* in 30 feet of water over coral sand.

Such an amazing place! Looking out over the ocean there was to be seen only the surf breaking on the reef a half mile away to windward. We were as if anchored in a pond, although the wind was E 20-25.

I swam. Later Deb was worried and called. Looking over to *Chyka*, she had seen my stern swim ladder was down and that I had rigged a trailing safety line in case the current would drift me away from the boat. But there was no Henry. Well, I had already had my swim and was back on *Chyka*.

In the morning Al and I wanted to snorkel the reef. It was then high tide. Some waves came over the reef to us. It was too rough for me to lower Li'l Rudy to my dinghy, which I had launched. So Al came by with his larger dinghy and in it we went to anchor at the reef and snorkel. Even with swim fins, it was a job to keep from being washed away by the current. We admired the reef fish and the coral heads with huge clams attached to them. A sand shark swam slowly under us over the bright clean coral sand bottom.

Tuesday morning we departed Beverage Reef as soon as the sun was high enough for us to see the shallow reefs at the entrance. We two captains each had one eye on the depth gage, and the other reading the colors of the water until we were out and safely at sea.

It was then to Niue a fast, downwind, overnight sail of 130 miles with a strong tail wind requiring double-reefed sails. Having not seen any vessel other than *Different Worlds* since Rarotonga, I felt comfortable taking one hour naps after first having a quick look around the ship, the horizon, and a radar scan before going back to my bunk. I heard on the shortwave cruisers' network that *Vindela* was there at Niue. That's Jack Oldenburg.

Niue

(Pronounced NEW - ay)

With an area of only 100 square miles and a population of 1,400, Niue is the smallest country in the world. It is associated with and under the protection of New Zealand about 1,300 miles away.

We arrived June 4, 2003 taking moorings in its lovely bay near the main town. After launching *Li'l Chyka* I was preparing to lower the outboard down to her. Then in perfectly calm waters the outboard mounting came loose and the motor plopped quietly into the sea. Well, this is not a good place to lose your outboard. Shops are few and basic. I called Al, moored right behind me, and told him I would need to buy a new outboard. Al said he would dive and get it.

The next morning he came over with his scuba gear. The water was so clear that with his mask on, he could see the outboard fifty feet below. He dove down to attach a line to the engine, and I could then haul it up.

There is a complicated procedure for treating a drowned outboard. I worked on it for over an hour then tried to start it. Nothing. *Oh well, Henry*, I thought, *you did your best*. Then it dawned on me: The fuel valve was still shut off. I opened it, and with one pull on the starter rope Li'l Rudy sprang alive.

We went to town. There was no dinghy dock, only the high long concrete pier used by the supply ship which comes once every three weeks. So, you have to hoist your dinghy up with a crane and park it on the pier.

Clearing in here was odd. I dug up Chamberlain, the customs man, and brought him out in my dinghy to inspect *Chyka*. After bringing him back to town he drove me to the man who is the Immigration Department amongst other things.

The next morning on my way to town with *Li'l Chyka* I stopped by *Vindela* to say hello to Jack Oldenburg. Torben was there playing his clarinet.

That night we all went to the Matavai Resort Terrace Restaurant overlooking the sea. Torben always brought along his clarinet whenever we went out to dinner. He played some solo jazz for everyone there.

For two days Al, Deb, and I toured the island. Most important are the limestone caves and how they open out to the ocean over lovely coral pools.

Someone told us we could get the best fresh vegetables on the island at the island prison, which had only three prisoners. One of them, Joe, greeted us, showed us the prison farm, and sold us a lot of stuff, for me the most important being wonderful tomatoes and cucumbers.

Joe was prisoner in charge. It was his job to lock up the place including himself at night and open up in the morning. Don't be surprised. There is no way one could hide on - or escape from - this small island.

Why was Joe in prison? Some man had raped both of his two young daughters, and Joe killed him. He told us that with their legal system being so lenient, the man would not have been given any real punishment. "So I had to kill him," he explained.

That night Jack and I joined Deb and Al on *Different Worlds* to discuss Tropical Storm Ginny predicted to pass 600 miles to the south of us two days later. We saw that we then would be on the windward shore with strong west winds and large waves coming to us from the ocean. I decided to move to the protection of the other side of the island and wait there. The others said they would stay put.

Early in the morning of June 10 the wind was already strong and the sea choppy. I loaded diesel from three jerry cans into the main tank. I should have first taken the outboard and the dinghy out of the water. Doing so later with higher waves and the bowsprit plunging into the water was a hard job.

In the early afternoon *Chyka* left to go to the other side of the island. There on the lee side of Niue, I hove-to in fairly smooth waters. I worried about the others who stayed on the trouble side. It turned out they did have a rough night with waves rolling them badly.

Five months after our visit there, Niue was devastated by Cyclone Heta. As of the time that *Chyka* completed her circumnavigation in 2008, Niue had not yet fully recovered.

We all departed June 13, 2003. Our destination was Tonga 240 miles away. It was a dream voyage: four days of mostly easy sailing.

A Lost Day in My Life - Crossing the International Dateline

On the way to Tonga, as *Chyka* crossed the International Dateline, I lost a whole day in my life. June 24 became for me instantly June 25.

Mark Twain in his book *Following the Equator* complained about this. He was on a large ship also crossing the International Dateline. He wrote, "We shall be a day behindhand all through eternity. We shall always be saying to the other angels, 'Fine day today,' and they will be always retorting, 'But it isn't today, it's tomorrow.'"

On the other hand, Phileas Fog in *Around the World in Eighty Days,* a marvelous movie from the novel by Jules Verne, while going in the opposite direction across the dateline, gained an extra day enabling him to return to his London club just in time to win his bet.

The only way I can possibly win back that lost day in my life is to go back and cross the dateline going the other way. Just flying west to east around the world would take most of a week, an inefficient way to gain back a day.

Tonga

The Kingdom of Tonga is an archipelago stretching north to south over 500 miles. Most of its islands are small and uninhabited. It is the only Pacific nation to have never been colonized. We had all decided to meet in Neiafu in the northern Vava'u group of the Tongan islands.

I entered the Ava Pass into the Vava'u group with less difficulty than I had anticipated. After passing about 30 forested, limestone islands, I motored into the quiet harbor of Neiafu. The mooring I took was next to *Different Worlds* and near the boats of Jack and Torben.

There, *Chyka* was as steady as being on land! Neiafu Harbor is nearly surrounded by land. The wind was light. For the first time in five weeks *Chyka* was not rolling or pitching. I could put anything down free standing and not worry about it tipping over. Cleaning up the clutter from the last passages took a few hours. I planned on staying two or three weeks in these islands. Well, they turned out to be too marvelous and fun for us all. I stayed five weeks.

Our hangout was the Mermaid, an outdoor shore bar and restaurant with its dinghy dock in view from our boats. We often met there for lunches, on our way to or from town, and usually in the evening for beers and sometimes dinners.

On the dock of the Mermaid, Bev Tensen did haircuts. The first day ashore she gave me one. I met her two adorable daughters, Andrea and Ashley, aged five and seven. We had waved to each other as *Chyka* passed their boat when entering the harbor. They asked a million questions. Finally, I took them out to *Chyka* and we went for a small run around the harbor with the girls taking turns steering. We became good friends. Often the girls walked with me to town. One day a lady stopped me and asked, "How long have your granddaughters been sailing with you?"

Tongan School Girls - Neiafu

In my opinion you cannot relax and enjoy being in these island nations unless you accept their ways. In the Caribbean it is to know that all agreed appointments are to be at Island Time, which usually means much later than the time they say.

Here I quote from the *South Pacific Handbook* by David Stanley:

> *Fakatonga - The Tongan Way*
> *Most things will be late or lost.*
> *Yes can mean no.*
> *No can mean maybe.*
> *Maybe can mean anything.*
> *To display anger or even frustration will get you nowhere fast.*
> *And it is very bad form.*
> *Better to shrug your shoulders and*
> *adopt Fakatonga yourself.*

Sunday Morning. As happened every morning, there was the Local Cruisers' Network on VHF radio. After announcements there was time for us all to exchange information and ask for help and advice with problems.

The Christian community here does not allow work to be done on Sundays. So no one did boat jobs on deck in view of people on shore. By doing a few jobs below and out of sight I felt as if I was getting away with something, more of a reward than I usually get.

Al and Deb asked me over to see how English muffins are made. In the afternoon Al came by to play chess. Throughout the day we were serenaded by choruses from the beautiful Catholic church high above us.

The German Cemetery

When Germany possessed what is now Samoa, about 400 miles north of here, 1900 to 1914, many Germans came from there to settle on this island.

I visited their cemetery overlooking the beautiful scene of the harbor far below with *Chyka* clearly in view.

Grave stones tell a lot. I spent a long time thinking about what was written on them. On the one of Lucy Guttenbeil, who died in 1918, was engraved in old German, "*Droben werden wier uns wiedersehen.*" (There above we will be with each other again.)

I tracked the Guttenbeil family along their graves until the death in 1999 of Maile Guttenbeil, wife of Richard Guttenbeil, leaving four sons with English and German first names.

Before leaving to visit Island #11, I shopped in town. Bev had asked me to buy chicken, some frozen fish, roast beef, tomatoes and cucumbers.

When we were there and well anchored, Bev and family came to *Chyka* for dinner. Her husband, Henry, soon returned to their boat to drink alone. Bev and the girls stayed overnight on *Chyka*.

In the morning I swam with the girls to the beach. In the late afternoon Jack blew in and anchored near us. He joined us for dinner and conversation until late. Ashley stayed over.

After brunch for all on *Chyka*, we departed for Island #7. Ashley was my crew and steered most of the way. Al and Deb were already there.

The girls and I swam under *Chyka* with our fins as practice to be ready for the underwater entry to Mariner's Cave the next day. That evening Bev made most of the dinner for all of us. Included was Beef Stroganoff prepared by Chef Extraordinaire Henri.

Mariner's Cave

When fifteen years old, William Mariner's ship, the British privateer, *Port au Prince,* was captured by Tongan natives in 1806. Mariner was spared and lived in the Vava'u islands for four years.

I have not been able to find out why the cave is named after him. Did he somehow in his years there find it? The entrance to it is six feet under water, depending on the tides. Even now it is difficult to find.

Our three boats motored to a bay a short distance from Mariner's Cave and anchored. The others came over to *Chyka*, and she brought us all to where the entrance was supposed to be. Fortunately a local boat happened by and showed us exactly where to find the underwater tunnel into the cave.

Each of us with snorkel masks and fins, after taking six deep breaths to build up oxygen, dove down four feet to the entrance of the tunnel, then swam ten feet under water to the bottom of the cave, where we could then surface and finally breathe.

Bev and the girls were so happy to make it in. Bev did it on her third try with Al shining a light for her from the inside of the cave. Jack made it in also. The afternoon sunlight came through the tunnel illuminating the fish below and projecting colored images on the limestone ceiling above. The air alternated between clear and foggy as it was compressed and released by outside swells pushing water through the tunnel every ten seconds or so.

The next day we all, now including a boat from New Zealand, dinghied to Swallows Cave. This one was much easier. You just paddle your dinghy into it. Again, the water in it was illuminated by the sun shining through the entrance showing a tightly packed school of small fish.

The Entrance to Swallows Cave in Tonga

Our excursion through these tiny islands lasted much longer than expected. Most of the time, there were five to six for dinner on *Chyka*. So we were scrounging and asking people to bring food. And Bev was good at combining whatever was around.

In the early morning the girls annoyed me. I had asked them to speak quietly so Bev could sleep, but they would not. Bev slept anyway.

Later Jack came over for brunch. We had run out of everything. All we could provide was oatmeal, canned fruit mixed with peanuts, and coffee.

Back to Neiafu - June 30, 2003

There we all recovered, shopped, and tried to check email, but the Internet here was down.

FM 89.3 is the local radio station. Their theme is, "The first radio station in the world to give you news and music all day every day." And they are right - the International Dateline bends just east of Tonga, making it the first place on earth with a radio station to greet the new day. They play classics and 1950's music.

The Tongan women I met were pleasantly gentle. They spoke quietly using well chosen words often using only facial expressions in place of words.

The next day I had lunch at the Mermaid. Bev was giving haircuts. All she earned from noon to 9:00 PM she donated to the small, local hospital even though she could ill afford to do so. The girls were selling shells.

Jack and I decided to sail to nearby Island #4. In about 45 minutes we were there in its beautiful bay and the only ones there. At sunset I went over to Jack's boat for two of his amazing rum punches. Back on *Chyka* I slept 11 hours.

I sailed to the most remote of all in the group, Island #17. It is an unusually difficult place to anchor; few sailors ever come here. I entered and found myself between two mean looking reefs, many rocks, and coral heads. My first attempt to anchor did not hold. The next did, and it was worth the effort. Such a beautiful place. Of course, *Chyka* was the only boat here.

At sundown, village children came out to me in a small outrigger canoe. They serenaded me in Tongan and school English with a tune something like Jingle Bells. They all were dressed in pretty colorful shirts. I was impressed by the girl who was at the stern. She sat so proudly erect and looked at me with a confident smile. I was sure she was the leader of the group. I gave them all pencils and pens which are so much treasured by children in remote or third world places. *Chyka* always had these and other gifts on board.

Children in their Outrigger Canoe - Remote Island #17 of the Vava'u Group, Tonga

A Tongan Feast

I motored to Island #7. We had made reservations for a Tongan Feast to be provided by a family there. Jack was already at the anchorage. *Rare*

Earth, Bev and family, joined us. In the evening we all dinghied ashore. We walked along the beach to a path in some woods over a hill and to the only home there on what they call Barnacle Beach.

While we waited for the pig to be roasted, we enjoyed the animals they had, the shore views, and their children. Knowing there would be no alcoholic drinks available, Bev had told us to bring something to drink.

Some people came without reservations, so they ran a little short of some food. Still there was plenty to eat. After the feast, young girls dressed in costumes danced for us with music from a ukulele and a guitar.

After paying and saying good-bye to all the people, we went off with two flashlights in total darkness stumbling along the path back to the beach where we had left our dinghies. When we got there, Bev said, "Let's build a fire." We did. The fire attracted people from another boat anchored off. They came in to join us bringing with them a guitar. A good beach party. But after awhile I got tired of the music and returned home to *Chyka.*

In the morning Bev and the girls swam over to *Chyka* for eggs and biscuits. Bev was badly hung over. I gave her strong coffee and she took a hot shower. While she did, Murphy (See Murphy's Laws after the end of Part II) chose that time to have my water pump fail for the first time, leaving her fully soaped up. I brought her a bucket of warm water from the galley. The kids swam off *Chyka*. Bev slept soundly until noon.

We all returned again to Neiafu. One of my jobs was to get more gasoline for Li'l Rudy. I had just enough to get to the town dock, but not back.

At the gas station I filled my two gallon can. Stupidly, I had forgotten to bring outboard oil to mix with it, which you must do for a two-cycle engine.

I stood there awhile wondering what I should do. In one minute as if a godsend, down the hill to me walked Rob Dubin having just arrived from Samoa. He was the Island Packet expert who had advised me to make a major improvement back in Raiatea.

Rob had also come to get gasoline for his outboard, had the outboard oil with him, and gave some to me!

The Sinking of *Skywalker* - July 7, 2003

David and Steff had built *Skywalker* in New Zealand and did everything to equip her well for ocean. But they lacked training and experience in anchoring. They sailed from New Zealand to Tonga.

One day's sail short of us, they anchored inside a remote barrier reef. Bad weather moved into the area. Late at night with increasing winds and waves they were dragged onto a reef where their boat sank. They spent the night on deck just above the water holding onto the mast. They called for help on their handheld VHF radio. A passing freighter heard their call but had no way to assist. However, the freighter did inform us of their situation.

Paul and Julia on their *Sabina*, anchored near them, also heard their distress call. In the dawn hours when they could see what they were doing, but still in rough seas, they came to rescue them in their dinghy and brought them back to *Sabina*. David was dangerously depressed. They immediately gave him a sedative, probably Alprazolam (Xanax), which some of us kept on board to treat people for anxiety and panic.

They cared for, fed, and clothed Dave and Steff. The strong winds and rain prevented them from moving.

Twenty of us met at the Mermaid to discuss what we could do to help them. Bev volunteered to assemble donations of food, and she did. But for nine days the weather was terrible keeping us from bringing it to them. We checked with them every day on VHF radio.

The weather suddenly quieted. *Sabina* was able to sail north to us. We all were so happy to see them sail in and take a mooring. At cocktail hour we waited at the Mermaid hoping they would come ashore. They did. We expected them to be a pathetic, exhausted foursome.

Instead, they arrived in *Sabina's* dinghy, well dressed, radiating huge smiles. It was a celebration.

The next evening they were with us again at the Mermaid. Dave and I talked alone awhile. Dave felt crushed by the loss of his boat and said, "Now I understand why the captain goes down with his ship." Steff, who was strong and well, and the *Sabina* people happened by at the time, overheard some of what he was telling me, and told Dave he should let it go.

I asked Dave to speak to all of us the next day at the Mermaid to tell us their complete story. But he declined to do so.

There was later an attempt to refloat *Skywalker*, but it failed. Eventually, back in New Zealand Dave and Steff built a new boat.

A Rainy, Blowy Day

On the day we learned about *Skywalker*, the weather was windy and rainy for the whole area. I went to *Different Worlds* to play several games of chess with Al. As we played, Deb, who is a neat freak, went around the cabin with a smile wiping down every surface.

We had dinner at Ana's, a shore restaurant right next to the Mermaid. With us were Rob and Dee Dubin and a Belgian family.

The next morning Deb called me on VHF. Al's father had died. Could they possibly use my satellite phone to call home? I brought it right over to them. The next day they were gone, and I never saw them again. Certain friends are hard to lose. I emailed with them for some years.

Late one night Bev called on VHF. Her Henry was drunk and difficult. He had gone back to the Mermaid to drink more; the girls were upset; "Please come." I did, calmed them down, kissed them all good night and returned to *Chyka*.

I ran into Bev and the girls in town. We shopped, bought fish for dinner, and were together the rest of the day. Back on *Chyka* Bev cooked the fish in fried onion tomato sauce. Jack joined us. I made pasta. After dinner we played Yacht Race. The girls went to sleep, Andrea in the forward cabin and Ashley in my arms. Jack left at 3:00 AM.

Late the next evening Baker, on a nearby boat, and I were having drinks on *Chyka*. Bev radioed. Henry had hit her; she felt desperate, could I come to help? I said I would bring Baker with me in case I needed him to help control Henry. Immediately, Ashley called back and said I should come alone.

When I arrived, Henry was gone. I brought Bev and the girls back to *Chyka*; and so there in my cozy home they felt safe and sound. Soon it was to bed for us all.

After breakfast I brought Bev and the girls to shore and left them there to go on a whale watch. I then went to *Rare Earth* to drop off some stuff for Bev. Henry awoke to tell me a few things. "Bev attacked me and I had to defend myself." *What rot!*

Bev and I said good-bye. I told Bev to leave Henry ASAP, and eventually she did.

Departing Tonga

The first step for me in leaving for Fiji was to stage *Chyka* for an overnight at the western island of the Vava'u Group, #7, where as you know I had been before. I left Neiafu at noon and was comfortably anchored at #7 by 3:00 PM.

Soon I realized I had a bad chest cold. I slept through the night and most of the next day feeling so weak and hoping it was not bronchitis.

Bev called me after the VHF Cruisers' Network saying, sorry that I was sick and insisting I eat garlic. *Nonsense!* But then I thought, *I have some, why not?*

I radioed back to ask how much I should eat and how to peel and cut it. But by then Bev had gone ashore. Ashley answered and sagely advised me exactly how to prepare it and that I needed to eat it with water, juice, or any liquid. So I did as she told me, downing it with Scotch.

The next morning I felt ready to sail on. I radioed Bev to again say good-bye. I was worried about her. I was so sorry that I had to leave her when she and the girls needed me. But it was certainly time for me to go.

A friend of ours in Neiafu, Graeme, had been our expert consultant as to our options for the *Skywalker* situation. His wife some days before had come by *Chyka* to tell me she was leaving him, and that she was on her way to the airport.

Eventually Graeme and Bev married, were happy together living in New Zealand with the girls, and have built a large cruising sailboat.

Five Days and 500 Miles to Fiji

I first listened to Weather Honolulu. There was going to be a cold front and a shear line between Fiji and Tonga. Why I did not take that warning, I have no idea. It was an exception to my usually being so careful.

Departing Monday the wind was light and the sky overcast. The wind gradually increased. I kept reefing in more sail. By noon the wind was against me 30 to 35 knots, and there were strangely confused breaking waves. This was the worst sailing for me so far.

The next day I was seasick, so I decided to heave-to and rest. While doing so and tacking under power to backwind the genoa, I forgot about the trailing line to the trolling generator propeller. *Chyka* crossed over the line, the engine propeller cut it, and the trolling propeller was gone. (I later bought a new one.) Then it was too rough to sleep, so I sailed on with triple-reefed main, staysail, and just a bit of genoa.

The wind calmed to 15-20 knots. Sailing slowly on with the autopilot in control, I slept waking every hour or so. My speed was three or four knots which in headwinds is fine with me.

Thursday the wind went up to 20-22 knots ahead. I motorsailed into building waves. Late afternoon the sky cleared and there was a colorful sunset, a sign of better weather for the next day. The saying goes, "Red Sky at Night, Sailor's Delight; Red sky at Morning, Sailor Take Warning." (There is actually a valid explanation as why this tends to be true.)

After passing south of the Lau and Ogea Islands, southeast of Fiji, I was able to then head 20 degrees more north, and so with a favorable angle to the wind I sailed smoothly along without the engine.

Friday was the best, most glorious, fast, easy, downwind sailing ever for me. *Chyka* glided quickly along between the beautiful volcanic islands, Totoya and Matuku. There was a golden sunset with pale blue and pink all around to welcome me to Fiji. Strange it is, that in one passage I had experienced both the worst and the best times of sailing for me so far.

Fiji

During the whole of World War II, Patricia's father, Raymond Holtgrieve, was in the First Marine Division in the Pacific. Prior to the battle of Guadalcanal they practiced for the beach landing of it on Koro, one of the many small islands that surround Fiji. I am so sorry I never had the chance to get to know him.

Sunday I sailed through the entrance of the barrier reef to Momi Bay on the west coast and anchored. It was a remote place with no houses or other boats. All was quiet. I heard only birds.

At 5:00 PM I saw a sailboat entering. It came over close to *Chyka* and anchored. It was Dieter, whom I had known in Raiatea and Tonga. Incredibly, for any cruiser anywhere, especially for a German, Dieter had no detailed charts! So I agreed to lead the way for us the next morning up the coast to Lautoka, where we could clear in. After we did so, we sailed back down the coast and went into the comfortable Vuda Point Marina, where I stayed for a week.

Here in Fiji I was in Melanesia. The indigenous people are darker than Polynesians. Almost forty percent of the people are East Indian, being descendents of laborers brought here from India by the British to work on the sugar plantations.

Klaus Wall

Klaus was coming to join me for some cruising in the Fiji Islands. We had been coworkers and friends in Germany, and we had sailed from north of Venice into the Adriatic Sea and along the coast of Croatia. After I retired, we sailed with some of our German friends in the Caribbean Windward Islands.

My intention for us in Fiji was that Klaus and I would sail to a few of the Mamanuka Islands as well as the remote volcanic Yasawa Islands. The natives of the Yasawas are simple and poor. They live in small villages protected by the government; one needs a permit to go there. (This is similar to the situation of the Hill Maria aborigines in India I had visited many years before.)

It is a long way flying from Germany to Fiji. It took Klaus 35 hours.

We toured the west side of Fiji including a Hindu temple and the South Pacific Culture Center. There, so essential for the success of our trip, we were taught and we practiced how to properly present the traditional gift of kava root to the village chiefs of the Yasawa Islands. They make a mildly intoxicating drink from kava. During the practice ceremony we had to drink a cup of it. It was awful. But if you are not accepted into a village by its chief, you cannot stay or meet anyone there.

Klaus and I went to Lautoka to get the permit to sail to the Yasawa Islands and to buy the kava root. At lunch Klaus became afraid of the food, was upset at how dirty everything was in town, and that there were all these Indian people around. (Lautoka was a miniature Bombay with all of its color and energy.) Klaus worried about what might happen to us anchored out alone at remote places. It was culture shock. Our cruise was to be a learning experience for him.

Off to the Little Islands - August 6, 2003

After sailing west for three hours to the small island of Malolo Lailai, we moored in front of the luxurious resort, Musket Cove, and stayed two days.

I became a life member of the Musket Cove Yacht Club, an exclusive one. It says on the back of my membership card, that in order to qualify for life membership, "you must have sailed to or from a foreign port to Musket Cove, Malolo Lailai Island, Fiji." The nearest foreign port is about 300 miles away.

The cost of life membership is one dollar. I don't mean an American dollar. It's not that expensive. It's a Fiji dollar, about fifty American cents.

Sometime later I entered the exclusive Milwaukee Yacht Club and presented my card. I had invited Dave Barret to join me for lunch. You cannot do that unless you are a member of that yacht club or a member of some other recognized yacht club. They had a listing of such yacht clubs in North America and Europe, but not of the Pacific. They were so impressed that I was a member of some yacht club in the Pacific.

Dave was a senior member of the club. I had crewed for him many years before. Later he crewed for me on *Chyka* from Milwaukee to Lake Huron. My yacht club, not being a recognized one, Dave was sure they would not let me buy lunch.

I waited for him at the bar. When he joined me we went to the dining room, Dave grinning. To Dave's astonishment the hostess welcomed us with, "Oh, Mr. Holt, we are so glad you are visiting us. Your table is ready for you, Mr. Holt. We reserved the one for you with the best view of the harbor, please come this way, Mr. Holt." then quietly sideways, "Oh, hello Mr. Barret." Dave trailed behind shaking his head and rolling his eyes.

Patricia and I did it again at the St. Petersburg Yacht Club with friends of ours who are members there. And again it worked at the same club when Jack Oldenburg visited us in 2013.

Sailing from Musket Cove between narrow passages to Mana Island we ran hard aground on a reef under the surface of the water. There were only sketch charts of these islands, and they were often wrong. A tourist dive boat came by and pulled us off. I gave them two bottles of wine.

Entering the reef to anchor at Mana was an exercise of extreme caution. We motored at about two knots with Klaus looking out from the bow. He yelled back to me, "There is a mast ahead." I stopped the boat assuming he had spotted a sunken sailboat. But it was a navigation beacon. We were speaking German. The German word for both mast and beacon is the same.

The next day we sailed to Navadra Island. We anchored in such a beautiful place under high hills in 80 feet of water! Again I was glad I had learned how to deep anchor. We took *Li'l Chyka* to the beach for snorkeling. We rolled just a little, but it made Klaus sick. I gave him two Bonine tablets, probably too late to be effective. Klaus made cucumber and corn salad for dinner and I made ham pasta, but then he could not eat any of it and soon went to bed.

Sunday morning we sailed to Yalobi Bay on Waya Island, the first of the Yasawas, and anchored in calm waters. Klaus did not want to go ashore saying he was afraid of getting sick again. I went alone. There was a primitive beach resort for tourists staying in tents. I spoke with a few of the customers. Judging from what was there and the food they were getting, I think this resort was a fraud.

On the beach I found a stranded boat full of locals not knowing what to do. They had run out of gasoline for their outboard. So I gave them plenty of fuel to get back home.

I returned to *Chyka* and swam ashore to snorkel while Klaus wrote postcards. I made a pasta dish and he ate some. We talked about his life. Eva, his wife, whom Sonja and I knew, had left him, saying to him she needed a new life. Klaus said he was afraid to start a new relationship for fear of being hurt again. But soon after, Klaus and Heidelore became - and are still - loving partners.

Soso Village

We anchored, the only boat there, in front of Soso Village in the bay of Naviti Island, the largest of the Yasawa Islands. Behind us was a hungry looking reef with the wind and waves wanting to take us there. Klaus was worried. I explained to him that in such places and with strong winds I always power set the anchor, which then securely fixes the boat to the ground with an anchor and chain, both well oversized for a boat the size of *Chyka*.

It was through the reefs just north of this island in 1789 after the *Mutiny on the Bounty,* that Captain Bligh and 18 crew frantically rowed their 23 foot open launch to escape cannibals chasing them in canoes. From the mutiny to safety in Timor they traveled 4,200 miles in 47 days! Bligh had basic navigation instruments but no charts! He did have the advantage of having learned navigation under Captain Cook, who, of course, usually was sailing to where there were no charts yet made.

It was only early afternoon so we took *Li'l Chyka* to the beach. There we were greeted by about ten children. We could not go into the village, not yet having been accepted by the village chief. A pleasant young man, Ralolo, speaking perfect English, came to greet us. We arranged with him to meet the chief the next morning.

As planned, Ralolo met us at the beach. We asked if we could give candies to the children. No, not until we had been accepted. He took us to a place in the village, I don't know what to call it, a roofed platform. Four village elders were already seated on the floor waiting for us. We sat down with them. In front of us was a fancy upholstered chair for the chief. The elders spoke good English.

Ralolo and one of the village elders. In front of me is the presentation we had brought for the chief.

The Chief of Soso Village

The chief came and seated himself. He did not speak English. The ceremony was formal and mostly in Fijian. We presented him our offering of kava roots in the way we had been taught. I knew I had to place the kava on the ground in front of the chief, not handing it to him. We knew that we were to clap hands at certain times, I was not sure when, and that I had to give a little speech.

After the ceremony Ralolo gave us a tour of the village introducing us to people as we strolled along. The people were well dressed in colorful wrap-around dresses for the women and clean shirts and pants for the men. They were friendly, and most spoke some English. (Fiji had been a British colony.) They all seemed proud, speaking quietly while looking straight at us.

Soso was in the woods along the beach. Their houses were tiny, neat, and primitive. The yards, gardens, and pathways were beautifully maintained. There was no trash to be seen anywhere. Ralolo showed us their school and the church.

At night on *Chyka* I said, "Klaus, there are no lights in the village!" In the morning when ashore we learned they had run out of diesel fuel for the village generator. So I told Ralolo to come back with us to *Chyka* with empty fuel cans. I gave him enough diesel to certainly last the village until they could next send their boat to Lautoka for supplies.

Klaus was not happy with this kind of cruising. He had expected to be at a marina every night, as in Europe, where one can usually walk to a town and restaurants. He does not read books and so gets bored.

Back to Vuda Point

In two days we were there again. For Klaus it was a great relief. He now felt safe. Dieter was there. In the evening a bunch of German cruisers with Klaus and Dieter went for dinner at a bar somewhere. I declined to join them, wanting to give Klaus time to discuss things with the other German blue water cruisers. There was a western-movie-class bar fight that Dieter thought amusing. Soon Klaus returned to Germany.

Nine years later, Klaus sent me an email birthday greeting telling me, that for him our adventure in Fiji had been the best ever for him!

And so often it is in life, especially so during adventures, that we experience a dangerous or unpleasant time wondering, "Why in hell am I doing this?" Then later we remember that it was a moment of drama in our lives for which we are proud.

Returning to the marina whom did I see! It's Jack Oldenburg on *Vindela!* For one week we both prepared for our next passages, his to Vanuatu and mine to New Caledonia, a 240 mile long island located about 930 miles east of Australia. It belongs to France.

The marina office had good weather information and it looked OK to go. While checking out, they gave me a letter just received from my daughter, Karen.

An easy five hour sail brought me back to anchor in Momi Bay, where Dieter and I had first anchored in Fiji. The next morning after bacon and eggs, I put away supplies, reviewed more the cruising guide to New Caledonia, and did the prenavigation (what I call plotting a route and entering its waypoints into the GPS). I checked everything, relaxed, and was ready for the next morning's departure.

Six Hundred Fifty Miles to New Caledonia

Day One - E-12, so downwind. Smooth sailing.

Day Two - South wind and choppy seas.

Day Three - I had to reef down sails. This was made so much easier, by my now always having at least a single reef in the main.

Day Four - Smooth fast broad reach. Blue sky. Wonderful.

Day Five - SE-12, lovely broad reach gliding along at four knots. A sunset of pastel colors. Almost no swells.

Day Six - Approaching New Caledonia I took naps of only 30 minutes checking radar before going back to bed.

At 4:00 AM I was ten miles offshore, hove-to, and slept until dawn when I could see where I was going.

Day Seven - I sailed through the infamous Havannah Pass and was glad to get through it in one piece. There were strong currents driving Chyka sideways and reefs on both sides with wrecked boats on them. I anchored in Bonne Anse (Pleasant Cove in French.)

The weather the next day was really bad, so I gladly stayed put for another night before going on up the west coast to Noumea, the capitol of New Caledonia, arriving there on September 5, 2003.

New Caledonia

Guess what, folks! It's Captain Cook already again! He discovered this island on his second Pacific voyage in 1774 and named it New Caledonia. It reminded him of Scotland, which the Romans called Caledonia when England was a province of the Roman Empire.

The people are mostly Europeans. And there are the indigenous Kanak Melanesians. Being part of France, the official language is French. It was in September and well south of the Equator; the weather was pleasant, cool, and dry.

Noumea, is modern, cosmopolitan, and the most westernized city in the South Pacific. It is called the Paris of the Pacific. The Port Moselle Marina was super: facilities excellent, the staff friendly, and was right there in the city.

The day I arrived I met a most amazing sailor, Nils Bjoerkman. In 14 years he had sailed alone from Sweden to here in his tiny 21 foot sailboat *Peter Pan*. On his way he spent long times in Brazil and Panama. He was 74 years old, heavy, had a pony tail, and reminded me of Torben. I later learned he had been with Jack in Moorea.

Peter Pan was so small, that Nils could not even sit up straight inside. We spent a lot of time together.

Going to town from the marina, the first thing you see is a park. There is an impressive garden memorial with American flags thanking the USA for keeping the Japanese away from New Caledonia during World War II.

Noumea was our military headquarters in the South Pacific. The city districts still now had names like Motor Pool, Receiving, and Robinson. France was then unable to do anything to defend New Caledonia, having been defeated by Germany early in the war.

From here our navy, with significant help from the Australian Navy, was able to stop the Japanese advancing south to New Caledonia in the Battle of the Coral Sea just north of here. There were heavy losses of ships on both sides.

Mike Wetson

I met Mike at the airport September 19, 2003. We had planned to spend a month touring New Caledonia and cruising its islands.

When I joined Torrington International in Belgium in 1965, Mike was there and we worked together. He was then a bachelor and spent a lot of time with our family. I knew Mike would love New Caledonia. He spoke perfect French.

Violetta was the secretary at my boat yard on Raiatea. She was young, tall, beautiful, and charming. The marina here passed on to me a note from her, saying she had seen me in town, giving her local telephone number, and asking if we could possibly meet. New Caledonia is 2,800 miles from Raiatea. What a coincidence! She was here to visit her three year old son, who was living there with his father.

They and friends of hers joined us for a visit to *Chyka* and lunch. Violetta told me she and her boyfriend in Raiatea had purchased the 43 foot sailboat of my friend, Jean Claude Bocher, the man who had written newspaper articles about me in Raiatea.

Mike and I made a three day tour of the island with a rental car generously paid for by Mike. The plains and mountains reminded me of Wyoming. Spectacular winding roads led us through the mountains and along rocky coastlines. Twice we picked up a Kanak hitchhiker.

Nils made pea soup for us. Being heavy and normally eating a lot, I wondered, *how did he ever carry enough food for the long passages on little Peter Pan?*

Then in the morning he departed waving good-bye to us. His heart was bad and he had been seeing doctors here. Eventually he made it as far as Malaysia. There he had to give it up and return to Sweden.

Mike and I sailed south anchoring first at Ilot Maitre (Small Master Island). We went on for a six hour upwind motor slog to anchor two nights in Baie Ouie, a lovely quiet spot, no houses or people in view. *Chyka* was the only boat.

We anchored, the second time for me, in the cove called Belle Anse. *Li'l Chyka* brought us along the forested coast, into an inlet, and part way up a narrow stream they call New River. It was so shallow we had to raise the outboard and paddle along under the overhanging trees. We climbed up the 620 foot hill for a grand view of New Caledonia, the Havannah Pass, and the Isle des Pins (Isle of Pines) to where we were to sail.

We sailed through the Havannah Pass heading for the Loyalty Islands east of New Caledonia. But after the pass we had light wind on the nose with uncomfortable swells. We were getting nowhere, and with no safe anchorages on this side of New Caledonia, we returned back through the Havannah Pass. There we were met by a strong tidal current coming towards us causing turbulence. The sea was a washing machine. That was my third time and more than enough. Rather than do it again I would sail south and around the Isle des Pins. In the bay on the west side we anchored off a beach.

It was a nice sail to anchor with some 20 other boats in the Baie de Kuto of the Isle des Pins. On the way Mike asked, "Is it OK to pee off the stern?" I said yes, but only at anchor. (The reason is that most men lost overboard are found with their flies open.) After a while there was no Mike around. I quickly prepared to have the autopilot retrace our route to find him. But he was in the head (bathroom).

What Was for Dinner On Board *Chyka*?

My journal notes of what the crew and what the captain cooked during our time together yield an amusing contrast. Mike had lived for many years in France and Belgium and loved to cook. I was a mechanical engineer used to cooking simple meals. For me cooking was a required means to an end. Examples of what we cooked now follow:

Mike prepared *cassoulet, merguez algerian* with hot peppers, *choucroute garni*, pasta *aux poissons provincial*, steaks, and fried prawns with tournedos and French fries.

I made pasta with hot dogs, cucumber with tomato and pepper salad, spaghetti and hot dogs, canned ham with vegetables and mixed fruit, and fried hot dogs with spinach and rice!

The fresh water pump failed. I took Mike to shore so he could climb the mountain Pic Nga, which was too high for me, while I worked on the water pump.

Friday the wind was NNW 20-25 so right into our bay. The chop was too much for us to take *Li'l Chyka* ashore. We moved *Chyka* around to the Baie Kanumera on the other side of the island where we were well protected from the wind, and the water was calm. This was the third time I went from one side of an island to the other to escape bad winds. The next time was to be two days later.

The propane solenoid failed. I needed to go to Noumea to look for a suitable replacement. We bought food that does not need to be cooked and canned goods that can be eaten cold.

The next day the wind reversed again. We and most other boats went back around to the Baie de Kuto. We watched huge sea turtles around our spot surfacing to breath and look us over.

Twins Edwina and Teddo from *Desert Rose* came by to give us a written invitation to come to their beach birthday party the next afternoon when they would become 13 years old.

The party was great, about 35 boaties. Mike and I brought candies for the kids, hot dogs, snacks, and wine. Their dad, Mick, organized the BBQ, games, and when dark, a bonfire.

I flew to Noumea, where I bought the correct solenoid, did email, flew back, and installed the new solenoid, all in one day. Soon we were cooking with gas.

Damn! What's next? I wondered. The outboard died. The carburetor was plugged up. One thing after another: That's boating.

We sailed back north to the Baie de Prony and another quiet beautiful anchorage. We paddled up the river past ruins of the old penal colony used by France in the nineteenth century. At anchor, *Desert Rose* was near us. Teddo and Edwina came over to give us drawings and thank us for the candies. Great kids.

Later we sailed around to Baie Ngo. Sailboat *Shallong* was just leaving, came along side to tell us the anchorage was too rolly (where sailboats at anchor are rolled), and that they were turning back to Ouen. We went in anyway to look around, tucked in behind a spit of land, and were fine.

Noumea Again

At the slip next to *Chyka* was *Avalon,* Jim and Rosie Zoro. You will read about them often as we go on with this story.

After four days of visiting more sights in Noumea, Mike departed for home October 17, 2003.

Ellie on *Desparado* gave me a haircut. She had learned haircutting from Beverly in Tonga. Ellie knew the Island Packet people, Rob and Dee Dubin, whom I told you about.

It rained, and that was fine with me. I had quiet time to do jobs for the long passage ahead. I decided to land in Australia at Bundaberg, Queensland, and did the prenavigation to get there.

Jim and I went to an Internet café to check weather. We saw light or no wind out there for five days, so I thought I should not go and just drift. But in the evening I rechecked and then saw strong northeast winds after four days. I thought it would be good to catch them and decided to go.

I departed for Australia 930 miles away. Looking later at the chart of the entrance to Noumea I saw why it had been so complicated for me the times before, entering and departing. There was a cloud of tiny islands and reefs to negotiate. One marker was way off from the chart position, which caused me trouble the first time arriving.

The first days were pleasant sailing with spectacular sunsets. Other sailboats were talking on VHF radio complaining that the wind was too light. But I loved it. *Chyka* was a steady platform moving serenely along at about three knots. The only birds were boobies. They glide over the water looking for fish, as the shearwaters do.

Sixth Day - Hit by a Rogue Wave

If I had known about rogue waves, unusual, exceptionally high single waves, and what causes them. I would have understood what was developing and how to prepare for it.

The wind had shifted to NW 20-25 bringing to me fairly large waves from the north. Clashing into them from the opposite direction were large swells coming from a gale in the Tasman Sea - perfect conditions for the making of a rogue wave. And I was sailing perpendicular to both the waves and the swells, the worst possible direction.

Two months later I wrote from my notes:

> *As of 2:00 PM the wind had increased to 27 knots, which is not normally so troublesome, but the seas were rough and confused. Chyka, a boat that usually swims happily like a dolphin through the waves in heavy weather, was moving awkwardly, as if she had become timid, trying to pick her way with care, but being repeatedly surprised and stumbling.*

Around 6:00 PM I was in the galley when it hit. I was thrown across the boat, through the aft cabin doorway, and headlong into the cabin's hanging locker door. There I lay, wondering what had happened. There was blood everywhere.

I had a severe pain in my back. I was able to move my feet, so thank God my spinal cord was not broken. There were still 350 miles to go to Australia. I managed to heave-to, climb into my bunk, and sleep through the night.

The next morning I checked my *Onboard Medical Handbook*. It said I had a lumbar strain, that it would be painful, but that the structure of the back and the nerve system were probably OK. I managed to load ten gallons of fuel into the main tank from two of my jerry cans.

I was up to look around every 30 to 45 minutes. Getting into and especially out of bed was terribly painful. Every move was a struggle. Thunder storms from the northwest were predicted for the night. So I again hove-to to sleep through it.

Day Eight - Suddenly my VHF radio came alive. It was an Australian Coast Guard airplane calling me to find out where I was going. I told them my situation. They asked if I needed to be rescued. I said I thought I could make it, but that I would need help when I got to Bundaberg. The Coast Guard called me frequently from then on to check.

Day Nine - The wind was against me at 22 knots, so I motorsailed tacking into it. Without an autopilot I could not have done this. I loaded another ten gallons into the fuel tank. There was a strong wind warning from some office in Bundaberg. I thought I would be there before it happened.

Day Ten - October 31, 2003 - Approaching the coast I told the Coast Guard that I could not leave the cockpit to anchor or to dock. They instructed me to just sail to outside the Bundaberg Marina and that everything was arranged.

Australia

I heard on VHF that Jack and Torben, having been part of the Vanuatu to Bundaberg Rally, had just arrived with all the other boats. The marina was completely full. Still, I was sure the Coast Guard and the marina must have figured out how to help me.

I slowly approached the marina and stopped. A launch came out and tied up to *Chyka*. Crew jumped on board. They told me to do nothing except sit there and keep the steering wheel centered. The launch moved *Chyka* to a slip where about fifteen people including medical people with a gurney were waiting.

Usually, clearing in to Australia is an all day job. Now, Officials from the Quarantine, Customs, and Immigration departments all jumped on board. Papers flew, rapid loud stamping of documents, signatures scrawled, and in ten minutes it was done. While all that was going on, Elisabeth from the Bundaberg *News Mail* and a photographer interviewed me.

Jeff, the Marina Manager, drove me to a doctor. He gave me pain prescriptions and sent me to a hospital for x-rays. There I endured the most terrible pain for me ever while moving as the technician required.

Back on *Chyka*, the wind increased, as I told you was predicted, and then was howling. With my pain medication and some Scotch I went to sleep for the night. A few times I woke thinking I needed to get up and check things on deck. Each time I said to myself, *Henry, you don't need to do anything. This is your refuge. Just sleep.*

Jack Oldenburg and Torben visited. They had loved Vanuatu and had a rough crossing to here. I spent a lot of time with them. When people visited, I had to lie on my main cabin port settee, because sitting or standing was painful. However, I was told walking was good for me, so I could get to the marina showers.

Rosie and Jim, who had sailed first to another port south of here, finally arrived. They hauled out *Avalon*. Its steel hull had serious rust problems. They started the long job of removing all wooden parts, sandblasting the rust away, and painting.

After two weeks Jack came by to use my marina net connection to do email and to say good-bye. He was leaving the next day. The next time I saw Jack was in Thailand. Torben stayed.

Rob and Dee Dubin on *Ventana*, whom you know, arrived and took the slip next to me. She brought me the groceries someone in the marina office had bought for me. She is so pretty and kind. I was sorry they left soon after. Many others brought me gifts and food supplies.

New friends, Rene and Sabine, came by. I stood in the companionway for support as we talked. Knowing I was always in pain, she started to cry, and so they left. She brought me food the next day.

The report from the doctor was that I had a compression fracture of thoracic vertebra T8 and needed to see Dr. Van der Walt, an orthopedic consultant.

He was confident and thorough. We talked about all aspects of the problem and what I should do. It would not heal. I needed to return to the USA for a special, recently developed operation. But I could not travel by air until three months from the injury, and it had be with at least business class with the advantage of being able to recline to an almost lying down position. For the meantime he recommended an abdominal compression support. I went to town to have one fitted to me.

This modern marina had wonderful facilities. There were shops including a marine store, a mechanic, and a restaurant. They had weekly tent BBQ lunches on the house. Jeff was always ready to help. Samantha, a beautiful blond, brought me flowers from the marina and my daily mail and messages. Lee was the driver of the shuttle to town. Eventually Rosie took over the job of delivering my mail and messages from Samantha.

Christmas Eve

Rosie and Jim came by with three balloons, a card, and three gifts. We went with others to the marina restaurant for dinner. Rosie chose for me an excellent fish dinner. Torben's wife, Helle, was visiting. My back held up OK and I was happy to be able to sit there and enjoy dinner with them.

I flew to Milwaukee at the end of January 2004. I was glad to spend time with my family there. The operation, called kyphoplasty, was on March 23. Vicodin was great for me, and I was fine. There followed three weeks of physical therapy.

On my way to daughter Susan and family in Sarasota I visited Patricia at her condo on Treasure Island. Her daughter Amy was there. As when with Patricia many times before, I admired her but had no idea that she would ever someday want to be my wife.

I returned to Australia in late April. My physical therapist had told me to have massages for a month. Twice a week Christa came to *Chyka* to set up a folding platform in the main cabin to give me wonderful *Ka Huna* massages.

I spent time with the others including Jim and Rosie. They were still working in the really hot weather sanding and painting *Avalon*. I was busy getting *Chyka* loaded and prepared for the next passages. I waved good-bye to Torben from the dock as he departed north.

To the North End of Australia

From Bundaberg it was to be 1,200 miles, almost all of it inside the Great Barrier Reef to Thursday Island at the top of Australia. This reef is more than twice the length of the second longest reef in the world. I anchored or was sometimes at marinas 31 times over 56 days, and so way too many places to tell you about. When at anchor I was usually the only one. The trip required heads-up navigation to avoid islands, innumerable reefs, and trawlers at night.

I departed Bundaberg at midnight with only stars and no moon. In the morning I watched the pretty mountain coast go by. I had been too long ashore; my abdominal muscles hurt. It was good to feel again the alertness of a low level of adrenaline. I came to anchor in Pancake Creek at 3:00 PM.

From then on most of the way up the coast it was with a strong wind from the south as I sailed north. So I scooted along downwind usually requiring a double-reefed main and varying reefs of genoa and staysail as speed control.

I was sailing along one day on my way to Port Clinton. When approaching it, the Coast Guard radioed that the entire area was closed for military exercises for three weeks. Either I had to go back and wait all that time or go on to arrive somewhere in the dark.

I decided to go on to High Peak Island another 35 miles, described as suitable in settled winds, which now was not the case. I went anyway.

Winds were S 30-35 with rain patches. At nighttime the cloud cover darkened everything to black. Arriving, I could see only the vague, slightly darker shape of land. I swore that if I could not be sure of what I was doing, I would give up and heave-to to ride it out for the night. I rounded the west coast of the island and headed to what I thought from the chart must be a protected cove on the north side. I had programmed into the GPS the waypoint to the entrance of the cove from the cruising guide. It proved to be slightly inaccurate. It would have put me onto a reef. With infinite care I entered the cove unable to see anything but having confidence in my radar and my depth sounder.

From the tide program Jack had installed in my computer I knew I was coming in at high tide. That meant I had to allow for a drop of 14 feet! When I found the depth I wanted and in the middle of what the radar showed to be the center of the bay, I dropped anchor. The wind blew some, but the cove was protected from it and the waves. Wonderful. I was too tired to eat dinner. I brushed my teeth and went to bed.

The next day I wrote, "Every muscle complains and my hands are sore. I will rest here. This is the prettiest cove for me ever." (I think I say that often.) I stayed two days.

During the near gale winds, the port genoa sheet had escaped its rope clutch because I had neglected to tie a stopper knot at the end of it. It had then gone wild and snarled itself around the active starboard sheet ripping up the foot of the genoa. I trimmed and taped it hoping it would hold awhile until I could get it repaired.

The fresh water pump failed again. I wondered, why could it not have failed in all the time I was in Bundaberg Marina where repairing it would have been so much easier?

Then I realized it was not because of Murphy. The answer is that the boat motion when at sea stirs up sand and debris from the bottom of the water tank. The sand is then carried into the pump when water is turned on. (The same thing happens with dirt or water in the fuel tank, when sea motion stirs it up and it makes its way to the fuel filters, as happened to me later in this story.)

The coast is like that of New Caledonia. Hills descend steeply to the shores with pine trees and pretty pink and gray limestone cliffs.

After an overnight in the bay of tiny Cid Island just off Whitsunday Island I headed for Daydream Island. I had told daughter Susan I would visit the place. She and her friend, Debbie, were one time at the resort there, where Debbie met her future husband, Neville Croft, an Aussie who had a water sports business there. I had visited them twice when passing through St. Augustine on *Chyka*.

I motored all around Daydream Island to look at the resort but found no place to berth *Chyka* and so moved on to Abel Point Marina near Airlie on the main coast. Jack was then in Cairns further up the Coast. Torben was here.

Townsville

Having had a rough night anchored at Cape Bowling Green and now with winds predicted to become north at 30 knots for two days I went into the marina at Townsville.

I wrote then:

> *I really don't like this. It's too rough and cold. You cannot swim. Anchorages are rolly. Sailing requires constant adjustment to changes in wind direction and velocity. My muscles are still sore and my hands raw. I am worn out. It is not just*

my age. This coast is just an unpleasant cruising area. I often love and wonder at what I see and feel, but too often it is a struggle.

I had dinner at Molly Malone's Irish Pub. I asked the waitress if she knew about Molly Malone. She thought I didn't know and ran off to find out for me. She returned to tell me that no one there knew. Strange! They work there and apparently never thought about it, and Molly is mostly very popular in Australia.

At the end of the 19th century about one-third of the settlers in Australia had come from Ireland. In a Dublin street there is a large, bronze statue of pretty, busty Molly and her wheelbarrow. In 2013 there was a plan to move it to Melbourne, Australia for awhile. But as of 2014 it seems it probably won't happen.

Most of you will recognize at least some of these words from the Irish ballad:

In Dublin's fair city where the girls are so pretty
I first set my eyes on sweet Molly Malone.
She wheeled her wheelbarrow through streets broad
and narrow
Crying cockles and mussels alive, alive - oh

(Chorus):
Alive, alive - oh, alive, alive - oh
Crying cockles and mussels alive, alive - oh.

She was a fishmonger and sure 'twas no wonder
For so were her father and mother before.
They wheeled their wheelbarrows through streets broad
and narrow
Crying cockles and mussels alive, alive - oh

(Chorus)

She died of the fever and no one could save her
And that was the end of sweet Molly Malone.
Her ghost wheels her wheelbarrow through streets broad and narrow
Crying cockles and mussels alive, alive, oh

(Chorus)

On my way here I had thought about how often I had to use the engine when negotiating my way along and between reefs and islands. What if ever it would not start when needed? So here I rehearsed the emergency engine start procedure recommended by Island Packet Customer Service. (They helped me with technical problems all during the years I owned *Chyka*.)

What they told me worked, which gave me confidence in case I ever needed to do it. And soon afterward, I did.

Wolfgang and Inge on *Stella Maris* invited me for morning coffee. Stepping down into their main cabin, I was surprised to see sitting there a pretty blond woman looking at me. Her name was Maureen. She lived alone on her nearby boat. She was an interesting woman. She and her husband had spent years in the Kalahari Desert on a foreign aid program. We talked a lot.

Awhile later I was invited for drinks on *Stella Maris*. Maureen was again there. As she did before, she looked at me intently the whole time. She and I did most of the talking. I invited her to join me on the next leg up to Cairns. We agreed to discuss it on *Chyka* in the morning.

She came for coffee. She said she wanted a day more to think about it, was concerned about possible seasickness, and that she had only four or five days until she had to return, which I could not guarantee. (Being required to arrive somewhere at a certain time can be dangerous. You then feel obligated to sail out into possibly bad weather.)

Maureen and I were attracted to each other. It would have been so nice to stay and spend a long time with her. But I did not want to risk the circumnavigation, and Maureen could not have joined me on it.

In the evening she came again to *Chyka* for drinks bringing cheese and crackers. We talked for a long time. I invited her to dinner. It took her a long time to answer. She said no. I thought perhaps it was because she did not want to deepen our relationship, knowing I would leave the next day.

To Mourilyan Harbor

Anchored at Dunk Island I woke at 6:30 AM. As was normal with me, it took two hours to get ready to go. Before departure, there often was a navy shower (get wet, stop the water, soap, and rinse), shave, breakfast, clean up, check the latest weather on radio, review navigation and instruments, if need be hitch the hose to the deck wash to clean the chain as it comes up, clear decks for action, warm up Big Rudy, and raise the anchor.

In four days I was in Mourilyan Harbor and rested a day. I wrote, "These 20 to 40 mile day sails are good for me. I am never tired and love the coast hills and the mountains beyond. After arriving each time I have time to do jobs and plan for the next day."

One night I woke up thinking, *What would I do if I became blind?* I had never even thought of that before. So I practiced with eyes closed how to find the nav station VHF and activate the EPIRB, which would signal by satellites exactly where I was to the people responsible for the area.

Cairns

(The Aussies pronounce it *cans*.)

This is a major tourist and boating center located at the mouth of the Trinity Inlet. As I approached, calling the marina, Ingrid on *Harlequin* answered. They were just leaving. So sorry to miss them. But I spent time with them later in Darwin.

Wolfgang and Inge on *Stella Maris* also responded. They were just then returning back to Cairns with an engine problem, came in first, and helped me dock. We killed two bottles of my finest wine, which just happens to be the very cheapest Chardonnay in Australia. They had no news about Maureen.

I was often at the In-Box Internet Cafe. As usual in Australia the people were friendly. They taught me some special terms: The crowds of people who come up here from New South Wales to escape the winter are called Mexicans. The girls from New Zealand are Kiwi Chicks, and the pretty ones from this country are Aussie Sheilas or just Sheilas.

Power boaters next to *Chyka* introduced me to an attractive lady from Stuttgart looking for a ride to Darwin, which was a long ways. We spoke German, which I liked. She said she would cook for us and help in any way she could.

We might have been good friends. But my knowledge of cruisers picking up crews at random warned me. I did not know her at all.

It is difficult to judge how someone you do not know might behave under stress. I had learned this: After days of living in tight quarters, people not used to it can become frustrated. Under the additional stress of heavy weather and facing serious problems, people can react with courage, or they may flip out, making for dangerous situations. In long distance cruising one should not volunteer to take such chances.

After two days sailing north of Cairns, I crossed behind a freighter. I looked down and saw the depth sounder dropping suddenly to ten feet! Alarmed, I threw the engine into reverse to stop. *What was this?* I checked the chart. The seabed was deep all around.

The cause of the false reading was that the signals of the depth sounder, instead of going to the bottom, were bouncing off the turbulence created by the propellers of the freighter. It happened two times more during the trip, but at those times I then knew the probable cause.

I carefully entered the reef of Hope Island. It was here in 1770, before charts of the area were made, that Captain Cook's ship *Endeavor* ran onto this reef. They were just able to get the ship to shore and up a river to repair it.

There were two moorings and I took one. There was a yawl at the other. They departed but soon stopped at the entrance. I was worried they might have run into a 'bommy': That is what they call a coral head. Or perhaps there was an engine problem and they had anchored. I tried to call them on VHF. No response. I planned to stop by them on my way out the next morning, but then they were gone.

Late afternoon rounding Cape Bedford while preparing to go upwind into the bay to anchor, Big Rudy would not start. There was no time for the emergency start procedure. For the second time with no engine I sailed upwind to anchor.

The first time I did that was off Montserrat in the Caribbean. The propeller had caught a large Japanese fish net which tangled the propeller and stopped the engine. The sea was far too rough for me to swim and fix it. I had to drag the net under sail upwind fifteen miles into the smoke of Montserrat's then active volcano. Very late I hove-to just offshore to wait for dawn. Then I sailed, still dragging the net, into a quiet bay where I anchored. There I could go into the water with my snorkel equipment and free the prop.

Now back to the present. Quietly at anchor, I had time to investigate why the engine would not start. The booster solenoid had failed. I told you that I recently rehearsed the emergency engine start procedure, but sometimes when under way you don't have the time to do it. I rigged a cable connection I had on board since I started out from Milwaukee just in case of such a situation. With it I could start the engine by just turning on a switch in the aft cabin. And that was how I started the engine from there all the way to Singapore, where at last I was able to find a correct replacement booster solenoid.

And once more, it was Captain Cook! I came to anchor at Lizard Island where he climbed to what is called Cook's Lookout to search for a path through the reefs. Most of the shoreline was rock steeply plunging into the sea.

After six hours of lovely smooth sailing with double-reefed main and staysail, I rounded Cape Melville expecting light winds in its lee. Instead it blew 30-35 knots with choppy seas. I could not leave the helm to take in more sail, because the autopilot was overwhelmed; it did not have the strength to steer into the heavy seas. And there was no open water to heave-to because there were nearby islands to avoid.

At last as I approached the bay, I was able to take in all sails and motored into the bay to anchor. *Can I go on like this? I am so exhausted.*

I stayed an extra night to rest.

Cape Melville is an out-of-the-way national park. Only four-wheel drive vehicles can handle its rough dirt roads. And even then it is risky, as no help is available. The shore is mostly hills of huge smoothly rounded boulders. I have not been able to find a good explanation as to how their round shapes developed.

Due to a lack of upcoming places to stop I prepared for an overnight sail. For this I rigged the radar reflector, difficult to do with the wind still gusting up to 35 knots. The next morning it was a job to raise anchor with such a wind. It required repeatedly engaging the engine in forward for some seconds, jumping forward to bring in chain, then back again to the wheel and engine controls.

The overnight to Night Island was downwind but difficult due to there being no naps allowed by *Chyka's* captain. The Great Barrier Reef was closing in. There was too much to watch for, islands, reefs, rocks, only a couple of cargo ships, but scores of brightly lit trawlers. It's hard to know what to do with them. They drag along in loops never keeping a course. One of them, thinking sailboats should not be allowed anywhere, came alongside then barged ahead right into my path so that I had to jibe to avoid hitting him.

This was the Cape York Peninsula which points north off the northeast corner of Australia. The peninsula is amazingly remote. The general map shows almost no roads. No one lives here, so there are no shore lights. There was no moon. At night I was sailing blind. Thank God for charts, GPS, and radar. They and the depth sounder were all I had to guide me.

By 8:00 AM I was anchored at Night Island, the only boat as usual. At last the weather was pleasant, the wind was gentle, there was no rolling, and the water was warm enough for swimming. The only sound was the cooing of the Torris Strait Pigeons, all white with black tipped wings. This was the first peace and quiet since Cairns two weeks before. For three days I slept a lot, read some, and swam.

Crocodiles - A Coast Guard Warning

I woke the third morning to see a Coast Guard Cutter anchored next to me. As expected, at 8:00 AM crew came over in a large inflatable launch with two huge outboards.

Many cruisers are annoyed and afraid of any country's coast guard inspections. Not me. The visit by the U.S. Coast Guard off Puerto Rico had been fun. I will always be grateful for the help given me by the Australian Coast Guard when I injured my back. And during this visit I learned from these people something critically important.

After finding my papers in order one of them pointed to my snorkel mask and asked, "Sir, you haven't been swimming here, have you?"

"Yes, I had a wonderful swim yesterday."

Then his answer, "Sir, you must not swim here or anywhere in this area. The salties (saltwater crocodiles) and sharks are everywhere. A saltie attacked someone right here last week."

I said, "I had thought this island would be too far off the coast for them."

I later found out that salties are the largest of all living reptiles and swim long distances out to sea. Along this coast only one or two people per year are killed by them. That low number is because the rule against swimming is so widely enforced.

Of course, the fresh water pump failed again. After three hours I gave up trying to fix it and replaced it with the new Sureflow pump I had purchased in case of this. The original was finally eaten up by Panama sand that came with the water there.

At Portland Roads there was one other sailboat. It was *Odyssey* manned by the Texan we all had known in Noumea, Steve. He spoke loudly and confidently, but his cruising was one long mess of everything going wrong, none of which could ever have even possibly been his fault!

In the morning Steve departed before I did. We both had 50 miles to go to Margaret Bay. I soon passed him. We could only talk on Channel 16, because his VHF was not working well. His GPS got wet somewhere and wasn't working. He was going too slowly. It was a long way to go before dark. I suggested he put up more sail, but he did not.

Late afternoon I anchored comfortably, had a sundowner, and waited for Steve to round the cape. A half hour before sunset I called him. He said he was on his way in. Night falls quickly near the equator. I told him I would have my bright foredeck light on for him. Like a ghost ship in the dark *with no navigation lights on,* he followed my light into the bay and anchored next to me.

How did this man ever make it this far? There was no helping him. He did not consider any suggestions. I never saw him again or heard anything more about him, and I wonder what happened to him.

There were then four day-sails from there to the top of Australia. After Bushy Islet I anchored in a special, quiet place up the Escape River with nothing there but woods. I thought it looked like what most of our East Coast rivers would have in the 17th century.

The Top of Australia

I had worried about currents, rocks, reefs, and commercial traffic when entering the Torres Strait. But it was easy, and at 5:30 PM *Chyka* glided in to anchor off the tiny town on Horn Island. Here anchoring is far better than off nearby Thursday Island, the main town.

This for sure could have been another movie set for a Josef Conrad novel. I wrote, "One day's sail from Queensland and I seem to be in the East Indies."

Thursday Island is the administrative and commercial center of the Torres Strait area having a population of around 2,500. Every day I took the short ferry ride over to Thursday Island. The ferry looked like the *African Queen* with a flimsy second deck put over the top of it.

In the 1951 movie *The African Queen* with Humphrey Bogart and Katharine Hepburn, they puttered down a narrow West African river during World War I in the *African Queen*, a pathetic, broken-down, old mess of a boat.

First I cleared in. Even though I had not left Australia, and this was Australia, I still had to. I needed a cruising guide or some information about the north coast of Australia. I had tried since Bundaberg to find something about it and could not. I thought, surely, there must be lots of books about it here on Thursday Island with so many boats heading to the north coast from here. I asked everywhere around, the officials, a news agent, and the library. There was nothing.

Neighbors joined me on *Chyka* for a BYOB evening. I saw children swimming off the beach, which I thought showed it must be safe from the salties. The next day I happened to mention to someone that I would swim. The reply was, "Good God, do *not!*" I was then told that the children had lookouts posted for the salties. With a blow of a whistle the kids would be out of the water in one second.

Jack emailed me suggestions for three places to anchor he had liked on his way to Darwin. He must have found them somehow on the Internet as he was a computer wizard. The company he owned in Sweden consulted other companies about computer systems.

I planned to leave the next day but first needed groceries. On Horn Island I found that the small store there had all I needed, tomatoes, cucumbers, eggs, English muffins, cheese, and bread.

To The Wessel Islands - 335 Miles

I timed departure to avoid the contrary current. So instead of it, I caught the current going west and sailed through the reefs between Horn and Thursday Islands zipping along at 11 knots over ground!

By late morning I was out into the loving arms of the Arafura Sea. It is called the reward to all those who have crossed the Pacific. The wind was perfect, ESE 10-12 with smooth seas. I had all three sails out gliding along smoothly.

And so it went for four days sailing across the top of the Gulf of Carpentaria. The sunsets were pretty. The moon was almost full, so I could see all my sails clearly at night. I often received calls from Coast Guard airplanes. They were on the watch for people trying to cross over from New Guinea. It was always nice to talk to them.

On day four I rounded the north end of the largest of the Wessel Islands and anchored in Two Island Bay recommended by Jack. It could be a place in the Bahamas with limestone hills and even casuarina trees everywhere. But there were no houses, no people. The water was turquoise.

A swim was called for. I was then so far from Queensland that I thought it must be safe to swim. But when looking at the chart of the area I found that nearby were Crocodile Island and Shark Point!

I stayed another day to change engine oil, clean sand out of the water pump, as usual, and rest. A second boat was there. The man had fished and brought over two fish fillets.

On to Darwin

August 3, 2004. My 70th Birthday. And what a special one!

In perfect, warm weather I departed and sailed west. Darwin was about six days away. The wind was E-10. I sailed wing and wing doing three to four knots. Brunch was the fish fillets, fried, with cheese, an apple, anchovy-stuffed olives, and a beer.

Then, what a gift! About eight pilot whales came from behind and followed just off the stern of *Chyka* for awhile. It was wonderful.

Two nights later a ship full of lights ten miles ahead suddenly turned off all lights. They called. It was the Australian warship *Melville* with which I had spoken before. They wanted my course and speed. After they passed me they turned all lights back on. Strange.

I was lucky to catch the south tidal current between Melville Island and the Coburg Peninsula to bring me into the Ian Dieman Gulf and to Cape Don where I anchored in Alcaro Bay, recommended by Jack. With its limestone cliffs and forest all around, it was like Tonga's Vava'u Group #7 from where we all had visited Swallows Cave.

I was really tired again, and it's no wonder. Four nights with only short naps due to potential traffic was too much. I should have hove-to, put on the anchor light and slept a few hours at least. Later I did that often.

Another lesson learned: I needed to be more careful of my knees. They were sore. I was too often up and down the steps from the main cabin to the cockpit. So from then on, I planned to use my arms and handholds to help lift me up, and to not make more such up and down trips than necessary. It worked. Observing this lesson for the rest of the trip, I had no more knee problems.

Sailing around here, and later on this trip, I needed to consider carefully the timing of tidal currents, which run up to six knots, with you or against you. Also of importance, especially when anchoring, is the tidal change in depth of up to 18 feet! So if you anchor at high tide and draw five feet, you need to anchor in at least 25 to 30 feet of water.

Having slept 14 hours I was up in time to leave at 7:00 AM and catch the south tidal current. My next stop was Cape Hotham, also suggested by Jack. With the help of the current I started out doing eight to nine knots over the ground. It was 64 miles which I did in only 10 hours! I felt great all day, but after the anchor was down I was again exhausted.

To leave in the morning would have required getting up at 4:00 AM due to the current, which I could not do. So I stayed another day.

Incredibly I ran out of sugar, and later out of beer. *Who the devil on my crew was in charge of stocking essential provisions? It's against regulations!* I only half learned my lesson. I never again ran out of sugar, but one time later I did run out of beer.

Darwin

I anchored off the city anchorage with many other boats. Before being allowed to go near land, *Chyka* had to be checked for mussels inside and out. A Fisheries man did that the next day. He then drove me to town, where I had brunch, a haircut, and did shopping.

A little north of Darwin was Tipperary Marina. The owner, Peter, on VHF talked me up the river and into the entrance lock, which raised *Chyka* ten feet and into his little marina.

Wolfgang and Inge were there with a friend of theirs, Hubert. He cooked lamb chops for the four of us, and we ate our meal on the marina terrace. We were later joined by Ingrid and Norbert, mentioned before. It was nice we could all speak German, because Norbert spoke very little English.

On Friday Peter hosted a Marina BBQ. Peter called on each of us to tell our stories. I sat with Alf and Sally from Norway.

I was there for two weeks. I often walked to town to do email, shop, and sometimes have lunch in the pleasant beer garden of the tavern called Rorke's Drift.

One day walking to town I stopped at a small marine store. There I happened to see a display of Sureflow water pumps, one of which I told you I had recently installed.

How very fortunate for me, and here of all places! Right there were displayed water filters that attach to the intake side of their pumps. I had not known they existed. I installed one the next day.

From then on, whenever I saw the water begin to flow a little slowly, I cleaned sand out of that filter. Eventually I had to do it seldom and then never more as the last of the sand from Panama came through. I did have another new pump on board ready, but it never was needed.

On August 24 I departed for Indonesia. I first sailed north to Fanny Bay, my getaway point, from where I could look back and see the high buildings of Darwin. I planned to leave early to go out into the Timor Sea.

Battery Problem

As I was dropping anchor in Fanny Bay I noticed the windlass was operating slowly. When it became dark I turned on a cabin lamp. It immediately became dim. All other lamps then failed. I tested all my batteries with my volt meter. The three house batteries were stone dead. I had not known they were failing, because I had been on shore power at the marina.

I had a separate battery dedicated to only starting the engine. There was a switch to connect that battery to the house circuits. With it, and having shut off the dead house batteries, I was able to have the anchor light on for the night, one cabin light, and still have power left to start the engine in the morning. It was fortunate this happened so close to Darwin to where I could easily return and find new batteries.

Early morning I locked into Darwin's Cullen Bay Marina, where the day before I had refueled. It is a pleasant marina with shops, bars, and restaurants. When I first came to Darwin the lock to it was closed for repairs.

I had three new house batteries delivered. There were no new batteries exactly the same size as the old. Again, I had to redo the carpentry of the battery compartment. (Batteries on an ocean sailboat must be tightly secured into position including above them in case of a rollover.) These Group 27 batteries are not like your car batteries. They are much larger and weigh almost twice as much. We had tested the engine start battery and it did not need to be replaced. And in case it would fail, I had another switch dedicated to allowing the house batteries to start the engine.

On to Indonesia

After two days of mostly motorsailing into a light breeze, I hove-to 130 miles into the Timor Sea for the night. There in the middle of this huge sea, I was more comfortable than in most Queensland anchorages.

The anchor light was shorting out. No problem. Al had made for me a portable cockpit light which I rigged as an anchor light off the boom. I slept all night. The rest of the way was easy light wind day-sailing. I hove-to each of the four nights the rest of the way.

I entered the harbor of Kupang, capitol of West Timor. There were many local African Queens and lateen rigged sailboats. I anchored. It was really hot. First thing was to put up the tarps, the larger one over the boom covering the main cabin and the smaller one over the staysail boom protecting the forward cabin.

To think I even doubted at all if I should spend so much money in Raiatea to have the lady make those tarps! In the tropical sun they lowered the interior temperature of *Chyka* by about ten degrees. And with them you can usually leave the hatches open when it rains.

Here in Kupang, Captain Bligh and his crew in their 21 foot open launch landed, at last, after their 41 day epic ocean ordeal starting with what I hope you have read in *Mutiny on the Bounty*.

My agent to arrange clearing in was Napa Rachman. He was also the Harbor Master. With only *Chyka* and seven other sailboats, he didn't have much to do. He had a VHF radio, but it did not work. He had no boat, so we few visiting cruisers had to dinghy him to our boats from the beach and back.

The people were friendly and helpful. But the city was a mess with so many buildings falling apart. Traffic was tightly packed with speeding mopeds and streams of bemos (minivan busses) all constantly blowing their horns. With no traffic lights to interrupt the flow, crossing a street was a dangerous challenge. The sidewalks were too narrow or nonexistent. Anyway, they were difficult to use with crowds blocking them while waiting for the bemos.

When going into town I always had to hire one of the boys to guard *Li'l Chyka*, which cost me about one dollar a day. Napa went with me to arrange that some boys would help me load four of my diesel jerry cans at the gas station and haul them back to the beach and onto *Li'l Chyka*. He came back to *Chyka* with me to have tea.

Karl, a German single-hander, sometimes rowed over to talk, one time with Napa, who had more papers I had to fill out.

After three days in Kupang I departed and enjoyed an easy two day overnight sail on the Sawu Sea finally deciding to settle into the quiet bay of Ende on the south coast of Flores Island. I stayed there two nights to rest and do engine maintenance. *Chyka* was the only boat.

What a pretty setting it was with the little town and its children playing on the beach! Behind the town rose the dramatic view of green hills ascending steeply up to sharply peaked mountains over 7,000 feet high and clearly in view! Sometimes children came out in small boats to say hello.

The only thing I did not like were the prayer calls. Indonesia is mostly Muslim. Their prayer calls are a sort of dissonant yodeling, always piercingly amplified from the minarets of mosques, up to five times a day.

Prayer calls annoyed me in otherwise pleasant places through much of Indonesia, Malaysia, and Egypt. Of course, Muslims must appreciate the calls. But it is hard to imagine that they are as charmed by them as we are by the sweet melodic ringing of church bells.

Often, after some serious action on deck in heavy weather, I would find a wound and have no idea how it happened. Now I had a large cut on my right leg that had not healed after ten days, even though I had cleaned and bandaged it regularly. It became infected and swollen. So I took Cipro twice a day for six days. Then it started to drain and build new skin. I continued with Cipro five more days.

From now on through Indonesia to Thailand, I will not describe the sailing conditions unless there is some exception to the normally light air weather and the occasional need to reef down with increasing wind.

Rinca Island

Another overnight sail on the Sawu Sea brought me to this remote tropical fjord. No one lives here: It is part of Komodo National Park. There were only quiet waters and steep, wooded mountains around. I swam and snorkeled.

I did not go ashore, but from the cockpit I saw monkeys and two wild pigs. All was quiet. The only sounds were of the gentle wind, the distant surf on the rocky shore, and birds. At sunset I put on a sweatshirt. One mosquito appeared, the first one in a long time. He won't be around here any more.

Five young boys came up to *Chyka* in a small African Queen with an ancient one lung engine. They tied up to the stern of *Chyka*. One of them was cooking their dinner over an open fire in the stern. They were here to catch shell fish and offered me some. Using sign language they begged for whatever I could give them. They wanted to come aboard, which I did not allow, but I gave them what they requested: shirts, crackers, and sugar.

The strait between Rinca and Komodo Island was turbulent. I tried to time the trip to catch a favorable current, which helped, but not much. Entering the bay I was met by some men in an ancient boat. They told me to follow them to the "best place to anchor." It ended up being two miles from the pier of Komodo Park Headquarters. I realized they wanted me over there so I would pay them to take me back and forth. So I declined and motored over to anchor *Chyka* just in front of the park pier. As was becoming increasingly common, *Chyka* was the only boat anchored here.

Ashore I checked in at Park Headquarters. There was an English speaking staff of 20 people in a small community, a small mosque, a snack bar, one sleepy Komodo dragon, and a few, mostly tame deer. Tourist boats brought visitors here during daytime.

Komodo Dragons

Komodo Park is home to the Komodo dragons, huge monitor lizards up to ten feet long and 330 pounds. They are strong and fast, making them good at ambushing their victims. Their saliva is venomous. They eat deer, pigs, horses, monkeys, water buffalo, other smaller dragons, and occasionally a human being. They swallow their victims whole up to the size of a goat taking 15 to 20 minutes to do so. The smell of dead or dying animals attracts them from as far as six miles away. They fear no other animals.

A short time before, a tourist was eaten by a dragon. Contrary to instructions given to all visitors, he had gone into the interior without a guide.

Two guides escorted me and another man into the park. Dragons have a fear of long sticks, and our guides had long pointed poles to defend us in case of trouble. We climbed a steep hill for a view of the forested hills.

After taking a picture, I saw a dragon a little below and behind a bush. The guides said I might climb down to get a good picture of him. Doing so I slipped on loose gravel and fell in front of the dragon cutting open a two inch long, deep wound below my right elbow. We all were concerned that the smell of blood would interest the dragon, but he must have already had his breakfast and did not move.

Back in headquarters they wanted to take me on a boat to a larger island to see a doctor. I refused and went back out to *Chyka*. There I cleaned the cut carefully, treated it with iodine, and started taking Cipro. Being a deep cut I left it open with protective bandaging which I changed every day. It was amazing to see how in time it gradually came together and finally healed completely.

Komodo Park Guides and Henry

The next day my guide, Jack, short for Jakarias, took me into the hilly forest of the park for an incredible three hour walk. Because the forest was thin, we could see wildlife fairly far into it: green jungle fowl, at least forty deer, many wild pigs, orchids, pigeons, cockatoos, and four dragons, one of them plodding along across our path ahead of us.

This Komodo dragon is about nine feet long.

During my days there, I often visited Eustis, the park ranger in charge. He always had time for me and enjoyed talking about anything, including politics, American or Indonesian. Eustis was young and spoke perfect English. His grandparents would have spoken Dutch instead. Indonesia was a colony of Holland until 1949.

The weather was perfect, warm and dry. Anchored alone in calm waters just offshore of Park Headquarters surrounded by steep hills, I relaxed using my wound as an excuse to stay and enjoy it all longer.

Four Days To Bali

From here north through the Linta Strait and then west over the north coast of Flores Island, there were difficult currents and confusing eddies.

Fortunately, I had the track feature on my autopilot. With this, *Chyka* could follow the exact direct line from one waypoint to the next in spite of side currents and wind variations.

An overnight sail brought me to Kananga on Sumbawa Island. Here again, I was reminded of the Bahamas. There were goats, chickens, dogs, and children on the beach. After a nap I swam. Then it rained pleasantly.

Next was Medan Island, described in the cruising guide as being an idyllic anchorage. The author must have never even entered it. Although from one mile out it seemed to be a postcard pretty beach, I found the bottom of what he called an anchorage to be only rocks and coral reefs. I tried anchoring in the only possible place far from shore. The anchor chain was pulling on rocks and there was a sunken reef downwind I had not seen.

Staying here was not a good idea. So off I went for another overnight sail. The wind was a perfect NE 15-20 as I went on into a fine sunset with shearwaters entertaining me.

The next morning I rounded Penny Purnawati's favorite resort island, Gilli Trawangen and went on to anchor in Lombok Island's Teluk Komal Bay.

Penny had lived with us in Wisconsin one year as an exchange student from Indonesia. A few years later she visited us. We have been well in contact all these years. I visited her in Jakarta soon after this, as you will read.

For days I had been studying the crossing from here to Bali. It is not easy because of the strong tidal currents. Here again, correct timing is essential.

Leaving at 6:00 AM I had to watch out for the many early morning fishermen all over the place in their narrow double outrigger canoes, which they row, paddle, or sail with a lateen rig.

I had timed the crossing well. Off the coast of Bali I was sailing five knots through the water with a five knot following current, so ten knots over the ground. Trying to sail or motorsail in the opposite direction at that time would have been impossible.

Bali

It is amazing how often I ran into old friends along the way. Here at the Bali Marina were Ingrid and Norbert, the Germans of my times in Australia, Rene and Sabine from Bundaberg, and three others I had met before. Our reunion was at the lovely bar overlooking the marina.

A local driver, Mahdee drove me up through hills and villages to a terrace restaurant overlooking Lake Batur, Mt. Batur Volcano, and beyond it the other sharp peaks of Bali. These would be respectable mountains in our Rocky Mountains viewed from the 5,000 foot level of Denver. But here, from a short distance away they soar up right out of the sea to over 10,000 feet!

We stopped at a tourist shop. I bought a hat. It fit well and was completely in the Indonesian style. Later, on *Chyka* I looked at the label and read, "Made in USA."

Returning to the marina we stopped at Mahdee's mother's house to meet her and her brother. Although most of Indonesia converted to being Muslim, the island of Bali remained solidly Hindu. Her house, like most others in Bali, had a tiny Hindu temple in the yard.

Near to the marina is the beach resort town of Kuta. In October 2002 two nightclubs packed with tourists were bombed killing 202 people and injuring 240. It was the work of the violent Islamist group of al-Qaeda called Jemaah Islamiyah.

I explored the shops of Kuta, did email, had a back massage, and visited the nearly completed Terrorist Victims Memorial.

Later Torben docked at the marina. We had dinner with Joe, whom I had met in Muscat Cove, Fiji, and others.

An Overnight to Kangeon Island

Departing early, I sailed back north, staying as close to the coast of Bali as I dared, in order to catch the countercurrent. (Often strong offshore currents produce small currents along the coast going in the opposite direction.) That actually added one to two knots to *Chyka's* downwind speed for most of the day.

Silent Runner had departed just ahead of me. They started out heading north. But they went out too far going into where the current would be strongly against them. I tried to call them on VHF. They did not answer, being true to the name of their boat.

When about 20 miles north of Bali and clear of local boats I was able to take brief naps.

Kangeon Island is between the Bali Sea and the Java Sea. *Chyka* spent two nights anchored alone in the lovely quiet bay just off the village. If this had been in the Caribbean, there would have been 50 boats with plenty of room for all. There was a pleasant spicy smell of the island, a combination of vegetation, wood fire smoke, and the seashore. I reorganized, prepared charts, planned the future, rested, and swam off the boat.

The only negative was the prayer calls screaming out five times a day. There were two mosques there. They competed with each other as to which of them could annoy me more. I was able to mostly drown them out with CD music.

350 Miles in Five Days to Serutu Island

That is only 70 miles per day. The reason why so few is that I hove-to every night, not being able to see the constant traffic of fishing boats. They are built of light wood and so do not show up on radar. They do not use standard navigation lights and don't know how to use VHF. Anyway, I enjoyed getting lots of sleep.

Chyka stayed anchored off Serutu for two days. The last night there, a menacing thunder and lightning storm came directly towards *Chyka*. I shut down the circuit breakers killing all electrical systems that could have been destroyed by a lightning hit. The only lamps remaining were battery lamps and my emergency, battery powered anchor light.

Six Days - 320 Miles to Batam Island

I crossed the South China Sea. There was either light or no wind. A current constantly drifted *Chyka* south. If I had lost the engine, I would have ended up anchored off reefs far to the south to await, perhaps for many days, a helpful wind. Each night I hove-to. I worried about fuel. I kept five gallons in one jerry can as an emergency reserve only to be used to avoid dangers and get me in and out of tight places. Then I would have dealt with light wind sailing and no power, the way all sailors had to do until modern times.

On October 15, 2004 I crossed back to north of the equator. I wrote that I was "motoring smoothly over a mirror-like sea joining a cloudless sky of the same light blue."

At night a large faster sailboat came up from behind. It would have been a collision. I called on VHF, but they must have been asleep. I had to go sharp to port and let them pass. Good thing someone was awake!

Batam Island

Finally I came to Nongsa Point Marina on Batam Island. It had been 1,100 miles in 18 days since Bali.

This small island is about 60 miles northeast of Sumatra. From *Chyka* the tall buildings of Singapore were in view 20 miles to the northwest. Most cruisers on their way north stop here to clear out of Indonesia. (To clear out is to get permission from the officials to depart a country.) I arrived with only eight gallons of diesel.

Chyka rested here five weeks. Norbert and Ingrid were here, of course, and others showed up including Torben. We all spent happy hours at the marina terrace restaurant. One night Torben entertained everyone there playing his clarinet, as you know he likes to do. I often went with the ferry for day trips to Singapore.

Singapore

Singapore is a modern city-state with the third highest per capita income in the world. Most of the people are Chinese. There are beautiful parks and large department stores. In a huge book store I had my pick of travel books for all the places I planned to visit. The streets were the cleanest I have ever seen anywhere. I never saw anything like a single cigarette butt or a scrap of paper on the ground. The reason for this is that the law against littering is effective. The first offense costs $50, the second $500, and the third costs you a Saturday working in the parks. So no one litters. Wonderful!

I had been in Singapore in 1962. The only building I recognized now was the colonial-style Raffles Hotel built in 1887 under the British, described in novels by Kipling and Somerset Maugham. Now I had my second drink at the Raffles Bar, the first having been 42 years before.

I took the train to Kuala Lumpur, the capitol of Malaysia, 300 miles north of Singapore. The most striking sight is the super modern styled Petronis Twin Towers, the tallest *twin* towers in the world at 1,183 feet. (They always were, before and after the destruction of the World Trade Center with its twin towers of 1,368 feet.) The city is a mixture of Muslim influenced, modern, and British colonial buildings.

Jakarta

Some days later I flew to Jakarta to visit Penny Purnawati, our exchange student I mentioned before. Penny was still full of fun and love. Now she had additional poise and confidence. Her husband was Ricky. She apologized for not having corresponded enough with Sonja and me, but cherished memories of Sonja, her "Mummy" and the rest of us. I was her, "Daddy," and I still am.

We three had dinner at the classic old Café Batavia in Kota, the original Dutch port near Jakarta. The next morning I had breakfast at Penny and Ricky's apartment overlooking Jakarta. Then being so interested in the history of Indonesia, I returned to Kota.

Kota - Later Called Old Batavia and Old Jakarta

In 1603 the Dutch established a trading post here. As the Dutch colonized Indonesia, Kota was their capitol. Europeans called it, "The Jewel of Asia." From here the Dutch expanded their control to all of Indonesia's vast archipelago of some 14,000 islands, spreading over about the same width as that of the USA. Josef Conrad's novels describe life in those remote islands of long ago.

Years before, Penny had given me the marvelous *Buru Quartet*, a historical novel in four volumes telling of life in Java under the Dutch. It was written by Pramoedya Anata Toer during the ten years he was in prison on remote Buru Island during the Suharto regime.

In the middle of Kota was a canal with an Amsterdam-style drawbridge and old Dutch buildings everywhere. The scene of it looked like a Van Gogh painting. After visiting the Watch Tower and the Maritime Museum, I went back to the Café Batavia, where we had been the night before, and had a beer.

The café looks over an open square to a beautiful white bell-towered hall built in 1627. It was the seat of the Dutch government in Indonesia and is now the Jakarta History Museum. Its exhibits were for me so interesting.

That night we had a farewell dinner at a traditional Jakarta restaurant.

Back at the marina on Batam Island, I installed the new booster solenoid I had purchased in Singapore and then could start the engine by just turning the ignition key, for the first time since Australia. The parts I had ordered from West Marine arrived, as well as 90 charts from Bluewater Books and Charts.

The Malacca Strait runs over 500 miles northwest of Singapore between Sumatra and Malaysia. It has heavy freighter traffic, so one must sail outside the shipping channel. Most cruising sailors choose the Malaysian side. After leaving Batam Island, I crossed over to that side. Then the challenge was to avoid fish nets and fishing boats. My first stop was the bay of Kukup Island off Malaysia. Sumatra was clearly in view across the strait about 25 miles to the southwest.

A Sumatra Southwest Squall

In the morning the wind turned from northeast, normal at that time of year, to southwest. Then it quickly built to gale force blowing into my bay from Sumatra. I couldn't believe it. I checked my cruising guide. It said this was a Sumatra southwest squall, that they occur rarely, but that when they do they last three hours. It did exactly that.

The shore was behind. Steep waves were pitching *Chyka* violently, the foredeck bobbing between being under water and high in the air as the anchor chain yanked on *Chyka*. Either this would cause serious damage on board, or the anchor would be pulled out. I let out most of the anchor chain with a long snubber line, which is a strong nylon line attached part way down the chain and cleated on deck. Nylon rope stretches, so a snubber line acts as a shock absorber.

I worried that the snubber line might fail so I rigged another. The first one did break. I backed up number two with a third to also share the load. Past that I could do no more, because putting on another snubber would have required letting out more chain, and I didn't have more.

The work was exhausting. Several times I tried to rest below. But each time I did, I heard a crash or some strange noise and so crawled up and forward on deck again to see about it. Doing so repeatedly was a struggle with waves boarding and the driving rain. Of course, I was always attached to the boat by a jackline. My strength was running out.

At last the wind died. I wanted to stay and sleep all day. But the steep remaining waves were still coming in rolling *Chyka* dangerously. With no wind there was no way to point *Chyka* into the waves to stop the rolling while being at anchor.

I picked up the anchor and headed out. With her sails up keeping *Chyka* steady, she then moved along nicely with little rolling.

Late, in the black of night I saw ahead a tug-tow, a tugboat pulling barges, coming toward me. I tracked him on radar. I altered course. So did he, but in the wrong direction. He came really close. With all sails out and the engine turning at high RPMs I managed to get out of his way.

Unfortunately, there is no system to navigation lights in these waters.

Having had the struggle with that Sumatra squall and an overnight with no naps, I came to the marina at Port Dickson, Malaysia, to collapse and sleep until whenever.

Somewhere I had taken on board a rat. I never saw him, but I could hear him at night and saw his calling cards in the mornings. I starved him by sealing all foods in strong containers. Some people say you should not do it this way, because a rat may try to eat through the water hoses. But what else could I do? I didn't have a rat trap. One morning I saw he had tried to gnaw his way into Barry Groves's second peanut butter plastic bottle, but the Canadians make them super strong, and he failed. Here at Port Dickson he became discouraged about the food available on *Chyka* and jumped ship.

Along the way north, the coast became increasingly beautiful with dark green hills and rock cliffs rising straight up out of the water.

After five more stops, sailing only in daylight so I could see the fish nets and small local boats, I arrived at the Langkawi Yacht Club, still in Malaysia, on December 6, 2004. I stayed there eight days doing errands and boat jobs.

As usual wherever I sailed, Ingrid and Norbert were there, also Lucka and Bernd on *Minivado*. While sailing together into Singapore, both their boats were struck by lightning; the electronics on their boats were destroyed. Fortunately, Singapore was right there for them. Dieter showed up. I had not seen him since Fiji. Torben came over to visit from nearby Rebak Island Marina, where his boat was hauled out for repairs.

Rebak Island Resort

Going on, I sailed 12 easy miles to Rebak Island Marina where Torben's boat was. There was the luxury Rebak Island Resort. Torben and I swam in their huge pool. We had drinks at the pool bar, one of those built low to the water to serve guests lounging in the pool.

After we got ourselves ready for dinner, we had drinks at their tropical style bar and a *mee goreng* dinner, spicy fried noodles. Then there was entertainment. Torben with his clarinet joined Fuart on the keyboard and Sheila, a beautiful 24 year old singer. I had met Sheila a few days before in a store in Langkawi.

The three of them were wonderful, doing sweet love songs with an easy beat and smooth modulating harmony. She sang with a voice like Julie Andrews swaying softly to the music. They joined me between sets. I bought her a Bailey's Irish Cream. Sheila was Muslim from a small town in Eastern Malaysia. Her family did not approve of her dressing like a Western singer, but they accepted it. She dedicated one song to Henry, after which I went up to thank her and kissed her on her cheek.

The place was full of locals and Westerners. They must have wondered, who is the old man to whom the Rebak Trio goes during breaks, as they also did for awhile after the performance? The people obviously loved the show. A few met me later and commented how much they liked Torben's playing.

Thailand

I sailed north and immediately was in Thai waters. I anchored in Ko Khai Yai, a spectacular anchorage between two islands.

The next day coming into Ko Muk there was another sailboat anchored. They called. It was *Alkira,* Andy and Kerry. We had seen each other twice since the beach birthday party a year before on Pine Island, New Caledonia, for Teddo and Edwina. We were all there to go into the Emerald Cave.

The Emerald Cave

In the morning I dinghied up to the tunnel and went into it. It is 250 feet long. You have to time it for low tide, because the tunnel is below water at high tide. And you have to paddle your dinghy. There is too little depth to lower an outboard into the water, which is a blessing, because it prevents the horror of engines spoiling the serenity of the place.

In pitch dark I worked my way through the tunnel with flashlights. I turned into a tunnel that went nowhere and turned back to take the right one.

The tunnel opened into a small emerald green lagoon with a white sand beach. From here rock slopes covered with vegetation rose straight up 300 feet making a round frame for the blue sky above.

I was alone. All was silent and wonderful. After a while Andy and Kerry popped out from the tunnel. We swam in the lagoon.

Jack Oldenburg's Party - December 19, 2004

I departed for Ko Phi Phi Don Island. At the resort there, Jack had assembled 16 or more of his family for a grand reunion. He had long before invited me to attend the banquet, which was to be this night. Often on the way with all the delays, I had thought I would never make it in time, but I did. I met Jack's wife Kerstin, his children, and all of their people. There were hors d'oeuvres and cocktails outside followed by dinner, toasts and speeches. It was a wonderful celebration.

Seven days later the tsunami destroyed everything on this little island killing almost 1,000 of the people who were here. More of this later.

Phuket Island

Arriving at dusk off Phuket's Ao Chalong Bay I hove-to to sleep and wait for a clear morning entrance. But this time it did not work. There was a fast current and it became rough out there. So at midnight I decided to motor on in and anchored safely away from the many other boats.

The next morning I took a mooring off Jimmy's Lighthouse Bar and Restaurant. Over the next four weeks the Lighthouse turned out to be a great place to meet locals and other cruisers.

I motored around the south coast to Nai Harn Bay to meet up with Jack and Torben. As I was towing *Li'l Chyka,* its floor came apart from where it was attached to the tube. Later at anchor, I was able to tie an old inflatable floor from a previous dinghy to the tube, and with that I was able to get to shore.

The next day I got a moped ride back to Chalong. Boris and his wife showed me around the town. This included Cholamark Boat Company, where I ordered a new dinghy. They built it for me in only three days.

Christmas Eve - 2004

Chyka was anchored just off the nicely rustic Ao Sane shore restaurant by itself in the woods under a hill off to the side of Nai Harn Bay. They had agreed to provide a Christmas Eve party for all of us, about eighty sailboats anchored in the bay.

Jack came over early for drinks and we moved ashore for the party. It was a buffet dinner, dancing, and kids running around. I sat with Jack, Torben, Peter, and the *Avanti* people, Ola and Signy, whom I mentioned in the South Pacific. I thought, *I'm getting to be a party animal.*

After lunch Christmas Day at the Lighthouse, the big event for me was a Thai massage, two attractive young ladies working on me. They knew the standard oil stroking massage, but I wanted to try their way, which concentrates on deep static and rhythmic pressure spending extra time on the feet. It was wonderful.

The next day, December 26, 2004 the tsunami hit. There was devastation here and throughout the shores of the Indian Ocean. About 230,000 people lost their lives. I will tell you about that in Part Two.

END OF PART I

Part II

From Thailand, Back to the Bahamas, and Some Closing Stories

2005 to 2008

Believe me, my young friend, there is nothing - absolutely nothing - half so much worth doing as simply messing about in boats.

Wind in the Willows
— Kenneth Grahame

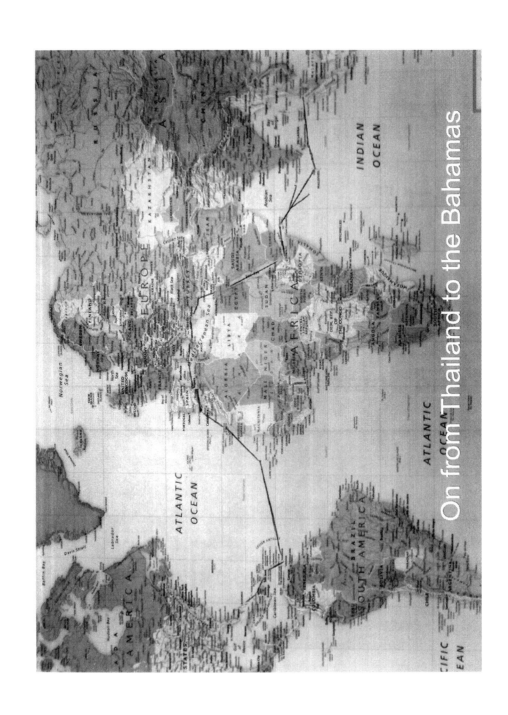

Tsunami - December 26, 2004

At 9:30 AM all was quiet. I was below on VHF radio planning lunch ashore with Jack and Torben. Suddenly, I heard the sound of rushing water and felt the boat shifting around. In one second I was on deck. Water was streaming past. The dinghy was straining at its tether. I looked at objects on land close by and could tell that *Chyka* was not actually moving at all over ground. *What the hell?*

The VHF came instantly alive. Other cruisers with better tech resources than mine immediately found it was a tsunami caused by an earthquake under the Indian Ocean west of Sumatra about 500 miles away from us. Tsunami waves travel remarkably fast. Coming to us at 330 miles per hour it hit with no warning.

Our bay opened exactly southwest, being from where the tsunami waves came. This first wave lifted *Chyka* about 22 feet up, then down, and went on to shore greatly increasing in height as the depth of the water under it diminished. It wiped out most buildings including our dear Ao Sane restaurant. Soon the wreckage of the town floated out and past me. On shore there were cars and trucks that had been thrown around. Some ended up perched on rocks above.

Fortunately, I had long before learned the advantages of anchoring further away from shore than most other boats. *Chyka* was anchored in a deep 50 feet of water with about 160 feet of anchor chain. So she rode the wave well. Most of the other boats, being closer to shore, dragged anchor and were washed around doing damage to each other. They headed out to sea to remain there until the end of the day to be sure it was all over. We few being deep anchored, including Jack and Torben, did not have to move.

The earthquake that caused the tsunami was the third strongest ever recorded. It lasted ten minutes, the longest of any known earthquake. It caused the entire earth to vibrate 0.4 inches.

The tsunami waves struck Sumatra, Thailand, Sri Lanka, India, and Africa. Of the some 230,000 people killed, about 250 of them were here on Phuket. Jack's Ko Phi Phi Don Island was ruined; 1,000 people there died. The Rebak Marina on Langkawi, where Torben had his boat when I visited him, was totally destroyed.

After the first wave, an Australian went ashore with a friend to go to town. He did not know there can be more than one wave to a tsunami. His daughter stayed on board their boat and later told me what happened:

They landed their dinghy at the ruins of the Ao Sane Restaurant under the steep wooded hill behind it. The second wave arrived and carried the two men and the dinghy half way up the hill depositing them at the top of a tree. The girl's father was hanging onto a limb with his friend hanging onto one of his legs. The friend managed to swing over to the trunk of the tree. They both carefully climbed down. It took a long time. Just as they got to the ground, the third wave came ashore and carried the two of them up the rest of the way to the top of the ridge, both of them amazingly unhurt in any way from all that.

Even the concrete foundation of the Ao Sane restaurant was broken up. The people had been so sincerely kind to us. I wrote in a long email report to all my people:

> *We are cruisers from Sweden, Germany, Norway, Denmark, Belgium, England, Australia, New Zealand, Poland, and our two boats from the USA. There was immediate aid organized. Some of our men were previously in the construction business, builders and carpenters. All day and even at night they were working to rebuild the Ao Sane with flood lights, mixing concrete, sawing and hammering. The local women were cooking for everyone, children and dogs wandering around adding cheer. It took many days. There was always a huge bin full of iced drinks and beer for sale.*
>
> *Today little Luna, a 12 year old girl from Belgium, speaking perfect English, organized a donation program. People have*

lost their houses, belongings, and money. They need clothing, blankets, shoes, and toiletries.

I donated to Luna lots of stuff from Chyka including towels, blankets, two sleeping bags, and old clothes. The greatest need was for blood. I could not donate mine, because I once had hepatitis.

Perhaps it is their Buddhism that helps the Thais to be stoic. The people in Phuket City and Chalong were calm and smiling. I was talking to a man who seemed fine. Only by asking did I learn, that his house and all his belongings were gone; only his car survived, and he was sleeping in it.

Friends and family emailed if they should send money to me or some place in Thailand. I responded, "Please donate to the standard reputable relief organizations. And I wish people would stop canceling reservations at Thai resorts, almost all of which are fine. Thailand needs the tourist dollars."

New Year's Eve - December 31, 2004

Although the restaurant was far from ready, the Ao Sane people planned a New Year's BBQ dinner for us all.

Some of the cruisers annoyed me very much by saying they were too upset by the disaster to attend, as if sniveling into your crying towel alone on your boat is going to help anyone! And here, when the Thai people were trying to get on with their lives and earn a little money!

I came ashore early to help others land their dinghies, which was not easy. Coming ashore here you had to steer carefully as the following surf washes your dinghi to the beach between the rocks.

The Ao Sane people had set up the beach area with whatever tables there were, and more tables cobbled up from benches, boards, and rocks. Torches around the area provided a soft warm light. We had quiet background music, and Torben played his clarinet. Dinner was shish kebab, chicken, potato salad made by our Germans, fresh veggies, sliced tomatoes, cucumbers, etc., then melons.

A German/Polish couple were staying in a simple cottage up the hill from Ao Sane. Instead of running away after the tsunami, they stayed and helped with the reconstruction. They sat with us tonight. Their seven year old, Livia, came to me several times to play games. We spoke German. When it was late she fell asleep in my lap. Her parents offered to take her away.

"Oh, No! I'll keep her," I assured them. So I held her in my arms until midnight while talking to the others.

A little after midnight it started to rain lightly. We all wished each other Happy New Year and one by one went back to our boats. I searched for and found my little Livia to kiss her and say to her Auf Wiedersehen.

New Year's Day we had lunch on *Avanti*, Ola and Signy. Then Jack, Torben, and I sailed back to Ao Chalong Bay, where on *Chyka* we had drinks and dinner, my World Famous Caribbean Fish Pasta.

The three of us went to Kuta Beach one evening. On the shore Bo met us with his dinghy and brought us out to his dive boat. There was his wife, Shamnien. Bo was a Dane, who had lived here many years operating a dive boat business. His boat happened to be near Jack's Ko Phi Phi Don Island, almost too near, when the tsunami first wave hit. He had difficulty keeping his boat upright. Then he was able to fish six people out of the ocean. Shamnien had a massage shop. It was destroyed by the tsunami. She made us an excellent Thai dinner.

Many boats wanted to join us crossing the Indian Ocean. Jack was in charge of it. For many days there were discussions about it including what we would do about the pirates in the Gulf of Aden. We thought there should be two groups of boats.

On January 13, 2005 Jack, Torben, and some others left to sail to India. I was not ready at all, and anyway I was concerned about what debris was still floating out there from the tsunami. And there was a tropical storm forming just north of the path west.

With a rental car I shopped at a modern mall bringing back five shopping carts of provisions. While at the mall I treated myself to a haircut which included a manicure, a pedicure, a massage of hands to elbows, and another from feet to knees.

Indian Ocean

On January 24, 2005 I departed Nai Harn Bay to sail the first half of the way across the Indian ocean. From Thailand west the natural stopping point of choice was always Sri Lanka, which was called Ceylon when I was there long before. But the ports there had been destroyed by the tsunami. Jack and Torben were on their way to Cochin, India. Many years before I was in Cochin and found it to be noisy and unpleasant.

I had heard good reports about the small harbor of Uligam in the northern Maldives, southwest of India and perfectly on my way west. From there I planned to sail to Al Mukalla in Yemen and there meet Jack, Torben, and the others.

Pleasant days went by with fine downwind sailing. It took me two days to get across the shipping channel with a stream of tankers low in the water bringing petroleum from the Middle East to Asia and those returning empty, high in the water.

Again, I was so glad for my radar. I could track all of the ships day and night as I went along. Also, my radar reflector was a comfort. I knew since crossing Lake Michigan that ships see my radar image and think I am something like an aircraft carrier. They shied away from my path already when they were still 12 miles ahead of me.

I did not see a single bird for ten days. In the Pacific, even a thousand miles from any land, I could always look out and see at least a few shearwaters or storm petrels. So, I am going to write another book, *Holt's Comprehensive Field Guide to Birds of the Indian Ocean*. It will be the shortest book ever written and the only one having a title longer than the text. Page one will say it all, "There aren't any."

Suddenly, A Major Problem

It was a very busy early morning of February 4, 2005. I was south of Sri Lanka. While motorsailing in light wind the cutlass bearing suddenly came apart. It supports the drive shaft where it comes out of the hull to the propeller. The drive shaft was slamming around. It would have destroyed the transmission if I had not put it in neutral. So this meant I could not use the engine to propel *Chyka* until she could be hauled out of the water somewhere to replace the cutlass bearing.

I wondered where I should go. Uligam in the northern Maldives could not have helped at all. The facilities in nearby Sri Lanka had been wiped out. It looked like Cochin, India or return upwind the 1,030 miles to Thailand.

Considering Cochin, I worried that working my way up the west coast of India to Cochin with no engine, against the current and winds, and with heavy shipping traffic would be really difficult for a single-hander.

Coincidentally, both my daughter, Sandy, and my stepsister, Cathy, whose son-in-law had family in Cochin, received email from Jack saying that I should not come to Cochin, that there was no wind in the area, entering the harbor was difficult, formalities were frustrating, and the facilities terrible. I could not communicate directly with Jack. He did not have a satellite phone, and I could not broadcast on shortwave.

Sandy told Jack about my cutlass bearing problem. He relayed back that he knew a sailor who had been hauled out in Male (pronounced MAH-lay), capitol of the Maldives. I spoke with the man on my satellite phone. He recommended it and also gave me the name of the agent he had used there, Abdullah. Already by 8:00 AM all that had happened, and I had redirected course to Male 470 miles away.

Maldives

The Republic of the Maldives is a nation of 1200 coral islands and atolls southwest of India. Only 190 of them are inhabited. The highest elevation is about eight feet, so the rising level of oceans is a major concern.

During late morning February 8, 2005 I worked *Chyka* through the surrounding islands to outside the entrance of Male's small ancient harbor enclosed by walls of rock and cement. Abdullah had arranged for a local African Queen to tow *Chyka* in. There were no docks or any pier. The harbor was upset by a strong east wind. It was confusing and the people spoke no English. I did not like what they were doing and could only use sign language. Finally they helped me deploy my two large anchors and tie two stern lines to the wall.

There was no time to rest. I had to inflate *Li'l Chyka* to get the officials out from the wall to *Chyka* so they could clear me in. Abdullah was energetic and called me on VHF about every ten minutes.

After things settled down, I took the ferry, a ride of 20 minutes to Thilafushi Island, west of Male, where the Gulf Craft Services Boat Yard was located. With them I arranged for the haul out of *Chyka*. Back to Male and on board my home, I had dinner and looked forward to sleeping long and soundly until late morning. But it was not to be.

At about 1:00 AM I heard pounding on the deck and went above. Right alongside was a sailboat blown against *Chyka*. They had just anchored upwind of me and their anchor had soon dragged. A polite pretty lady and a man were pushing against *Chyka* trying to keep our boats separated. She asked if I could put out fenders to prevent damage to our boats. "Of course!" I replied and did so.

Theirs had been a really bad day. Their sailboat, *Harmony*, had been stuck for a long time on a reef off a nearby island. They had just been pulled off and brought here.

The wind blew hard. Even with *Harmony* doubling the load on my two anchors, they held and kept both our boats off the wall during the night.

I spent a day in town having a long meeting with Abdullah, two hours email, and shopping. Just after returning to the boat another sailboat was towed in, and again it was a monkey theater of confusion with snagged and crossed lines.

Abdullah had arranged for Hammid to help me sail *Chyka* to the boat yard on Thilafushi Island. I would have been far better off without him.

After *Chyka* was towed just a little out of the harbor entrance, and without asking, he stupidly released the tow line. *Damn!* The wind was ahead and was blowing *Chyka* towards the rock wall. Remember, I could not use my engine. I scrambled to raise sail and was just barely able to get *Chyka* going and sail away from the rocks.

Hammid thought I wanted to go to Palm Tree Marina, which I had checked and did not like. He had no idea how to get to Gulf Craft on the other side of the island. I remembered enough from my visit there two days before to be able to sail there. We anchored 20 feet off the boat yard. It was so nice to at last be safe, protected from the strong wind, anchored calmly in a large atoll, and to get rid of Hammid, who soon took the ferry back to Male.

The boat yard hauled *Chyka* out and put her on jack stands. They did it with a huge 150 ton travelift, suitable, I thought, for small ships. Mohammed operated it by a hand-held remote control while he walked around. It was a more advanced travelift than you would have seen in most USA boat yards.

Thilafushi Island was created by dumping Male's trash in the ocean within well planned sand barriers to lock it all in. Soil was added on top. Vegetation grew over it yielding trees and bushes. There was not much: some residents, two small, primitive stores for them, and a few places making things. But important to me was that in the year 2000 Gulf Craft, based in the United Arab Emirates, established here their boat yard and factory to manufacture power boats. The yard was well equipped.

I went to the boatyard office to discuss all that should happen. I already knew Shareef, the Manager. There were a number of women secretaries sitting in front of their computers. This country is strictly Muslim and they wore the traditional *hijab* dress. Only the assistant manager, a confident beautiful young woman, wore western dress. She had a way of smiling at me, then looking away and then back to me, that was charming.

Shuwaida

Her name was Shuwaida Shameem. She became my prime contact at the boatyard. We became good friends. Shuwaida sometimes visited *Chyka*. One morning we showed the boat to the office staff. I met her for dinners in Male.

My first job, of course, was to get going on replacing the cutlass bearing. A mechanic came over from Male to look at the problem. He told me that the rudder would have to come off, a very big job, in order to get the drive shaft out. I checked with Island Packet about that. They sent me detailed instructions on how to do it without removing the rudder.

A marine store told me a new cutlass bearing could be found in Singapore and an inquiry was sent out for a quote.

From the boat yard I often walked the 20 minutes to the ferry landing for the trip over to Male to do shopping, lunch, consulting officials, seeing Abdullah, email, and sometimes meeting Shuwaida.

About all I purchased on Thilafushi was beer, non-alcoholic, because except for resorts, in the Maldives alcohol is not allowed.

Male was crowded with traffic in narrow streets. The public toilets were Muslim having hoses for washing your behind. The floors of the toilets were covered with water. I always brought my own toilet paper along.

An exception was my favorite place in town, the modern first class Nasandhura Hotel. On their patio overlooking the ocean, they served wonderful meals.

During a brunch I admired how the chef broke eggs over his frying pan. He held the egg up in his left hand, cracked it sharply in the middle with the edge of his spatula, pulled the shell apart, and dropped the egg nicely into the pan. Since then I have always broken eggs his way.

The only other sailboat hauled out with *Chyka* was *Sir George*. They were Rick, a Kiwi, and Toy, a cute little lady from Phuket, Thailand. She cooked two meals for us. I treated them to a dinner in town. Rick and I always talked politics. Toy gave me a haircut.

Rick's sailing history was a long series of super troubles. He reminded me of the hopeless Texan, Steve, on *Odyssey* I told you about in Australia.

Just off Cochin, Rick's boat was hit by an Indian Navy vessel. (And close to Cochin? Gross negligence is suspected.) The damage required over a year to repair. On the way here from Langkawi his bilge pump failed, the stern tube hose cracked, and the generator quit as he limped in for repairs.

I had problems; everyone on a sailboat does. But too many at one time is an indication of poor general maintenance. Rick asked me to check something on his boat. As I walked around the deck I saw why he had so many troubles. Everything was corroded or about to come apart. He noted down what I said needed attention.

After ten days I learned that no one, not even in Singapore, could find a correct replacement for the cutlass bearing. I immediately ordered two of them from Island Packet, one to be a spare. By the time they arrived and the failed bearing was replaced, it was March 4.

Sailing the 1,600 miles north through the Red Sea is always difficult due to strong head winds. To avoid the worst weather in the Red Sea, one must enter the south end of it by early March. My problem was: It was already early March!

To get *Chyka* in the water and ready for the long trip would take ten days. And then, sailing to the entrance of the Red Sea from Male would take three weeks. All this meant that I was way too late to do it this season. The next chance was to be in December.

So for eight months *Chyka* had to stay put. Keeping her on the hard would have cost $700 per month. I asked Shareef if we could put *Chyka* back in the water and on a mooring. He said that would be good, quoted a price, and that they would install the mooring for me.

Only, they had no idea how to design a mooring. From a book on board I found a recommendation from the New York Yacht Club as to how to design one. I gave it to Shareef. He said they would do it. When later we launched *Chyka* they asked me to tell them where to drop the mooring. I was not impressed with the thing, but I thought it adequate.

While on the mooring I prepared *Chyka* for whatever bad weather might come. I stayed two nights in the Nasandhura Hotel and then departed Male for Colombo and London on March 18, 2005.

Home Leave - 2005

For many reasons it was actually good it had to happen. I spent time with family and friends. There were the usual doctor checkups. I stayed with daughters and fixed things in their homes and in Sonja's. I met often with the old chess group.

I was often in contact with Shuwaida. She kept me up to date about *Chyka*.

Shuwaida told me the mooring had not held in a wind. *Chyka* had drifted away and up against a reef. They found her, towed her back, and put her back up on land. The hull was OK.

Island Packet owners meet annually in various places with their boats. Each meeting is called an Island Packet Rendezvous. There was one in Racine, Wisconsin. They asked me to speak to them after their Saturday dinner about world cruising.

Patricia

On my way to visit Susan in Sarasota I visited Patricia as usual. Her second husband, Warren, had died two years before. Warren and I had been friends since we were five years old. We three had been together many times.

Patricia and I agreed to meet for brunch at the fancy Don CeSar Hotel in St. Pete Beach. When I showed up, the host asked me with a bored tone of voice what I wanted. I told him I was there to meet a tall, beautiful blond. I gained immediate respect. He politely escorted me to Patricia.

The time flew for us. I never knew a brunch could last two and one half hours. Walking back to our cars we held hands.

Return to Male - December 14, 2005

I stayed at the Nasandhura Hotel three nights. Shuwaida and I had lunch there. She made dinner and gave me a turtle key ring.

Chyka was ready to get a bottom paint. All was well, except someone had stolen my handheld GPS. It had served as backup for the main built-in GPS. Without any GPS I would have to go back to celestial navigation, which is difficult and inaccurate. So in Male, I bought two Garmin handheld GPS units, one as the next backup and the other hidden away as a standby for the backup.

The next destinations were the Gulf of Aden and the south end of the Red Sea. To get to them I had to cross the Arabian Sea.

It took many days to prepare for it, stocking supplies, final maintenance of engine and systems, paying charges to the government, and clearing out with the officials. I loaded 100 gallons of fresh water and brought my diesel fuel up to the full capacity of 80 gallons, 50 in the main tank and six jerry cans each holding five gallons.

Two days before intended departure, there was an after hours goodbye party for the office staff on *Chyka*.

A day before intended departure, *Chyka* was tied up against the seawall ready to go. The weather forecast was bad. That night waves were coming in against *Chyka*. At 2:00 AM one of the two lines holding the fender board had frayed and had come apart. (Whenever *Chyka* was tied up against a post, I hung my fender board horizontally against it and then positioned two normal fenders between the board and the boat.)

Now, the fenders alone between the post and *Chyka* held long enough for me to install eyelets at the top of the fender board and lower it back into position. The fender board, improved that way, remained so for the rest of *Chyka's* voyages. Departure was postponed.

I was not able to get weather on Shuwaida's computer. I went over to Male and there got a good forecast. It was OK to leave the next day.

My cruising friends were stopping in Aden, a former British colony, now in Yemen, to go from there into the Red Sea. I finally decided to go instead to Djibouti, a former French colony. It seemed to be more historically interesting, and I spoke fair French. A yacht club was said to be there, and that would make things easier. (When I got there the club was closed up.)

To the Gulf of Aden

Sunday January 15, 2006 I departed. First I circled a little offshore stowing lines and fenders. The wind was light. I raised the main and genoa and sailed slowly quite close to the boatyard office to wave goodbye to Shuwaida and the others.

I needed to get out of this atoll before dark. In it were about 50 islands, also sand bars, and coral heads. Then there were two more atolls I needed to go between before breaking out into the Arabian Sea. I did so in waning daylight.

During the first few days the winds were easy. I only saw two ships in five days. The winds picked up and I sailed with double-reefed main and staysail. As happened before, not having sailed in heavy weather for such a long time, my muscles ached and my hands were raw. I wore sailing gloves for a day.

I saw two shearwaters, which were so common in the Pacific. Well, that means I will have to add a whole page to *Holt's Comprehensive Field Guide to Birds of the Indian Ocean*.

Approaching the Gulf of Aden, the shipping traffic increased. A passing Russian motor tanker called me. He had seen the name on my boat. Of course, he knew that *Chyka* meant seagull in Russian. We had a pleasant conversation, but in English; at one time I spoke basic Russian, but by now it was mostly gone.

Avoiding Pirates

For years this was a common subject of magazine articles and conversations about it with us cruisers intending to sail into the Gulf of Aden. I had increasingly distrusted the wisdom of traveling through pirate waters in convoys. I concluded that a fleet of small boats would make a larger target, more likely to attract the pirates. And if there would be an encounter, I wondered just what would shouting and flashing of lights do to scare off people with assault weapons. I had decided the best would be to do it quietly in the dark and on my own.

And as to weapons, I have always recommended carrying no weapons on board at all. None of my friends did. What are you going to do with your pea shooter against a group of heavily armed robbers? Make them mad enough, and you lose your boat and possibly your life as well! Better to have some money badly hidden, and the rest buried deeply in the boat.

I had studied a chart plot of all the reported pirate hits in the Gulf of Aden during the previous ten years. They formed an hourglass figure between Yemen to the north, and Somalia to the south, with the most frequent attacks spread along their coasts. Then further offshore, the danger area narrowed down to the neck of the hourglass, 50 miles from Yemen and 110 miles off Somalia.

Pirates did not like to operate in the dark. Nor did they like rough weather far from shore. I timed my arrival to the neck of the danger zone for sundown. The shipping lane was 12 miles to the north, and so of no concern. The radar reflector was put away. It would have told every pirate in the Gulf where I was. All lights were off except for my deck lights. They were visible from only a very short distance, and I wanted them on in case some fisherman would possibly be near me. I did not broadcast at all on my radios.

The wind was strong from the ESE. With reduced sails and Big Rudy humming at high RPMs, *Chyka* was going over her hull speed, 7.5 knots, the theoretical maximum a boat can move through the water. I arrived at the other side of the pirate zone by dawn but kept going a few more hours at maximum speed to be sure.

Over the next two days the wind gradually increased to over 30 knots. The following waves were becoming higher and steep. I prepared the boat for a boarding wave. But *Chyka's* stern always rose nicely to such occasions. The waves passed under the boat, not into it. Island Packets have broad sterns, one advantage of which is extra aft flotation that better lifts the stern with high following waves. The other advantage is that the greater stern width provides much more storage room in the lazarettes, large storage compartments at the stern and under cockpit cushions.

The next night with only my double-reefed main, *Chyka* was still going way too fast risking an out of control situation. I needed to reduce the main to a triple reef. This required heading upwind to reduce pressure on the main. I should have used the engine to help do it.

The preventer snarled up in the sheet block making a real mess. With the violent conditions I could not untangle it, so it had to wait until I got to Djibouti.

Djibouti

On February 4, 2006 I rounded the cape north of the city, sailed nicely along in the lee of the cape, came into the harbor, and anchored just offshore the city.

In Male I had folded up the dinghy and stored it on *Chyka's* foredeck. Uncovering it I saw there were several large holes in it. The next day having no dinghy, but required to clear in, I brought *Chyka* into the inner harbor, worked her in between two huge ships at the pier, and tied up against a fender of one of the ships. There Mohamed from Port Authority met me. He helped me clear in with Immigration and the Capitainerie (office of the Port Captain).

I asked the Port Captain if I could take *Chyka* to the Yacht Club. "Oh yes, no problem." He called around and found that, "Sorry, the yacht club is closed up; there are no facilities and no docking." After I brought *Chyka* back to anchor, Mohamed came by to take *Li'l Chyka* off to be repaired.

Another boat had anchored, the British sailboat *Trompeta*, a Hallberg-Rassy 42 with Captain Peter and crew; Ken, his wife, Catherine, and friend Thomas. On their way here they had been confronted by three pirate boats off the coast of Yemen. They called on VHF for help. Most fortunately for them there was a container ship passing nearby willing to assist. It came onto the scene and blew away the pirates.

In the evening I went with them to shore. We walked around this old French colonial city admiring its large, beautifully designed stone buildings on wide streets and the large squares with monuments. We changed money, had some beers, and then had dinner at the Hotel Ciel Claire *(Clear Sky)*. Its French restaurants are a major reason to come to Djibouti.

In the light of the next day it was disappointing to see the reality of Djibouti, no longer the dream vision of grand old buildings in the soft glow of city evening lights. The buildings were mostly deteriorating and some falling apart.

Beggars were everywhere. I gave something to some, but each time quickly moved on, as others seeing me give money, rushed up to get theirs. Mothers carried their children around intentionally looking pathetic. In my journal I wrote, "Children beg. I stop and touch them, play hand games with them, and make them laugh. And then I give them a little money."

I met the Brits at the Histoire for beers.

Mohamed returned *Li'l Chyka* so well repaired. I have never seen such a good job. Each patch was covered by a far larger patch to protect it, because they tend to deteriorate from the sun over time.

My mainsail had a serious tear in it. With the awl and needles I had, I could not penetrate the cloth because it was reinforced at that place. Peter lent me a special awl he had which worked wonderfully. I later ordered one like it and used it often from then on.

Into the Red Sea - February 14, 2006

The south entrance to the Red Sea is called Bab-el-Mandeb, Arabic for "Gate of Grief" because of its often hazardous conditions that have doomed so many ships for thousands of years.

Having a good weather forecast, I left Djibouti at 9:30 AM and motor-sailed back east until late afternoon to the entrance. I had planned to do it at the time of a favorable current. With that and a helpful wind behind me, I sailed nicely through the dreaded Bab-el-Mandeb.

The next day I had to work my way through islands and fishing boats. Late at night a powerful light came from the water. I looked over the side. It was phosphorescence. I had not known it could be so brilliant. There were long, flashing neon blue-green streaks streaming aft.

I had benefited by perfect sailing conditions getting well into the Red Sea before the expected strong head winds took over and remained so almost all of the 1,200 miles sailing on to Suez.

Although strong winds and choppy seas make sailing difficult especially for north bound sailors, the Red Sea does have advantages. Temperatures at this time of year are pleasant. There are few insects. Swimming and snorkeling are good. The anchorages are beautiful usually with a backdrop of high mountains coming down to the desert coastline.

There are no storms and it almost never rains, which explains why so few people live along the shores of the Red Sea.

A special sight was of 20 to 30 baby dolphins playing alongside *Chyka* with their adults further away riding shotgun. There were shearwaters everywhere.

For three days and nights I worked my way through small steep islands. One night I almost ran into a fishing boat. As I said before, being made of wood they usually do not show up on radar. I took Sudafed to stay awake. Whenever they wore off I hove-to for some sleep. I did this also just off Massawa, where I wanted to wait for daylight before entering.

Eritrea

Massawa was at one time the grand capitol of Italian Eritrea. They built it to what became the largest and safest deep-water port on the east coast of Africa.

On Saturday February 18, 2006 I enjoyed an easy entrance. Officials were not available until Monday so I went on into the inner harbor. Many sailboats were anchored here. I found a spot to anchor near them. They were members of the Vasco da Gama Yacht Rally. Vasco was a Portuguese explorer. His ships were the first to sail from Europe around Africa to India.

The sailboats of the rally had come down from the Mediterranean and were on their way to Goa, the former colony of Portugal on the west coast of India.

John from Holland, the one in charge of the rally, came over for beers. Soon more of them came. They all wanted me to join them on the beach for a potluck dinner. I declined and that night slept 14 hours.

Sunday I had many visitors. Kosta and Amarina, a sweet, young Russian couple, came. They were on a small sailboat and part of the rally. They were naïve children. They had few charts of the Indian Ocean. There were no places here or ahead of them where they could buy charts. And they didn't have the money to buy them anyway.

I gave them 156 charts from here to Bundaberg, Australia. They gave me excellent Russian charts of the Aegean Sea and Cyprus.

On Monday I took *Li'l Chyka* in to the main harbor of Massawa to go ashore and clear in. At one time, from this harbor one would have seen a classic, beautiful, colonial port city. Now its remains were hidden behind an ugly, high wall built for security reasons following the war between Eritrea and Ethiopia. After taking our dinghies in to the city dock, we sailors had to walk to the guarded entrance off to the eastern side and then a long way around and into the city.

Massawa, had been built in the Italian/Arab style of architecture. It was bombed to destruction during the war. From the ruins I saw as I walked along, I could imagine how beautiful the buildings and the piazzas had once been. Among the ruined buildings were a few restaurants and shops. There was an Internet café that sometimes worked. Mike operated a small restaurant. I often had lunch there. He arranged for a lady to do my laundry.

Money Problems

Until that point I had always been able to get local currency with credit cards at ATMs or banks. I always had travelers checks and a reserve of dollars stowed away, which I replenished as needed whenever on home leave.

You can always change dollars into local currency, but now I was about to run out of dollars. There were no ATMs. No banks or any other places could take credit cards or travelers checks. The only way to get money was to have it sent by Western Union, and it had to be to a certain bank in Asmara, the capitol of Eritrea. I had to go there to get it. Sonja sent it to me at that bank.

So often in life, a bother turns into a blessing, like this time.

Asmara

The bus ride from Massawa to Asmara must be one of the most dramatic rides anywhere. In three hours forty minutes we went from sea level to Asmara at 7,600 feet, in only about 50 miles. The narrow road switched back and forth as we went steeply up giving fine views of the desert and the sea.

There was a rest stop at the small town of Ghinda. Children were selling baskets. They were students and spoke beginning English. I was sorry I had not brought pens with me from *Chyka's* gift supply. I was better prepared for them on the return trip.

I enjoyed walking around this beautiful Italian built colonial city. It was not at all damaged during the war that destroyed Massawa. The high altitude there provides moderate temperatures. It seemed to me too cool for palm trees, but they were all over. I had not thought to bring warm clothes, so in the early evening I retreated to my hotel.

The bank had the money Sonja had sent. They could not give me dollars. It had to be in nakfa, the local currency. I spent an hour to get a permit to travel back to Massawa. Then I had to go to a shop to get the required two copies of it.

On the return to Massawa, the bus stopped at Ghinda. This time I was loaded with a ton of pens I had bought in Asmara for the children. They were delighted.

Back at the anchorage the rally had departed. The only other boat anchored was *Trompeta*, my British friends I had been with in Djibouti. The next day we went to town and I introduced them to Mike, who organizes everything in town for cruisers.

I was preparing to depart. Mike arranged that a truck would deliver to the dock 35 gallons of diesel, 10 gallons of drinking water, and one gallon of gasoline for the outboard. It required three trips with *Li'l Chyka* to transport it all back to *Chyka*.

When close to departure, I had too much local money, which the banks would not change to anything else. Jacque on *Miscat*, a French single-hander, was tied up at the town dock for an emergency engine repair. He gave me dollars for some of my nakfa local money. (I will tell you later how I met him in Turkey.) And Mike, taking a risk breaking the law, changed most of the rest of my nakfa into dollars, of course at an attractive rate for his benefit. What otherwise would I have done with their money, which is worthless anywhere else? I used up the remaining nakfa buying supplies.

At a store I met a Swedish couple, Lars and Christine. Their boat was *La Brique*. They were friends of Jack Oldenburg.

Early morning, *Trompeta* and *Chyka* motored to the town dock. We walked to Immigration and waited two hours for the place to open so we could clear out. Ken wanted to wait longer. Peter and I did not want to do so, because after later clearing out we would have arrived at our destination after sundown. We decided to go back to our anchorage and try again the next day.

Then Immigration was open early. A man came with us to the dock to inspect our boats for stowaways. We had to start our engines and cast off as he watched. Our two boats went together 24 miles north to anchor for the night at Abu Island. I had my first lesson that old charts of the Red Sea are not accurate. There was no indication of a potential problem. I was overconfident.

While entering the bay the depth gage suddenly dropped, and *Chyka* hit a reef. I backed off from it, then carefully searched along in shallow water until I found a safe entrance and could then tell *Trompeta* what happened.

Sudan

After an overnight sail and just after dawn, we worked our way into Khor Nawarat, Sudan, a beautiful, quiet Bahamas - like bay with turquoise waters. People of some agency of the Sudan Navy boarded our boats to look around. They were friendly. *Trompeta* gave them cigarettes. I gave them beers. We anchored and were the only boats there. Catherine made dinner of a wahoo they had caught. (Wahoo is a game fish found worldwide in tropical seas.)

The next morning a Sudanese warship came in and anchored next to us. On VHF they said we should send representatives of our boats to them with documentation. Peter and Thomas picked me up with their dinghy and we went over. We climbed up the side of the ship by way of tire fenders. When we arrived on deck, we were cordially greeted by the officers. They brought us to the ship's day room and gave us tea and orange sections.

After checking our documents they told us how welcome we were, asked how they could help us, and gave us valuable advice on sailing north. The Captain spoke perfect English having been in California and Texas for naval training.

Going into anchorages for the night along this coast requires extra care. It must be done before the sun gets too low in the west and in your eyes making it impossible to see the colors of the water. And when departing in the morning, which is always going east, it has to be done early before the sun is blinding from that direction.

Difficult Navigation

Charts of the Red Sea were made over 150 years ago and so understandably with inaccuracies. Most of the time I was using charts having a scale of 1 to 500,000. On them a mile is seen as about 1/8 of an inch and so, of course, with no details.

Trompeta led the way through the Shubuk Channel between islands and reefs. The north end of the channel widened into rough, open water. We were motorsailing north into a head wind of 25 knots and a nasty chop. *Trompeta*, a larger boat, went ahead. I worked my way forward tacking back and forth trying to stay off a threatening downwind reef.

Our hope for a place to stop was an anchorage behind coral reefs called Marsa Esh. (*Marsa* means 'anchorage'.) In my *Red Sea Pilot* (a cruising guide) we had found the GPS location to its entrance. We hoped it was accurate. After working my way north to a point east of the entrance, I could then approach Marsa Esh on a steady beam reach. I put the autopilot on track to take *Chyka* exactly to the entrance. I motored slowly through the rough waves trusting the autopilot, only watching the depth gage, ready to back off and retreat if it became too shallow. The reefs were way offshore, underwater, and invisible from any distance.

There was nothing to see on shore but the mountains far beyond. I watched from the helm as the GPS distance to the entrance waypoint gradually dropped to zero, and the depth gage dropped to 15 feet. Suddenly, there was a small red buoy floating around in the waves. From it I thankfully followed buoys further on and into Marsa Esh. I anchored next to *Trompeta*. The wind was still strong, and land was far away. But we were in quiet waters protected from the waves by the underwater reefs.

What would I have done if I had not found the entrance? As I have told you before, there must always be a backup plan. The result was this: After checking on VHF with *Trompeta*, I would have gone on up the coast another 20 miles to Suakin. Progress would have been difficult and way too slow to get there in daylight. But it has a large harbor and would have night markers. And if that had not worked, I could have anchored in the lee of the entrance.

We stayed three nights waiting for better weather. I called Cyndie every day for a forecast. On Sunday March 20 the wind settled to only NNE-10. We had a pleasant sail to Suakin, entered its harbor easily, and anchored just south of the ruined city island.

Suakin

Long ago Suakin was the major port gateway for trade between Europe, Arabia, and the Far East. Caravans of 1,000 camels brought cotton, hides, and ivory from the Nile Valley to be shipped mostly to the East Indies. Ships returned here with spices, silks, rice, sugar, and teak. Suakin was built on an island within a bay and connected by a narrow causeway to the mainland, which gave the place excellent protection.

The beginning of its fall as Europe's connection to the East was the development of the sea trade route between Europe and Asia going around South Africa. This started in the late 1490s when Vasco da Gama sailed that way to India and back. His ships returned to Portugal full of spices from the East. Then, many in Europe hurried to do the same.

After the Suez Canal was opened, nearly 400 years later in 1869, ships became too large for the entrance to Suakin. In 1905 the British decided it would be better to develop Port Sudan to the north instead of Suakin.

That was the end of Suakin. And to make things worse, its buildings had been constructed of coral, which does not weather nearly as long as stone. This onetime grand city was now completely in ruins.

Soon after we anchored, a small open boat brought to us people from quarantine, police, and immigration. With them came the well known sailors' agent I had read about, Mohammed, dressed in a long white robe, speaking perfect English.

As they finished with *Chyka* and were leaving, their outboard started, but the propeller was not turning. I took it off and saw the shear pin had broken. My spare shear pins would not fit. So I made one for them from a short piece of thick wire, put it all together, and off they went.

Trompeta and *Chyka* stayed four nights. We went into the local town on the mainland to shop in the open stall markets. The place was dilapidated. Camels and goats wandered around not bothering anybody.

Mohammed arranged to have fuel and water brought to the shore to be dinghied out to *Chyka*. The water came in a cart pulled by a donkey.

I spent most of a day walking around ruined Suakin. To get into it you have to go through a small gate at the causeway and pay something. The guard showed me his historical manual of the place. I sat down for an hour to read most of it before going in.

The most interesting ruins of the city are those of what at one time was a large hotel. It looms over the entrance to the harbor like a ghost of what is gone. There was still enough of the buildings left for me to imagine how beautiful the city must have been. As I wandered the old places of Suakin I saw only two other people.

We bought a lot of Coca Cola. It was made in Khartoum, the capitol of Sudan. The oranges were excellent. I bought eggs, tomatoes, apples, cans of tuna, and pineapple chunks.

The weather now in March was perfect, but you don't want to be in this area in July. Then the average high for the day is 107 F.

I was at that time getting weather reports from daughter Sandy. From her information we saw an excellent weather window, and we departed. Then rounding the city island just under the remains of the old hotel, *Trompeta* ran aground and was stuck. A current had caught them. I passed one end of a long rope to a fishing boat to take over to *Trompeta*. With it fastened to the stern of *Trompeta* and to the stern of *Chyka*, I easily pulled them off. We then had a pleasant 12 mile sail to Marsa Ata followed the next day by a stop at Port Sudan. And so it went.

One day *Trompeta* went on without me. I had not liked the forecast Sandy had given us for that day. After they left, they radioed that it was blowing N 20-25. I was glad I had not gone with them.

It then took sixteen days for me to complete the coast of Sudan. One morning I departed with a good forecast from Sandy. At sea the sailing became impossibly rough. I returned to try it another day. When two days later I did so, again with a good forecast, I had to also then retreat back in and wait six more days. As you can see, the actual conditions are sometimes rougher than forecasted, especially in the Red Sea.

During these stops I had time to do boat jobs and prenavigation to the next places. I snorkeled on reefs, maintained the propeller, and cleaned the boat bottom. I loved the quiet sunsets with sharp mountains in view and the desert shores in front of me.

I worried about having enough fuel. The constant strong headwinds had required continuous motorsailing. I had to think about what I would do if fuel was too low or if the engine would fail. The answer to both scenarios was to sail back downwind to Port Sudan.

Egypt

Marsa Girid was the first stop for me in Egypt. It was out of the way to the west, but it was the nearest place where I could get fuel. The *Red Sea Pilot* said it was a good place to anchor and provision.

It took an overnight sail. I hove-to late and slept. I then anticipated an easy sail heading west expecting the usual north wind. Unfortunately, the wind was instead W-20, so exactly against *Chyka*.

Marsa Girid's harbor was protected by a seawall having a narrow entrance. As I approached, I received on VHF instructions on how to enter. Having done so, I motored up to the dock. Egyptian Navy people shouted down that this was now a naval station, and that I was not allowed to dock or anchor.

I told them I was exhausted, could not go on, and needed to buy fuel. One of them said, "Well then, come up here and have tea with us." There we discussed the problem. One of them called Cairo. He hung up and said I could stay one night. I said that would not be enough. So he telephoned again. "OK, you can stay two nights."

They helped me move *Chyka* to the protected side of the dock. It all worked out so well for me, because where the anchorage had been, the water now was rough. And I would have had to use *Li'l Chyka* to go ashore to bring back fuel and supplies in bad conditions.

They were a small group of Navy people and could not have been kinder. They all spoke excellent English, of course, and I think they enjoyed having another person to talk with. Ali, the officer in charge, invited me to join them for dinner. I said I had already started cooking mine and was too tired to move. He sent over a complete dinner of shellfish, spinach, and macaroni with meat.

First thing in the morning Mustafa brought me *chai* (tea.) Then he connected a water hose for me. It was RO water (reverse osmosis and absolutely pure), wonderful for filling my water tank, but it seemed a shame to use it to wash the boat. Mustafa said it was the only water they had and not to worry about it.

We were in disputed territory between Egypt and Sudan, Ali and Mazan had to escort me into the small town to shop. It was in Egypt but the people were Sudanese. I bought a ton of fresh vegetables. Ali and Mazan visited me on *Chyka*. Ali was quite impressed with my electronics.

At night they delivered to *Chyka* 25 gallons of diesel. I tried to tip them, but they refused. I planned to leave in the early morning; we said good-bye. I gave them my West Marine catalog and all of my fishing equipment, which I had never used. Why fish? I had other things to do, and you can find fresh fish right out of the ocean in every small food store anywhere, or you can buy it from local fishermen.

I felt great and was well rested. *Chyka* was full of fuel, water, and food.

Although I knew there would be rough sailing further on, the worst of the Red Sea was behind me.

I left Marsa Girid with a pleasant light wind into what became a double overnight passage across Foul Bay to Sharm Luli (*sharm* means 'cove') north of it. An unusual south wind helped me against a one knot current for awhile, but then it was business as usual with the wind against me N-23.

One time when turning up the throttle, the engine slowed down instead of going faster. I thought it must be due to a heavy wave that stalled *Chyka* for a second and didn't worry about it.

Fuel Filter Problem

The next morning while motorsailing into NNW 18-20 the engine just limped along at low RPMs. It would not go faster. So the engine was failing! This was really bad.

I consulted my book *Troubleshooting Marine Diesel Engines*. It had a system of analyzing the symptoms of problems. It said, "One or both fuel filters are clogged." That was impossible; I had just changed both fuel filters in Massawa. The *Boatowner's Mechanical and Electrical Manual*, which was on board most cruising boats, said, "A filter in the fuel line is clogged." The Yanmar manual said, "It is a dirty fuel filter." So, *damn it all, OK, I'll change them.*

I hove-to, so *Chyka* stayed mostly facing the waves. Still she was rolling and pitching some. I had to work very carefully to avoid losing parts and tools. I completed the job, bled the fuel line to eliminate any air in it, and started the engine. Success! Big Rudy was happy!

Entering Sharm Luli was tricky. Having entered, I was in this beautiful well protected place with green hills all around and bright coral reefs.

Three other sailboats were there. Locals, Mustafa and Saba, came by going fishing. I invited them aboard for tea and cookies. Mustafa was wearing a T-shirt with "Vasco da Gama Rally" on it. Mustafa explained:

When the rally arrived here, it was dark. He had prevented the Russian couple Kosta and Amarina, the young Russians I mentioned before, from running onto a reef.

The next day Mustafa brought to me two fish he had caught.

Port Ghalib, Egypt

It was 75 miles to get there. Cyndie gave me a good forecast, and I told the others. They left in the morning. But why did they do it in the morning, sail 15 hours, and arrive in the dark? Instead, I took a long nap and departed at 4:00 PM so as to arrive in the light of the next morning.

Through the night the wind was north, of course, but light. There was a three-quarter moon. Again, moonlight makes night sailing so much more pleasant. In the morning I motored quietly into the new marina of Port Ghalib, the first marina for me since Thailand.

I was relieved to have made it to a secure base, to where I could always retreat, if need be, when going further north from here. People at the marina helped me clear in with the Egyptian officials, refuel, and take on water. There was not much else near the marina. They helped me move to the dock of the luxury Coral Beach Diving Hotel.

The other boats from Sharm Luli were there. We took the airport shuttle to do an ATM, buy booze, and get supplies from a small shop. Back in the hotel we did email and had beers on *Calypso* with John and Margo.

The luxury of the hotel was such a contrast to the places where I had been since Malaysia. The lobby was our headquarters. We all had dinner at the hotel to celebrate Margo's Birthday. I basked in the safety and comfort of the place for five days.

The next stop was Abu Tig, 135 miles north located at the south end of the Gulf of Suez. At 5:30 AM I departed with a few of the others helping me cast off. During the day the wind was ahead but light. I motored along easily. I did not want to arrive in the dark, so I hove-to at 2:00 AM and slept.

Abu Tig Marina

Early morning I glided in. This is a popular, modern, world-class marina. Many boats come down here from the Mediterranean. I had made a reservation by email from Port Ghalib. All boats were moored stern to the dock.

A few steps from *Chyka's* stern was a long row of shops, hotels, restaurants, bars, a laundry, and the marina office building with toilets and showers. As in all Egyptian resorts, security was tight.

The weather conditions in the Gulf of Suez are known to become worse in May and June. I wished I could have then gone on to Suez. But I needed to get back home for several reasons and booked flights to depart from Cairo on April 26. I returned to *Chyka* one month later.

The others had left going north. The winds now were stronger. There was a huge sand dune just north of Abu Tig. The wind blew sand into town, into the buildings, and into our boats. It found its way into *Chyka* but never made it into the engine room, thank God.

It became too hot to stay on *Chyka*. I moved to the air conditioned Turtle Inn. Mornings, before it became too hot, I did boat jobs. I watched on the Internet for a weather window to go north. I played chess regularly with a young man who worked at the inn.

I was moored next to a Dutch couple. While I was gone, they had left twice to go north, both times found the weather impossible, and had to come back.

At last, I saw a brief weather window and decided to clear out and depart the next day.

Into the Gulf of Suez

Preparing to leave, I saw that the electronics displays of wind, depth, and autopilot were all dead. I worried that the repair might cost me days, perhaps the weather window, or in the worst case the whole season. But in two hours I found the problem. It was a loose connection, an easy fix, and I sailed away.

I negotiated the Tawila Channel in light wind and then into the normal N 20-25 to anchor south of Queisum Island. I swam around *Chyka* inspecting the bottom, the prop, and the zincs attached to it. All looked good.

The Gulf of Suez connects the Red Sea to the Suez Canal and so continues the division between Africa and Asia, as then the Suez Canal itself does further north to the Mediterranean.

The Gulf has a length from north to south of 190 miles and a width of only 12-20 miles. Being narrow and lying between mountain ranges, the funnel effect of winds blowing from the north continues to make sailing north about as difficult as in the Red Sea.

The winds on the east side of the Gulf of Suez are still from the north but generally not so strong. I mounted the radar cockpit display and hoisted the radar reflector, both of them to help me deal with the ships I expected to encounter.

Crossing the Gulf was like sailing in a washing machine. The wind was NW 18-20 with short steep waves. On the east side I anchored in Sheikh Riyah Harbor. The wind was blowing 20 knots, but the land to the north gave me protection from the waves, so the sea was calm.

The wind was full of sand which covered everything. I wondered, *why is it, that the sand of the desert over the tens of thousands of years has not already all blown out into the sea? And how do the few people who live here survive? Their homes, clothes, carpets, blankets, everything must always be filled up with sand.*

I departed very early hoping to get on up to Shab El Hasa in daylight. Fortunately, this was close to being the longest day of the year. It was 13 hours of bumpy motorsailing against winds of 18-20 knots. Heavy spray often blew over *Chyka* and me. I made an average speed to the destination of three knots. I arrived just one half hour before dark. It was dusk and too late to read the waters. So I went in behind the reefs, relying on the GPS and the depth gage. I found a good place to anchor behind a protecting reef.

I was glad I did not have to sail on through the night. My arm muscles were sore from two days' rough sailing; they did not want to go on.

Instead, I was secure. I had a beer and loved the spectacular view of the darkening mountains of Sinai. I was too tired to cook dinner. I had canned fruit and went to bed.

As I write this, I wonder why I did not rest a day more after all that. Perhaps it was due to a weather prediction. I don't know. My journal does not tell me.

The next day was not at all as rough, only some light spray and a little pounding. There was a lot of tacking through the oil rigs of the narrowing gulf. I sailed through the night. The north winds gradually became light as I sailed into the north end of the gulf.

Having avoided the shipping channel all this time, I saw there were actually only a few ships going past. So I went over and straight up the middle of the shipping channel where there were no oil rigs. Then I had an easy motorsail on to Suez.

Suez Canal

Suez is at the top of the Gulf of Suez and at the south end of the 101 mile long Suez Canal. Completed in 1869, it was built by the French under Ferdinand de Lesseps, whose company later attempted to construct the Panama Canal, as I told early in this book.

Sailing into the Suez Yacht Club was a moment I had looked forward to. Sometimes I had wondered if I could ever make it. Having read about my troubles with the Red Sea, you can imagine how great was the relief I felt.

I had arranged for Felix Maritime to be my agent for the transit of the canal. Their man, Magdi, met me at the dock. He had reserved for me the only place where one can tie up directly to the dock and so avoid the usual need to moor between pilings.

The next day Magdi took me shopping. The agency took care of the many complications for preparing the transit. These included a customs certificate, fees paid to a certain bank, Egyptian insurance, harbor clearances, pilots to come with me, pilotage dues, a security-clearance certificate, and a tonnage certificate - all issued in different offices around Suez.

Years later I read in *Cruising World* magazine about the Suez Canal, that it takes so many days of frustration to get the formalities done, and how difficult the officials are. The author did not have an agent. *Cruising World* published my response, which in essence said that the key is to have a reliable agent make all the arrangements.

The *Red Sea Pilot* sternly warns against trying to do it on your own, that your applications will get slow attention, and so it will take four days to a week. The reason for this is that the prime job of the officials is big ships. We small fry are just a nuisance.

Felix Maritime charged me $80. It was worth every penny, saving me the loss of many days as well as a lot of hair. My agent for the Panama Canal had charged $200.

A Canal engineer measured *Chyka* and inspected her, the engine, and my safety equipment. Magdi coached me as to what to do and what to expect during the transit. He told me how much to tip the people, that they would always complain it was too little, and that all I needed to do was to say that Felix Maritime recommended so much. I added a little more to it, and in that way the matter was settled nicely each time.

Ismalia

Nabil, was my pilot during the day from Suez to the Ismailia Yacht Club, which is about half way along the length of the canal. Arriving, we had to first tie up with a long bow line to a buoy and back in to tie stern lines to the dock.

Standing on the dock was Sebastian, who caught a line from us. I later lent him my *Greek Pilot* to make copies of some pages. He returned it to me the next day with a can of beer he had purchased in Malaysia! (On my boat it would not have made it to Thailand.) He and his Heike were like sweet children; yet they had sailed around the world in three years with their 28 foot plywood boat!

At a nearby supermarket, which really was super, I could not pay for the stuff I bought, because I did not have enough Egyptian pounds and they would not exchange any other currency.

A nice young man working there drove me to an ATM. After we came back and I paid the supermarket cashier, the young man was kind and drove me with all my groceries to the yacht club. He deserved the generous baksheesh (Middle Eastern term for tip) I gave him.

I had hoped to leave in the morning, especially to get away from the horribly amplified, screaming prayer calls coming at the same times from different mosques.

At 9:00 PM Ahmed from Felix Maritime radioed and told me, there were too many ships scheduled to come through the next day and *Chyka* would not be allowed to go.

So the next morning I went to town. Leaving the marina we always had to check with the Immigration officer at the gate. He did not have much to do. He invited me into his office. We sat and had a long interesting conversation about the wisdom one can find in the Koran.

I shopped more and had my second excellent lunch at the Nefertiti Restaurant. I did email and checked weather.

Ahmed came by at midnight to tell me my next pilot would arrive early to go with me to Port Said.

His name was Samir. We departed at 5:45 AM. He did most of the steering. I made for us eggs and toast for breakfast and tuna sandwiches for lunch.

We came to Port Said on the Mediterranean at 1:30 PM. A pilot boat came alongside to pick up Samir. I had no intention of stopping at Port Said. I had been here 45 years before and would have enjoyed walking around, but docking and anchoring in this place are famously difficult and uncomfortable.

The Mediterranean Sea

I motorsailed out into the Med. The wind was light, 9-12 knots on the nose, and with a light chop on the sea. My plan was to motorsail on through the night to get past all the trawlers, the shipping, and the oil rigs.

At 12:30 AM I was past all the trouble and well into the open sea. I hove-to and slept five hours, only checking a few times how much *Chyka* was drifting back south.

I planned on getting to Turkey in about six days. The first day was easy, pleasant sailing with a light west wind. *Chyka* took care of herself while I took naps, read my book, and studied some Turkish.

I had assumed the Med would be full of ships and boats, but it was not. After a whole day not seeing any other vessel, I had some diversion. *US Warship Number 58* made a wide circle around *Chyka* but did not call. I spoke with two approaching cargo ships. I asked them if they wanted me to change course or speed. Both said I was OK as I was.

The wind became west and stayed that way. By sailing close to it I was able to sail northwest. It began to look as if, with some motorsailing on the last day, I might be able to get all the way to Marmaris on the southwest corner of Turkey. But finally, I saw it would be too difficult to do so, and decided to go into Finike on the middle south coast of Turkey. It was within reach under sail. I was happy with this. At least I had sailed enough west of Cyprus to avoid having to stop there, where the ports are difficult for sailboats.

Turkey

I arrived at 3:00 PM on 5 July 2006. Finike Marina was one of the best marinas I have known. It had everything; shops, restaurants, a lady who does your washing and irons it for almost nothing, a boat yard, spotless, modern showers and toilets with marble floors and motion sensors to control the lights. The office had Internet and a helpful staff.

In the center area was a beer garden, called The Rose Garden, surrounded by trees and bushes. There, 10 to 20 of us congregated most evenings at five o'clock for beers sometimes followed by dinner at one of the marina restaurants.

From our boats we could see green mountains on three sides. Just outside the street entrance to the marina was the middle of Finike with shops for everything, better Internet places than at the marina, hotels, and more restaurants. And we were well protected from difficult weather.

One of the notorious winds of the Mediterranean, the meltemi, was developing. It occurs from June until October. After that, winter gales rapidly develop. So, as happened in me in the Maldives, it was then too late in the year to go on further. And I really did not want to anyway. There was on board almost nothing that did not need to be repaired, replaced, adjusted, cleaned, or due for serious maintenance.

Most of us wanted to keep our boats here for the winter. An exception was Jim and Rosie on *Avalon*. They had lingered a year in Australia. Moving along fast, they caught up with me here. I told them this is a better place to stay for the winter, but for some reason they went on the next 120 miles to winter instead in Marmaris. I caught up with them there nine months later.

Our group visited nearby Greek and Roman city ruins. One special evening ten of us were driven in a van the long trip to Aspendos. There, is the Roman "best-preserved theater of antiquity." It was completed in 155 AD with 7,000 seats. We had to split up to find places and then enjoyed an impressive performance of *Carmina Burana*. Back at the marina by 2:30 AM we had many beers in The Rose Garden discussing everything. I returned to *Chyka* at 5:00 AM.

Jack was already in Greece and planned to be in Croatia in September. Since Thailand, there was no more catching up with him. And I never did again. Later he and Kerstin did fly to join me in the Canary Islands as you can read later.

A Norwegian couple on their way to Israel had no charts of Cyprus which was on the way there. I gave them the charts of Cyprus the young Russians had given me, since I then had no possible use for them.

A group of us took a tour to the ancient Roman city of Olympos (Not spelled like Mount Olympus in Greece). With us was a German family: 15 year old Verina, her parents, and her grandparents. Verina walked with me as we explored the ruins and the harbor of Olympos.

The Chimera

After Olympos, our van took us to the foot of a nearby mountain. We climbed 45 minutes up a rough mountain path to a rocky elevation and the site of the Chimera, flames from methane gas coming from far below and out of holes in the stone. They have burned constantly for thousands of years. During the times when the Greeks and Romans were around, sailors used the Chimera as a night time beacon. In those days Chimera was the name of a mythical monster that spits fire.

The climb up to the Chimera was difficult for me. Verina stayed with me the whole way. She was worried about this old man. It became pitch dark. The flames were like camp fires. Over one of them our guide cooked kebab for us.

As is usually true, walking down was more difficult than climbing up. We had brought flashlights, but it was confusing. Verina held my hand over the rough places. We walked down carefully. At the bottom I had to sit down to rest with her awhile before walking to the van.

The ride back was fun mostly because of Verina. We spoke to each other in German, but she did speak excellent English.

I told Verina the riddle - but she repeatedly cracked up trying to say the whole of it - "How much wood would a woodchuck chuck if a woodchuck would chuck wood?" If you do not know the answer to this question, just ask Verina or any of my grandchildren.

Well, never mind. I will tell you the answer. "A woodchuck would chuck all the wood he could chuck if a woodchuck would chuck wood."

I was sorry when after some days she and her family departed.

Eumet, the manager of the marina, made clearing into Turkey simple for all boats arriving from other countries. He was always helpful with information. He spoke perfect English and often said, "Of course" instead of yes. One time he was on his way to Moscow to be at some celebration for a Russian friend. I asked him:

"Now, Eumet, you won't drink the vodka there will you?"

"Of course I will."

"But Eumet, you are Muslim."

"Of course I am."

"So you should not drink alcohol."

"Of course not."

"But you will?"

"Of course."

A key member of our group was voluptuous Sandra, who had arranged our trip to Aspendos to see *Carmina Burana*. She organized a large benefit for animals. There were all of our group, also local Turks, Germans, and more English people. It started at 11:00 AM and lasted all day and evening. For the whole time, there was beer, wine, food, and a BBQ, as well as what we brought ourselves.

It ended up late at night with five of us having had way too much to drink. Kate and Sandra got into an ugly argument that the rest of us thought was amusing. Anyway, it had been a great success and lots of fun.

Sandra and Bob had invited me to come to them the next evening. It was a delightful dinner at their home overlooking the town and the marina from their terrace. Sandra's friend, Helen, was there. Too often the conversation rehashed the tiff of the night before. Finally, I honestly told Sandra, "You and Kate were both skunked. Just clear it one on one with Kate." The next day she did.

There was a great party on board *Chyka,* but for the women only. I don't remember and my notes don't say why it was so, but I was allowed to be there; I guess because I was crew, and, after all, it was my boat!

Kekova Roads

Chyka headed out and sailed west along the beautiful coast of Lycia (pronounced LISH - ya) four and a half hours to Kekova Roads, a scenic almost landlocked roadstead. Along this coast the Taurus mountains are always in view. They plunge down into the sea making lovely fjord anchorages. After entering the east end of Kekova Roads, I sailed the four miles to the remote west end and anchored. I spent three weeks there.

On shore there were only a few ramshackle buildings. I launched *Li'l Chyka* to get ashore. But the outboard would not start.

A German boat, *Venus,* arrived and anchored near *Chyka.* The wind shifted resulting in our boats changing position to each other. They were then anchored way too close to me. This happens from time to time.

I asked the beautiful lady on their foredeck if they would please move. It is understood internationally that the first boat to anchor has priority of location. She gladly agreed, and they moved.

I worked on the outboard for two hours. There was a lot of trouble with a frozen bolt that had to be removed. (Frozen means it was solidly fixed in place by corrosion.) In the late afternoon I gave up for the day and had a swim. The air was 80 F and the water 78 F. Wonderful.

The next day started with a light rain and a slight breeze. All was serene with soft grey-green hills on every side. It was quiet except for a rooster. I finished the outboard. There had been dirt and water in the carburetor.

One of the few beach buildings was the friendly little Yoruk Restaurant. There I met Karl, another single-hander. Originally from Rosenheim, Germany, he was living in Cyprus and had been sailing to this area for 20 years. We had dinner together. Karl told me something important: Behind the Yoruk starts a trail to the next bay, where there are the ruins of Aperlae.

After lunch the next day at the Yoruk I hiked the 1.5 mile trail Karl told me about. It joined a path called the Lycian Way, which at one time connected the ancient coastal towns of Lycia.

Aperlae

This was a port city from the 5th century BC through the Greek and Roman Empires and into the Middle Ages. Now it is gone. Most of its ruins are under water. And there are no roads to the place. So the trail I took was actually the best way to get here.

I felt sad standing there looking over this pretty inlet and thinking about all that was lost, going from a busy Mediterranean port and now reduced to ruins and two stone houses.

Outside one of them I found a young man working on it, a hopelessly dilapidated place. It had once belonged to his grandfather. Every time that he came, he had to hike four miles along a path in the woods and over a hill carrying what he needed.

Hills rose steeply up from Aperlae. From his house I could see stone walls in the woods above. He told me those walls were part of an ancient castle and showed me where to find the path up to them. As I climbed I passed many sarcophagi, ancient stone coffins with decorations carved in the stone. They are everywhere along this coast. I ran out of strength at some large ruins that must have been part of the castle.

After resting on the grass 10 minutes I started back. Half way down, off to one side I saw a piece of a broken, red roof tile perched on a stone under a bush. In the woods there were a few, long ago abandoned houses with red tiled roofs.

Looking down at it I saw that in the tile was cast, "St. Henry." How strange! Henry is not at all a Turkish name. Well, I had no room for the thing on *Chyka* and walked on. One minute later I stopped and thought, *You fool, go back and get it.* I did so, and it now is on display in our condo living room.

My research guru, Patricia Holt, has found there was a French manufacturer of roof tiles called St. Henry Marseille and that St. Henry, who lived 973 - 1024 was Duke of Bavaria and later a Holy Roman Emperor.

Ucagiz

(For me the correct pronunciation of it is impossible.)

North of the center of Kekova Roads is the entrance to a small bay with the busy tourist town of Ucagiz. I sailed there and anchored just west of town.

In town I had a beer and did email at the Kabay Bar. There, doing the same were the couple from *Venus*, the boat that I had asked to move. They were Gisela and Uwe. We met that night for a delightful dinner with another German couple at the Onur dock restaurant.

Many Germans tour Turkey. With some of them I rode on a glass bottom boat to the south side of Kekova Roads to view the sunken city there. The stone buildings underwater were clear to see and amazingly intact.

Returning, they dropped me off at the dock of Kale Koy, an ancient but still living town at the entrance to Ucagiz Bay. Looming over it are the walls of the castle that once protected the entrance.

After morning tea I started up the path to the castle. A lady joined me and offered to help me find the way. I was not sure how to go and agreed. As we climbed up out of town and into the scrub area under the steep hill, I eventually saw what I thought was the right way to go. So I paid her something and let her go. That was a very big mistake.

The Most Dangerous Event of the Adventure

I took a wrong turn. What I thought was the correct path became increasingly steep until I was climbing up a rock front. I kept thinking just a little further it will level off, but it did not.

At some point I realized it was too late to retreat. I was wearing the worst kind of climbing shoes, sandals, and I had a heavy backpack. Slowly I gained handholds thinking each time, *if this rock gives way I will fall to my death.*

I made it over the top, thank God, to where it became a short steep walk up to the old castle. From it I had the wonderful view of Kekova Roads and Kale Koy below. I took an easy path to the east, down through a field of sarcophagi, around the east end of the bay to join the old Lycian Way, and back to Ucagiz where I had a celebration lunch with beers at the Onur.

Kekova Roads from Kale Koy Castle

Sarcophagi, down the hill from the castle

For two days it was thunderstorm weather. That did not slow down Jacque on *Miscat*. He came to *Chyka* to talk while it was blowing. I told you about how he helped me changing money way back in Massawa, Eritrea. He gave me advice on the Mediterranean. And then he went back to his boat, hauled his dinghy up, and sailed out into it! He had some obligation to be somewhere sometime, often a mistake in bad weather. With the wind howling I happily remained on *Chyka*.

After one more day the wind calmed. I went to town. The weather had wiped out electricity and there was no Internet.

After I sailed back to Finike, violent weather came. It lasted three days. I was glad to be safely docked at this well protected marina.

We cruisers survived it all with pleasant evenings at The Rose Garden. After the bad weather passed, the water in the marina was cluttered with debris, which took the marina people days to remove.

Home Leave - November 2006 to March 2007

Winter was closing in on Turkey with its cold windy weather, not good for sailing or living on a boat. We all retreated to our homes.

I don't usually tell you much about what happens during home leaves, but this one was very special. It led to love.

You know already I was interested in Patricia since that long brunch we had. On my way to Susan's I visited her. As I did for my daughters, I repaired things for her around her condo.

Patricia made lunch for me and a few of her friends. She was at one end of the table and I at the other. She was dressed all in white. During the meal we often looked at each other with smiles.

Another time Patricia and I went for dinner at Treasure Island's Sloppy Joe's. They said there would be a wait of one hour. No problem. The Gulf beach was right there, and in the trunk of her car we had beach chairs, a bottle of wine, and glasses. We watched the sunset. After a little more conversation, I looked over to her, and she to me. We kissed really well. We both said, "Wow!" We were in love. I stayed two days with her.

On my way back to Turkey I had to change planes in London. I made it a few days stopover to visit Mike and Susan Wetson. (A reminder - I had sailed with Mike in New Caledonia.) They lived near the pretty little town of Henley-on-Thames in a lovely country area that could not be more old rural England.

Susan informed us a few years later that Mike died of a knee surgery complication. It was so sad to hear this; he was otherwise healthy and only in his sixties.

I returned to Finike on April 3. Mike and Kate were already back. Some of us had dinner at a marina restaurant. Trygve Olson sat next to me. He had been with all of us on Phuket Island for our Christmas dinner and the tsunami. Trygve was part of the group of boats that had done the Red Sea in 2005 together with Jack Oldenberg, Torben, Ola and Signy, and another boat I did not know. In January Torben had arranged a reunion of them all in Denmark.

Patricia and I emailed every day, sometimes more than once a day. And we did so whenever I could find a place to do email until the end of the voyage and beyond.

Patricia has three hatboxes full of copies of my emails. We read them from time to time with such tender memories of our early love. I intend to write a book about us. The title of it will be *The Hatbox*. It will appear sometime after the publication of *Holt's Comprehensive Field Guide to Birds of the Indian Ocean*.

On April 28, 2007 I departed, with many friends on the dock giving me a great sendoff. Marge gave me a bottle of her homemade marmalade. Of course, Mike and Kate were there. I hugged and kissed Kate and told her I would miss her.

I sailed back to Kekova Roads and anchored again at the lovely west end of it just off the Yoruk Restaurant. *Chyka* was alone. All was still and beautiful. I stayed three days. I preferred this to the many other places on the way to Marmaris which require lowering the dinghy at anchor to take a long stern line ashore.

Taking up the anchor the windlass failed. I had worried about this possibly happening for years and had on board my emergency recovery handle. With it I slowly but easily raised the anchor.

It was an easy overnight sail to Marmaris during which I hove-to for awhile. Rosie and Jim were in the brand new, super Marmaris Yacht Marina. I went there.

Marmaris

This is a pretty tourist resort town on the southwest corner of Turkey. Two mountain ranges meet giving grand views of themselves from anywhere in the area. The buildings are white with red tile roofs. Overlooking Marmaris is a well preserved medieval fortress.

Rosie, Jim, and I often went to town to shop, email, check weather online, and dine out.

Patricia had seen pictures of Marmaris and asked me to photograph some of it. I did so as we walked around. Then we climbed up to the castle to enjoy and photograph the wonderful views of the harbor, the city, and the mountains.

The restaurant at the marina was impressive. It was on the second floor with a fine view. The food was excellent. As we ordered, the waiter entered it all on a touchpad that transmitted it directly to the kitchen! Are the Turks smarter than Americans?

Winds of the Mediterranean

The Med is surrounded by mountain ranges. At times they funnel and accelerate prevailing winds into the Med creating dry, strong to gale force winds over the sea lasting days at a time. The stories in literature all the way back to the *Odyssey* of Homer describe the loss of countless ships mostly due to the notorious winds of the Mediterranean. They are:

> 1) *The meltemi comes down through the Aegean Sea in the summer. We avoided it by crossing the Aegean before summer.*
>
> 2) *The scirocco blows off North Africa and can happen anytime of the year.*
>
> 3) *The bora comes to the Adriatic Sea off Croatia. One time Klaus Wall and I with others got hit by it when crossing the Adriatic. We had to scramble to keep a tear in the mainsail from destroying the whole sail.*
>
> 4) *The mistral blows off the coast of France mostly during winter and spring but can occur in any season. The French say its winds are strong enough to blow the ears off a donkey.*
>
> 5) *The levanter, which happens south of Spain, is known to suddenly occur at anytime of the year. How suddenly it strikes I learned the hard way in August.*

Greece

Chyka and *Avalon* left Marmaris May 14, 2007 to cross the Aegean. We did so in two weeks visiting six islands.

The Greek Islands extend all the way over to the shores of Turkey and include Rhodes, which was right in front of us. It is an important, interesting, historical place, which Sonja and I had visited 11 years before. But it is difficult to moor sailboats in Rhodes. We decided to skip it and go on to Kos.

With an overnight sail in light wind we arrived early at the modern Kos Marina. Clearing into Greece was complicated. I was used to all that, but here it was really funny to watch. People were coming and going shouting at each other. Whatever they needed, a stapler, a stamp, they didn't have and had to run off to another room to get it. Everything cost money, but they had no change. To get it, they scrounged around all over into safes, boxes, and friends' purses.

The town has an imposing fort and an agora, what the ancients called their public squares. It reminded me of the agora in Athens where Socrates taught his students. One of them was Plato, who taught Aristotle. He became the mentor of Alexander the Great, always encouraging him to seek knowledge.

After Alexander founded Alexandria, it became the center of knowledge of the ancient world, recognized as such and supported by scholars throughout Europe! (I write about Alexandria later in this book when telling you about Columbus crossing the Atlantic.)

We sailed to the head of Plakoudhi Bay on Leros Island and anchored. We were the only cruising boats there. It was a pretty little cove with a few homes and some small, local boats.

It had been cold sailing here; I was wearing jeans and a sweatshirt. So our timing to cross over was perfect, being after the winter but before the summer months of the meltemi.

I had planned for a long time to visit Miranda in Athens. Like Penny Purnawaty in Indonesia, Miranda had lived with my family one year as an exchange student. I called her to discuss the visit. Jim had picked up a forecast of bad weather. So I asked Miranda about it. In 45 minutes she called back with a forecast for our area that confirmed what Jim had heard.

Later it rained and the wind increased. We stayed four nights until it passed. On the morning of the third day, having heard the weather would improve, Jim wanted to leave. I had seen too many people going out into bad weather because of somebody's prediction and a lot of hope, and then getting slammed. Cyndie confirmed the weather would stay bad for awhile. I told Jim I would stay. They did also. I read a book Patricia had given me, *The Road Less Traveled* by Scott Peck.

After sailing all day and into the night with a wonderful SSW-15, we arrived at a bay on Naxos Island at 1:00 AM. With my radar, our depth gauges, and eyes we worked our way in and anchored. Early the next day we sailed the short distance around to the west side of the island to the Naxos Marina. It was difficult to Med moor there and the facilities dysfunctional, but it is a small, pretty port. We were able to shop and email. We were especially there to take the ferry to Santorini.

Santorini

The *Greek Waters Pilot* calls it, "unlike anywhere else in the world," and, "one of the places in the Aegean that must be visited." It was far out of our way, and anchoring there is difficult. So instead of sailing there, we took the ferry. Going 19 knots, we were there in 3½ hours.

Santorini is a volcano with its center collapsed deeply into the sea forming a four by six mile lagoon within its crater. Crossing the lagoon, we were awed by the views. The mostly brick red rock cliffs climb steeply on three sides up 980 feet. Way above us on the edge of the rim, we could see its pretty city of mostly white buildings.

The ferry docked. With others we took a bus to the top to explore the town, shop, have lunch, and enjoy the clear views of the lagoon and the rest of the rim facing us.

Santorini, Greece

This was a normal island until about 1,445 BC when under it occurred the most violent volcanic eruption in known history, about three times more powerful than Krakatoa in 1883.

Giant waves went out from the eruption to the nearby island of Crete, where with the following storm of ash deeply covering everything, the homeland of the Minoan civilization was destroyed. Part of their civilization had been on Santorini in the ancient city now called Akrotiri.

Excavations of it starting in 1967 have proven it was a prosperous advanced city with three story mansions and an elaborate drainage system. The people built ships. In 2005 the roof structure to protect the excavation site collapsed causing the place to be closed to tourists. So we missed the chance to visit the site by two years.

The Legend of Atlantis - The Vanished Civilization.

In the times when the volcano erupted and for three thousand years after, news traveled very slowly. It was only by word of mouth, with people being remote from each other, that news ever got anywhere at all. News became legends passed on through generations.

Over a thousand years after it happened, Plato called it Atlantis, an island civilization that disappeared from some disaster. As literacy developed, the story became a mystery with several possible locations as to where the Lost Civilization had been, including places in the Atlantic Ocean. We now are sure that what Plato wrote about was the destruction of the Minoan Civilization on Crete. And we know, that was caused by the eruption of Santorini.

Aliens

As is usual with extraordinary events, some without real evidence, like UFOs, and some real, like the construction of the pyramids, there are people who would like to think it must have been the work of aliens.

The alien theories picked up speed by the surprising news that when unearthing Akrotiri in 1967 they found no remains of any humans! All of the people there had vanished! Where did they go? What could have happened to them? Of course, it had to have been because of aliens! What more proof do you need?

One idea is that aliens caused it all. Another is that the people of Santorini themselves were aliens, and they decided to pack up and go back to their home, off in the universe somewhere.

The explanation is this: We know the people of Akrotiri had at least a thousand years of experience with seismic activity and its history of eruptive incidents. (They occur in Santorini from time to time, the last three being in the 19th century.) The people would have recognized from the forewarnings that something overwhelming was brewing, got on their ships, and sailed to other islands seeking safety. I think most or all of them probably sailed to nearby Crete, the center of their culture, and there lost their lives anyway.

After returning to Naxos, Rosie, Jim, and I planned eating out. On the ferry back from Santorini we had met a young couple, Ann Marie and Phil. As we were relaxing and thinking about dinner, Ann Marie happened by. We agreed we all would have dinner together. She went off to get Phil. He came along later alone; he had somehow missed Ann Marie.

We told him to go back to their hotel and leave a message that she should meet him at the original meeting place. They showed up much later, beaming. Rosie, Jim, and I were half done with our dinners but enjoyed spending time with them.

In the morning an easy day sail brought our two boats 24 miles to anchor in a quiet pretty bay on Siros Island. And the next day was a pleasant sail to Kithnos Island.

We intended to moor in the town, but it was full and too busy. So we went a little further around the north side of the island to check on a small cove. It was too small. (Sounds like Goldilocks!) That was at 3:00 PM. We had lots of time and so sailed on another 15 miles to the west coast of Kea and anchored in pretty Kavia Bay surrounded by green and brown high hills with windmills and stone walls.

The weather was perfect. But Jim once again heard something about bad weather brewing.

I called Patricia and asked her for a weather forecast. She looked at it for a long while. Then she gave me a comprehensive report. Patricia's forecasts from then on to the end of this journey were all that way.

Essentially, her report said the wind would pick up, shift to the southeast, and that it would rain. So we knew we could not depart for awhile. We went ashore to a beach bar for beers and lunch.

That night the barometer fell quickly. (A barometer measures air pressure. High pressure predicts fair weather. Low pressure indicates bad weather, and the lower it gets the worse the weather will probably be.) The weather did exactly what Patricia said it would. Southeast winds with waves coming to us from the west produced uncomfortable rolling of our boats most of the night.

With a strong east wind *Avalon* departed for Aegina Island to go on from there to the Corinth Canal and the Ionian Sea beyond. Jim later reported on VHF that their weather died to calm with later thunderstorms and strong headwinds. They were soaked and cold. I did not see them again until Sicily.

I left much later for a short sail with some lighting crackling to Olympic Marina on the mainland of Greece. Just as with the best marinas anywhere, they had floating finger piers (so much easier because they rise and fall with the tide along with the boats moored to them).

Miranda

After a day to reorganize the boat, Miranda, whom I mentioned before having been an exchange student daughter of ours, and her seven year old daughter, Alexsia, came to the Marina. After a brief visit on *Chyka* they drove me back to their beautiful home in Athens for an overnight. It was near dinner time. Kitty, Miranda's mother, greeted me with, "I see you need a strong Scotch." She was recalling the following story we had always remembered:

Eleven years before this visit, when Sonja and I were in Athens, Kitty invited us to dinner having assembled family people to meet us. She lived on a tiny street about 100 feet long. The first cab driver could not find it. After we let him go, we found a man in a store who spoke good English. He looked up Kitty's name in the phone book. The address we had was correct. It was nearby. He told the next cab driver how to find it. That driver dropped us off in front of some apartment building.

Now, which apartment? The names listed in front were all written in the Greek alphabet. Fortunately, I had learned Russian, which uses almost the same alphabet as the Greeks. We were very late. The others were to be there and waiting.

The elevator took us to the top floor and to the door of a penthouse. Before us stood a simple woman who spoke no English. We had never before seen Kitty, but we knew she spoke perfect English. Sonja said, "We have the wrong place."

But suddenly Kitty came from around a corner to greet us. The other woman was her cook. Kitty ushered us in saying to me, "I see you need a strong Scotch."

Three years ago Patricia and I visited Miranda in London. She and her husband, Costis, have a flat there as well as their house in Athens. Kitty was with her. When they greeted us Kitty, of course, said, "I see you need a strong Scotch."

Now, back to my visiting Miranda in Athens. Alexsia was sweet and bright. Her playroom was stuffed with toys as was her bedroom. But the girl was not at all spoiled. She had excellent manners. She was not allowed to join us until her homework was done and approved.

After breakfast Alexsia, remember, only seven years old, already speaking fluent English, read to me. We made paper airplanes.

Since college, I had liked Greek mythology. Miranda took a picture of me telling Alexsia the story of the Riddle of the Sphinx, the female monster that lurked in the woods near Thebes in Greece.

As told in the Greek tragedy, *Oedipus Rex* by Sophocles, every man who came near the sphinx was required to solve that riddle. If any man could, he would become King. But if he could not, she cast him over the cliff to his destruction. Below was an enormous pile of the bones of all those who had failed.

The riddle was this: What has four legs, two legs, and three legs? The answer is, a man. As a baby he crawls on four limbs, later walks on two, and when old, two legs and a cane.

Oedipus came by and gave the correct answer. The sphinx was crushed, and in her despair jumped off the cliff herself. Oedipus became the King of Thebes. He then married the Queen without yet knowing that she was actually his own mother.

Miranda drove me back to *Chyka*. We had lunch at a place next to the Temple of Poseidon perched at the end of the peninsula south of Athens. Poseidon was the god of the seas. From 200 feet above, the temple looks out majestically over the sea on three sides. The temple was built in the traditional rectangular form, like the Parthenon, in 450 BC to 440 BC, and so in the Golden Age of Greece. Back on *Chyka* Miranda and I said good-bye.

Across Greece

After a few days preparing, I departed on June 4, 2007. I would have been worried by the ominous cloud cover, but the barometer held steady at an optimistic 1014. Soon after departure I rounded the cape enjoying the passing views of the Temple of Poseidon way above, where Miranda and I had been.

After a pleasant 36 mile sail to the island of Aegina, I anchored in the bay at the west side of it. My family and I had taken a boat trip to Aegina in 1969 when we were in Athens on our way to Africa.

In the morning the barometer was falling. There was lighting and light rain. I saw that protection from the coming bad weather in this place would not be good. So I decided to immediately sail the next leg of 26 miles before a serious blow arrived.

In Kalamaki Bay just north of the entrance to the Corinth Canal I anchored in the early afternoon. Later, as predicted, it started to blow hard. *Chyka* was well anchored. I was not worried. The barometer continued to fall. Then there was a red sunset, an indication of good weather the next day, as I have already written.

Corinth Canal

The canal entrance was only a half mile away from where I was anchored. I docked at the headquarters, paid the fee, and went back on board to wait. The canal is too narrow to allow two way traffic, so delays of hours can happen. But in only 15 minutes they called on VHF and told me to go.

Completed in 1893 the canal connects the Aegean Sea to the Gulf of Corinth opening onto the Ionian Sea west of Greece. It saves having to sail all the way around the Peloponnesian Peninsula. Cut deeply into solid rock up to 250 feet above the water, it is 3.2 miles long and only 81 feet wide. With a head current and strong eddies swaying *Chyka* this way and that, it took careful steering to keep going along. From the canal I sailed northwest across the gulf to spend the night in Andikiron Bay.

Trizonia Island

The next day I came to this small, unique island off the north coast of the Gulf of Corinth. I entered its little harbor. With the help of a young lady, Jenny, I tied up to a dock next to her boat. It was from Norway, and Jenny was the girlfriend of the skipper, Sven.

Such an unusual place! There were a few sailboats and some local fishing boats. But there was no office to check into, no one to pay. I went ashore and walked the short distance into the picturesque town.

There were no cars and no motorbikes allowed on the island. All was quiet. The waterfront facing the mainland was a row of stone buildings with shops, restaurants, and tavernas. Sitting at tables in front of them and under the trees, old men lounged sipping drinks just like pictures you see of rural Greece. Small tourist boats brought tourists over from the mainland to walk around, visit the castle, and have a drink or a meal.

In the evenings on *Chyka* the quiet of the town enhanced the charm of the gentle church bells, which then struck me with the pleasant contrast of them to the shrill prayer calls I had endured in Indonesia and Egypt.

Jenny, Sven, and his cousin, Sara, twice joined me for dinner at tavernas. I gave Sven charts of where they were going. They were of where I had been. So I had no more need of them.

We were joined by 77 year old Vernon and his new partner, Ann. Both Vernon and Sven had done the North Atlantic Circle, which means sailing from Europe down to the Canary Islands, across to the Caribbean, north to Bermuda, and back east to Europe.

Sven asked me to help them cast off early one morning. I got up at 3:00 AM and found them all busy preparing. I was impressed with how super careful they were, even though the weather was predicted to be great for them. Sven was going around with a miner's headlamp slowly inspecting everything. Then gently off they sailed into the night.

I motorsailed the 22 miles to Patras passing under the new impressive suspension bridge, which crosses the one mile wide strait at the entrance to the Gulf of Corinth from the Ionian Sea.

Patras

Patras is the third largest city in Greece. It is a busy commercial port with ferries and fishing boats landing in their designated areas.

The marina was small, friendly, and comfortable. I stayed there eight days doing maintenance, repairing, loading fuel and water, and shopping for food supplies.

We were only 10 cruising boats. Nearby was an outdoor theater built in the ancient style. Kids practiced dancing during the daytime. In the evenings, shows gave us pleasant traditional Greek music.

In the city there were innumerable bars with people sipping drinks, water, and coffee. But strangely none of them offered anything to eat. Where were my tavernas? I finally found a sandwich at the ferry terminal.

Chris Swift on his Nauticat 33, a pilothouse motorsailor, was next to *Chyka*. We sometimes had sundowners and snacks on *Chyka*. My mainsail had a tear in it. There was no sailmaker around. I took the main down and used the new awl I had bought in the States to repair it. Hoisting it back up, the sail stuck in the mast track. I could not move it up with the main halyard, nor could I pull the sail back down. I was so glad for my mast steps, which I had installed at the beginning in Milwaukee. Up I climbed. Chris was tailing me with the spare halyard in case I fell. (That halyard was also used to haul the dinghy up on deck.) I broke the sail free and could then raise the main to the top.

Patricia was not getting all of my emails and I not all of hers. There was something wrong with my AOL. We sent short messages, she labeling hers number 1, 2, etc; mine were called A, B, and so on. One day, for example, I emailed to her, "I received your number five. This is my email G." If one went missing it was sent again.

With my email being so unreliable I called Patricia on the satellite phone at 5:30 AM her time, which she had told me would always be OK, to tell her I was leaving for Italy.

Checking out of the marina they did not want me to pay for the last five days; I had no idea why - perhaps something to do with our having been friends. I gave them three bottles of bourbon someone had given me. Scotch is so much better.

Messina, Italy

I sailed three days and nights across the Ionian Sea south of the mainland of Italy to its island, Sicily, the largest one in the Mediterranean. Heading north into the Messina Strait that separates mainland Italy from Sicily, I had to deal with a strong head wind and a three knot current against me. Jim and Rosie were way further south having similar conditions. While entering Messina and putting out fenders to dock, a squall hit with winds of 30 to 35 knots. Normally, squalls don't last long. When it passed I went in to a slip at the marina. Soon *Calypso*, John and Margo, arrived. You have read about my being with them in Egypt.

Maria at the marina office told me I did not need to clear into Italy. *What?* American boats not cleared in, or not having notified the Italian Coast Guard, have been fined. There were no customs or immigration offices in Messina. I went to the Port Captain and also to the Italian Coast Guard. Nothing. They said I could try the police. *Very funny.* So I gave up. If no one cared, why should I?

Staying there was bad. Half of the marina staff was unfriendly. It was the most expensive marina I had ever visited. The facilities were filthy; thankfully I had my own on *Chyka*. Our boats were always rocking around from the wind and the ships going in and out of the port.

It was June 25, 2007. Understandably, I was too anxious to leave - no excuse for what happened. When I cast off, *Chyka* did not get far. I was glad no one was watching, because I had stupidly neglected to release the two stern lines. I slunk back in, climbed ashore to release the lines, and cast off again.

This expensive, miserable marina had no fuel available! I stopped two miles north at the small port of Paradissa, where I was able to take on fuel. Just offshore from there I met up at sea with Rosie and Jim.

We then went on through the notorious Strait of Messina and into the Tyrrhenian Sea north of Sicily.

The Strait of Messina separating Sicily from mainland Italy is only two miles wide. There are tidal currents changing direction every six hours, counter currents, sudden strong winds accelerated by mountains on both sides, and in the middle of it are whirlpools.

As described in Homer's *Odyssey*, it has always been known for its terrible conditions and the destruction of countless ships. In Greek mythology it was ruled by female monsters. The sphinx was another of them. Are female monsters worse than male monsters?

We had planned the time of going through the strait so as to do it with a north running current and good weather. The wind was light and aft of us. We knew where the danger areas were and avoided them. Then we were free of it and out into the Tyrrhenian Sea.

The Aeolian Islands

These small islands are off the north coast of Sicily. Aeolus was the god of the winds. The Aeolian Triangle, as the islands are called, is far more a threat than the Bermuda Triangle, which is anyway a groundless myth.

Rod Heikell, author of the *Italian Waters Pilot,* tells of the several terrible times he has had with sudden unpredicted full gale winds and how he has known boats that were lost, and with them lives as well.

In these islands we often had strong winds when at anchor, otherwise we were fine. We were careful and patient. But really, we were lucky to get through them all without serious trouble.

Our first destination was Stromboli. It is a volcanic island. The peak of it rises 3,000 feet straight out of the sea. The volcano erupts gently every fifteen minutes or so with smoke and fire. This means the pressure in the volcano can never build up for a serious explosion. The some 500 people in the pretty little town under it have no cause to be worried. We sailed on past it, because it is a difficult place for cruisers. We hove-to north of Stromboli to have our dinners on our own boats and wait for night to see the fire of the eruptions.

When it was dark we sailed down the west coast of Stromboli. I was ahead using my radar. *Avalon* stayed behind me and a little further offshore to be sure she was in deeper water. We saw no fire, but because of a full moon we could see the smoke plumes belching up from time to time.

It was already late when we considered anchoring on the southwest coast of Stromboli. Instead of the predicted strong winds against us, there was no wind at all. It was only 22 miles on to Salina Island. So we took advantage of the easy weather and motorsailed on.

Five miles off Salina Island at 2:00 AM we hove-to, slept, and waited for daylight. When we could see, we anchored in a bay near to the town up against a towering rock slope. Rosie and Jim swam over to *Chyka* to visit and catch up. We had not actually been together since the Greek Islands. I swam twice in the warm, crystal clear, turquoise water. We went to the pretty town that sits under a high mountain. After beers at an outdoor bar we had dinner on a terrace overlooking the marina.

Then it was a day off for resting and projects. In the evening, from another restaurant overlooking the bay, we could see Stromboli over the horizon puffing smoke.

We sailed to the marina on Lipari Island. It is the largest of this island group and has a long history. Excavations have confirmed that people were here from prehistoric times, then Phoenicians, Greeks, Carthaginians, Romans, Byzantines, Normans, and Spanish.

At our slips we were blown around and rolled, which in these windy islands is to be expected.

We were planning the 280 mile passage to Sardinia. Rosie and I shopped for last provisions.

A Mistral

A long term forecast from Patricia, later confirmed on the Internet, predicted there would be a mistral wind in four to five days. Leaving the next day would give us enough time to get to Sardinia with good weather before it arrived. That is what we did.

The island of Vulcano is separated from Lipari by only a half mile. The views of it from offshore were stark. It is an island of mostly extinct volcanoes, one of them being active. On the way we could also clearly see the other high islands we knew, including Stromboli, still well above the horizon. We motored into Vulcano's northwest bay in quiet weather. Jim and Rosie liked it so much they decided to stay. I wanted to be sure to get to Sardinia before the mistral did.

So off I went into a light west wind motorsailing past the remaining Aeolian Islands and out to sea. The barometer confirmed there would be stable conditions for awhile.

At night a light wind from abeam developed and I had a delightful broad reach sail all night until daylight.

On the third day I came into Villasimius Bay on the southeast coast of Sardinia. Going into the marina I passed John and Margo anchored in the bay on *Calypso*. What is known to be a difficult heavy weather passage had been a piece of cake for me, because of Patricia.

Before leaving to sail the last 20 miles to Cagliari, the capitol of Sardinia, I talked to Patricia. She told me I had at least a full day more before the mistral would hit here. On the way out I stopped by *Calypso*. They said they would stay and wait out the predicted mistral winds. *Why?*

It was then an easy short sail to the harbor of Cagliari and to the Marina del Sole. A man met me in a dinghy to guide me to my slip. Their office and a bar were under a tent on their dock. I signed in and stayed several hours meeting the people and having Scotches.

Cagliari, Sardinia

The next morning before the mistral was to arrive, I moved to the nearby Marina di Sant Elmo, more expensive, but so much more comfortable and convenient. *Chyka* was then only steps from their office and the road to town. Rosie and Jim had told me they planned to come to this marina. The manager was Enrico Di Plano, a kind, interesting, and helpful man. Later he drove me to some place to fill a propane tank. Enrico had studied in London. He regretted having returned and said, "Nothing works here." His head secretary was Simone. She was charming, had a radiant smile, and was always glad to help me.

The next morning I walked to town to email Patricia and others, did some shopping, and returned to *Chyka*. In the late afternoon, the mistral, which Patricia had been telling me about for some days, finally started with winds gusting NW 20-25 – even at my dock in this well protected harbor! Having known from which direction the mistral would blow, I had chosen a berth facing north, so that the dodger could give good protection to the cockpit and the companionway down to the main cabin.

Of course, in the open sea it had to be rough going. I thought of Rosie and Jim out there slogging into it, and I wished they had come with me. It blew through the night and into the next day.

The mistral visited us again for two days the following week covering *Chyka* with sand and dust.

I stayed six weeks in Cagliari. It sounds like a long time, but it was really good. I had many major repairs, maintenance and improvements to do.

Maria came to visit. She is my daughter Catherine's Italian Mamma. Catherine stayed with her and her family a year as an exchange student in Oristano, another town on Sardinia. Maria could not do the climb over the bow to get on *Chyka*, so I packed up snacks and drinks and we went to a table in the shade near the marina office. Simone was leaving the office for the day, came by, and joined us for a wine, which was fortunate. She translated for us.

Many years before, Sonja and I visited Catherine at Maria's home. Knowing that Maria and her husband spoke only Italian, I had prepared for the trip by learning basic Italian. Every morning for six months before going to work I had studied Italian a half hour. It helped us very much during that visit. Now, too much of my Italian was forgotten.

Maria's niece, Paula, and her son Roberto came to join us. So when Simone had to leave us, Roberto took over translating. We went to the nearby pizza restaurant Rari Nantes for dinner. From there Maria cell phoned Catherine so we could tell her about our being together.

Every day I walked into town to shop and email, about 1½ miles each way, which was good for me. By each time lugging back food supplies, I was able to eat well on *Chyka* and gradually rebuild my stock of food.

Two weeks after my arrival, Rosie and Jim came and took a slip near *Chyka*. They had stayed two days in Vulcano, enjoying perfect swimming with bubbles coming up from the bottom, as they later told me, "like swimming in an aquarium."

During the first mistral they were rocked by waves at their anchorage in the bay of Filicudi Island. After an uneventful crossing to Sardinia, they rode out the second mistral in three places along the coast, working their way to Cagliari. Of course, we spent a lot of time together including dinners in the city.

A sailmaker came and we lowered the main to inspect it. It was more of a mess than I thought. He said he could mend it, but I could see the cloth was near to failing everywhere and that I needed a new sail, which he could not do, this being a specially shaped in-mast roller furling sail.

Island Packet put me in touch with their sailmaker in South Africa who quoted me. It would have taken them way too long.

I learned about a company right here in Cagliari, Andrea Mura Sail Design, a large team of sailmakers. They were world famous for designing and making sails for larger boats including America's Cup sailboats.

Everyone told me Andrea Mura would never bother with small fry like me, and even if he did, the sail would be very expensive. Anyway, I sent Andrea Mura an email describing exactly what I needed. He replied the next day with a detailed quote. I researched what he proposed.

The sail would be made of Bainbridge Ocean, an excellent cruising sailcloth. Mura selected it to be one grade heavier than used by Island Packet, and with special features I had never heard of.

His price was about the same as Island Packet's supplier, and he said they could make the sail in only a few weeks! By ordering the sail from Mura, there would be no expense and hassle of importing the sail into Italy.

It was always nice to know that I had my Winslow 4 Person life raft stored within reach in a lazarette. It had a canopy, insulated floor, some water, beginning emergency rations, a lamp, a pair of prescription glasses, a small first-aid kit; and it would automatically inflate when launched. All that otherwise would be needed was my getaway bag with more water, the handheld VHF, the satellite phone, a GPS, lights, warm clothes, and lots of candy bars. (The EPIRB would have already been activated.)

The life raft was overdue for an inspection. I emailed Winslow in Florida saying I had found a company here that does such inspections. They responded, "*Do Not* let anyone touch your life raft. It will be OK. Wait until you are in Florida and we will do it."

I would not have used it unless I was desperate. Too many people, being in a panic about something, have gone into their life rafts from their boats, later learning their boats were found washed up on a beach somewhere. The rule – You only step up into your life raft, not down into it.

My batteries, new in Australia, were now three years old and had been used a lot. I tested them and found they were in very bad condition. I ordered new ones.

When they arrived, the new batteries, as usual, were not quite the same size as the old. So again I had to rebuild the battery compartment. And the battery posts required inch size nuts, not metric! The batteries must have been made for export to the USA. No place in town had the right nuts. *Chyka* was a veritable small international hardware store. I had some nuts, not perfect, but close enough.

I spent most of two days doing a 100 percent maintenance of Big Rudy. If you ever sail to Italy, bring lots of diesel engine oil. I had to buy four liters, at twelve dollars a liter. Ouch!

My six winches were due for an overhaul. One of them had jammed. It took 4½ hours. And so it went. Rosie said, "Henry, I thought you said you would do the winches all in one day." I replied, "No Rosie, you misunderstood. What I said was, I would do each winch in one day." She knew it was a lie and a joke. It was because of Murphy's Second Law, "Everything will take longer than you plan." Why don't we just have our Navy Seals find Murphy and lock him up?

The motor to the windlass had long before failed. I had ordered a new one as soon as I arrived here. When it came, it was held up by Customs in Rome. They waited for paperwork from me, which I sent. They did not receive it. And so it went on. After another two weeks of faxing and telephoning, it arrived.

I needed help in getting the old motor out of the windlass due to frozen nuts. Liquid wrench and the usual tricks did not work. I had to take it to a mechanic who was able to back off the nuts. After I assembled it, the windlass worked well.

We had a dinner party on *Chyka* including Simone. After snacks and drinks Henry cooked his World Famous Caribbean Sea Food Pasta but had run out of mushroom soup. Jim came to the rescue. He went back to *Avalon* and got some.

Another party on *Chyka*. Of course, Jim and Rosie were there. Also invited were Simone, and the other secretary in the office, Tizana. It took awhile for Tizana to summon the courage to climb up on board. Also there were, Alexander, a local former exchange student, and an English couple on a boat near *Chyka*. We discussed Sardinia and all our histories. We ended the evening late with hugs and kisses all around.

The young women in town dressed well. They walked with poise and confidence, revealing up to half of their breasts; I mean half of each breast, not an entire one of the two.

On July 27 Jim and I went to town to check weather. *Avalon* departed in the early afternoon to Minorca, one of the Balearic Islands of Spain. The Balearics are the archipelago off the East Coast of Spain.

The new mainsail arrived. I installed it and found that I could set, reef, and furl it back into the mast smoothly. It endured a lot of rough weather with no damage at all, up to when I sold *Chyka* in 2012.

August 14, 2007 - I went to the office to say good-bye to Simone and Tizana. I gave them each a kiss and a small present. They came to the dock to wave good-bye. I was on my way to Majorca, another Balearic Island, where Jim, Rosie, and I had planned to meet.

Spain - Majorca

The sail to Majorca took three overnights and was mostly easy downwind sailing and motorsailing.

So I had time to review my Spanish, or rather the Spanglish I had used in the Caribbean. But when I landed in Spain I was disappointed to find I was stuck between Italian and Spanish and did not know which of them I was speaking!

In the morning of August 17, 2007 I came into Porto Colom, Majorca. I anchored next to Rosie and Jim. We had beers in town and dinner on *Avalon*.

I took Rosie to town in *Li'l Chyka*. We shopped and had lunch. Later we all had drinks on *Chyka* and dinner in town. I would have been glad to stay and relax, but a great weather window opened up for me and I jumped for it.

The next morning, after they gave me a card and gifts, we said goodbye. When retrieving the anchor, the windlass jammed. I couldn't even use my emergency recovery handle. Obviously, I had done something wrong installing the new motor in the windlass.

The wind was strong putting a heavy load on the anchor chain. Jim came over in his dinghy and tried to pull *Chyka* into the wind so I could lift the anchor. It did not work.

I used Big Rudy repeatedly to move *Chyka* forward a little, go quickly forward to haul up some chain, then back to the helm. Finally, huffing and puffing I lifted the anchor up and over its bow roller and secured it.

I did not again see Rosie and Jim for five years, until 2012, when Patricia and I met them in London.

It was then a fine overnight sail to Ibiza, another of the Balearic Islands.

Ibiza

In the morning I came into the large harbor of Ibiza. The marina was full.

After waiting out in the harbor four hours for the chance to do so, I went in and loaded fuel.

When entering the harbor I had seen a sign saying anchoring was not permitted. It was hard to believe. The harbor was huge and open. Other sailboats including one that flew a Spanish flag were anchored there. So after fueling, I did also. At 7:00 PM the Guardia came by and boat by boat told us that if we did not move out we would be towed in and fined. I never learned why it is they did not allow anchoring here.

Everyone obeyed except one boat. Its people were in town. I later learned their boat was towed in, and they were fined an enormous fee.

There was still daylight. I moved to the next bay, Cala Talamanca, and anchored. The next day I was happy to relax and rest.

An Alarming Forecast from Patricia

From what she told me, it was certain that in a few days a levanter would arrive. Levanters blow at gale force from the southeast, so it would be blowing directly into this bay. And they last three or four days.

There was no place on this island to hide. I stopped everything else and looked at possible places to find protection along the near coast of Spain and the nearby island of Formentera. Nothing looked good. I calculated I had a good chance to get to Cartagena on the southeast coast of Spain before it hit. And if not, I was sure I could survive the beginning of a gale at sea better than staying here at anchor, exposed to the full force of a gale, having no crew and a jammed windlass.

I departed early. The day was fine with a light east wind sometimes requiring motorsailing to maintain speed. The temperature was moderate. I was wearing jeans and a sweatshirt. Gradually the wind increased. Around midnight I entered and crossed the major shipping channel along the Spanish coast and used the radar to tell me how to get through the parade of ships.

Hit by the Levanter Gale

August 24, 2007 — In the wee hours I was moving along fast with single-reefed sails ready to take in more sail if the wind increased. At about 4:30 AM with a thunderstorm and lighting all around, it hit like a hammer.

At that time I had no idea that the wind could ever go in one second from 24 to over 40 knots. If I had known that, I would have been sailing with sails double-reefed, the engine on, and ready to turn upwind to go to a triple-reefed main and furl the foresails.

The autopilot was immediately overwhelmed. I had to hand steer for three hours. I could not leave the helm to do anything about the sails or the control lines.

Chyka broached twice. This happens when the wind overpowers the boat, the rudder cannot keep the boat on course, and a wave pushes the stern of the boat forward swinging the boat broadside to the wind and the waves. The boat stops. It then takes a lot of time and effort to get the boat going again.

Also, twice there were accidental jibes with the boom slamming hard over to the other side. As I said before, boats sometimes loose their entire rigging doing that. Island Packets are built strong.

Trying to ride it out by heaving-to was not an option. Nor was deploying my sea anchor. The conditions were to worsen very much over the following days. The waves coming from behind were already about 16 feet high and threatening to board. They would soon build higher and start to surf.

Eventually there were lulls in the wind down to about 20 knots. Then the autopilot was able to steer giving me a chance to take in the foresails and double-reef the main. Even with only that small amount of sail, *Chyka* was moving through the water doing six to seven knots.

Chyka rounded Cape Palos on the southeast corner of Spain with the wind blowing 32 knots from aft. I sailed west along the coast and in less than two hours I turned north and into the Bay of Cartegena.

I had suspected that many boats on this coast would by then have run for cover to the marina here. In case of being turned away, I had planned to anchor at a spot in the inner harbor near the marina. I thought it would be as well protected from the southeast wind as possible. There I would have put out three anchors.

That sounds as if I would wander in and stumble around in that foul weather to find some place. No. I had picked the best possible position for the predicted wind on my harbor chart and programmed the autopilot to take me exactly to its GPS location, if need be.

I was not turned away. Instead the marina welcomed me, gave me instructions, guided me in, and helped me dock.

Even with high hills on three sides protecting our boats in the marina from the levanter wind, it was blowing 25 knots at the dock. *Chyka* was moored with eight lines and bouncing around. I first checked around as to how *Chyka* had fared the gale. The rigging was fine. From what I could see damage was minimal.

The genoa was chewed up some and the Bimini was torn along one side. (The Bimini is a canvas cover rigged on a frame over the helm. For cruising it is essential for protection from sun and rain.) I stepped ashore to register at the office. The people were super friendly. Being able to speak some Spanish sure helped.

Below deck on *Chyka* the boat motion was as if I were at anchor in a blow. But *Chyka* and I were safe and sound. Before dark another much larger sailboat came in with plenty of crew on deck. The marina people helped them dock. With the wind so strong it was not easy, and they slammed against another boat before their docking was under control.

Cartagena

The center of the city was right outside the marina. Shops were just next door. Beyond them were beautiful classic buildings and churches all kept in excellent condition. The streets were clean. Some were for pedestrians only.

Cartagena has been an important city for almost 2,500 years having always been an easily defended port. Its time of power and glory was under the Roman Empire about 200 BC to 400 AD. I think of it as one of the few large living cities that have been significant since ancient times, as are Rome, Athens, Alexandria, and Damascus.

In 1533 the Spanish established the other Cartagena in present day Colombia. It became an economic center of the Caribbean. As mentioned when telling about Ecuador early in this book, Gold and silver mined in Peru and nearby places were brought across Panama to the Colombian Cartagena. There it was loaded onto galleons for shipment to Spain. I have not been in Cartagena, Colombia, but I know it is an impressive old city with four times the population of this Cartagena, its mother city.

From the shoreline the hills start their way up directly out of the water, and so does the city. Exploring on higher ground, I found a place where I could look out over the open sea. The waves out there were now breaking. With this Force 8 gale the waves would have by then developed to between 18 and 25 feet high with spindrift, which is streaks of foam and airborne spray.

I was in Cartagena ten days repairing damage, fixing the windlass, and cleaning the prop. It had been dragging for awhile. I knew it needed attention, but I had no chance to work on it until now. The shape of it was badly distorted by barnacles. I was lucky to have been able to get any propulsion from it at all.

After the levanter blew itself out, the wind shifted still strong to the northeast bringing a lot of dust. *Chyka* ended up covered with mud, but there was a water hose on the dock, so the mud was easily sprayed off.

August 27 was spent consulting my many books covering Spanish waters, of course Gibraltar, the Atlantic Islands, and crossing the Atlantic Ocean.

I decided to leave out the Madeira Islands. This greatly simplified the timing of it all. I now had all of September to get to Gibraltar, all of October to get from there to the Canary Islands, and there have time to wait until the right time to cross the Atlantic in late December or early January. I could relax, wait for weather before departing anywhere, and not feel at all pressed for time.

After the gale was gone a German boat came in. They were the ones whose boat was taken away in Ibiza by the Guardia. They told me they were fined the equivalent of $4,000 and made to leave. They went to Cala Talamanca, where I had been. There they were fortunate to ride out the gale, reanchoring from time to time as the gale dragged their boat toward shore.

Later Thoughts as to Serious Weather Problems

Up to this levanter gale I had escaped any real trouble from the other dangerous winds of the Mediterranean mostly by timing when to sail. The levanter in my opinion is the most dangerous.

Those who were in Cala Talamanca dragged anchor and had to repeatedly move into the wind and reanchor. It must have been exhausting for their crews. I was my only crew. My windlass did not work, so picking up the anchor to move into the wind would not have been possible. *Chyka* would have gone on the rocks.

What is more dangerous for a small sailboat, the Red Sea or the Med? The Red Sea was difficult and dangerous. There would have been no help if I had gone onto a reef, but I would have survived. In the Red Sea there are strong winds but no storms. In the Med a disaster can happen suddenly. The winds of the Med continue to sink boats.

What if Patricia had not warned me early about the upcoming levanter conditions? The other boats, probably most of them with better computer and communication systems than mine, relying on local and long distance sources, knew nothing of it or too little until too late. Perhaps some did know when I did but were frozen in place not knowing what to do.

Because of Weather Guru Patricia, I had avoided serious trouble in Ibiza. And I was given a chance to get to Cartagena and safety, or at least deal as best I could with the beginning of the gale as I approached Cartagena. One day out there later than I was would have been terribly difficult, possibly the end of the journey.

Others in Cartagena

In Cartagena other cruisers shared their stories with me. Charles and Robin blew in and gave me a huge piece of the swordfish they had just caught.

At the dock just behind *Chyka* were Tim and Ann, such dear people. They invited me to visit them in England. Their last name was England.

On September 3, I departed. Tim and Ann helped me cast off lines. We regretted having to say good-bye.

It was the beginning of a 114 mile pleasant, light wind overnight sail along the Spanish coast to Almerimar.

Almerimar Marina

This is a modern marina built on a bay of the south coast of Spain. It is protected by a stone seawall. Facing the docks were classic Mediterranean style buildings with restaurants, a small supermarket, a book store, gift shops, two laundries, Internet, and Kenny's Irish Pub.

There were several yacht brokers. They bought sailboats from those going west, having had enough of cruising in the Med, and from those going east, having had enough of it in the Atlantic. They both are often difficult.

Saturday I departed for another easy overnight to Gibraltar. At night I hove-to and slept. I approached Gibraltar at midday in a thick fog with my radar on. The fog lifted. Suddenly, looking down on me was the imposing Rock of Gibraltar rising nearly straight up 1,400 feet. I sailed around to the west side of it and to its harbor.

Gibraltar

Almost all small boats entering or leaving the Mediterranean stop at Gibraltar. It is busy. I had hoped to get a slip at the Queensway Quay Marina. Reservations are strongly recommended. I had asked for a reservation by email from Cartagena. They had replied, sorry, they were full.

Motoring slowly past the entrance I checked with them again on VHF. This time they told me, Yes, they could put me at the end of a pier. It was perfect. There were two other possibilities of places to stay, but this marina was by far the best. It was protected by outer breakwaters to the west and by all of Gibraltar from the other directions. The wonder of the Rock rose above, and the city was just steps away.

Now from my journal of that afternoon:

> The Med is done - not always easy - but I am glad to have visited its wonderful places of history, the good sails, pleasant anchorages, beautiful scenes, the marinas. And there were Miranda, Maria, their families, and my many dear friends with whom I had shared it all.

The Most Careful Planning of the Voyage

I was already thinking about when I should leave Gibraltar to sail through the Strait of Gibraltar between Spain and Morocco on the way to the open Atlantic Ocean. It was really complicated. If you do not get it right, there probably will be trouble.

The Strait is only 13 miles wide at its narrowest place. You can see Morocco clearly from a short ways up on the Rock. And the Strait reaches 30 miles west from Gibraltar to the Atlantic.

This narrow pass between Europe and Africa is the only opening from the Mediterranean Sea to an ocean. So with the changes of tides in the Atlantic there are strong currents and countercurrents that change strength and direction throughout the day, as the entire Mediterranean tries to empty and refill. And if the wind is against the current, the water will be turbulent.

To add to the difficulty of it, there is always heavy shipping traffic through the middle of the Strait.

In the *Mediterranean Spain Coastal Pilot* I had diagrams of the Strait showing the direction and strength of the currents every hour before and after high tide in Gibraltar. Figuring on maintaining an average speed of about four knots, I could see where I would probably be each hour after departure and the state of the current there.

It became clear to me that the best time to leave would be three hours after high tide in Gibraltar, whenever that would be on the day I left.

Another essential consideration was that I needed to leave during a morning, so that I would have time to reach the end of the Strait and the open Atlantic during daylight.

Every day Patricia kept me up to date as to upcoming weather in the Strait and into the Atlantic. I resolved I would not leave this place until all aspects of the sail out to the ocean looked solidly good even if I would have to wait a month.

Touring Gibraltar

Nestled up against the Rock and with an area of only 2.6 square miles, Gibraltar City is home to 3,000 people who enjoy British life in a warm climate. I wondered, *why don't more Brits move here?*

Tourists, of course many of them British, visit Gibraltar. The buildings are built of stone in classic styles. There are wide squares and impressive monuments. There is a street of Irish pubs. A cable car takes you to the top. This is the home of the only wild monkeys in Europe. They are everywhere outside the city and are quite tame.

The treaty of Utrecht of 1713 gave Gibraltar to Britain, "in perpetuity." It is a natural fortress, which the British fortified increasingly over hundreds of years and defended well against Spanish attacks from time to time, as well as air and sea attacks by the troublemakers of World Wars I and II.

Inside The Rock during World War II were barracks, offices, and a fully equipped hospital. From here the British and US Navies controlled the entrance to the Mediterranean.

On Tuesday it was engine jobs and a thunder storm. Thursday there were more storms. But between those days Wednesday was glorious. I took a minibus tour of the Rock. First we went to Europa Point looking out over to Africa, then up higher to the huge St. Michael's Cave. From a lookout far above the city I pointed out *Chyka* to the others. She was way below, just a speck at her dock in the harbor.

A narrow winding path took us on up to the entrance of one of the amazing tunnels the British dug. We walked through it. Many openings for cannons faced Spain to the north where the narrow land connection to Spain is flat. When the Spanish attacked in 1782 they had no chance against this fortress.

During an early morning T-storm I had morning coffee with Doug and Shanna on their boat just behind *Chyka*. When I returned to *Chyka* I found I had not closed the hatch over the main cabin table tightly enough. Rain had blown in and ruined a critical chart to North Africa.

Well, if something like that has to happen, this is the best place. In town I bought an expensive British Admiralty chart of the same area having much better detail than the one it replaced.

September 14, 2007. Everything suddenly came together. According to Patricia the weather for the next two days looked good. Everything pointed to a morning departure. I checked out of the marina and motored a few miles north to the pleasant Spanish bay of La Linea and anchored in 16 feet of water. During the quiet afternoon I rechecked everything on the boat, the conditions, and did more prenavigation to the Canary Islands. My plan was to depart the next morning exactly at 9:00 AM, which would be three hours after high tide. With all that done I could relax. I was confident.

The Rock of Gibraltar - Taken from *Chyka* **on the day before departure into the Atlantic.**

Into The Atlantic Ocean

In the morning I wanted to get going, but timing was so important. I waited impatiently. At the last minute I made a final check with Mission Control (Patricia). I was told, "Good to go!" At 9:00 AM *Chyka* started out.

The weather was clear except for the top of Gibraltar, which was then in its own cloud. I had to work my way through many fishing boats at anchor on my way out until I rounded Punta del Carnero and into the Strait with the wind behind me E 20-30.

I was sailing with a single-reefed main, staysail, and no genoa. Early, the current was not helpful as it was supposed to be, but it was not against me.

Rounding the southern most point of Spain, Tarifa, the waters were turbulent, confusing the autopilot. Once again, I had to hand steer, but only for a few minutes.

Approaching the end of the Strait I was going really fast. The tidal current was then behind me 7 to 8 knots and there was a tail wind of 15-20 knots. I did not check it on my GPS, but I must have been moving 12 or 13 knots over the ground. So in only about four hours I was sailing in the wide open Atlantic Ocean. The passage through the Strait of Gibraltar had gone so well.

My destination was the island of Lanzarote in the Canary Islands 490 miles south down the coast of Africa.

I passed Casablanca 80 miles to the east. In the 1942 classic movie *Casablanca* starring Humphrey Bogart and Ingrid Bergman, they were in Paris and deeply in love. He found out she was married, and fled to Casablanca where he established Rick's Bar. His flunky asked:

"Rick, whatever brought you to Casablanca?"

Rick replied in Bogart's crisp slow way of talking,

"I came to take the waters."

"But Rick, there are no waters in Casablanca."

Rick, "I was – misinformed."

I would have enjoyed sailing into old colonial Casablanca. Imagine having a Scotch with Bogart at Rick's Bar. But now Casablanca is a commercial and industrial city of three million people. The busy harbor is filled with freight and container ships. And anyway, Humphrey Bogart was probably never actually in Casablanca.

The wind went down to where the engine had to help for awhile until a west wind came up and provided a lovely broad reach in a calm ocean.

It took seven days to sail down to the Canary Islands. The winds became increasingly tricky as I went south. Of course, I talked every day with Patricia about the weather I was going into, and about us.

Canary Islands

This is an archipelago ranging 80 to 200 miles off the coast of Morocco. It is a birders' paradise with some 200 species many of them unique to these islands including canaries. Most people assume the Canary Islands were named after the bird, but in fact it was the other way around.

When troops from Morocco came here about 60 BC they were impressed by the large dogs roaming the islands. They brought back two of them to their king. From then on, the islands were called Insulae Canium, meaning The Islands of Dogs, which in Spanish is Islas Canarias. So the special birds found here were called canaries.

Spain conquered these islands one by one in the 15th century. Now it has been a province of Spain for almost two hundred years. The primary trade in the Canaries is tourism and with good reason. The weather is like late spring all year. It is a winter refuge for Europeans.

Jack Oldenburg had explored the Canary Islands early in his circumnavigation many years before. He recommended I stop at Puerto Calero on the island of Lanzarote. After consulting all I had on the Canaries, I decided to go there.

On the third day I was gliding along smoothly. I had forgotten that seas can be so pleasant in a fair wind. I called the Puerto Calero Marina asking for a slip reservation. They agreed.

During the fifth day I had to run the engine to charge the batteries. There had been too little sun for the solar panel, and the trolling generator had no chance with my loafing speed through the water.

As slow as I was going it was still too fast; I was getting close to Lanzarote and did not want to arrive in the dark of the next night. I changed the main to double-reefed, furled the genoa, and even reefed the staysail for the first time. That slowed me down just right.

Had my compass gone backward? Was I going north to the Arctic instead of south down the coast of Africa? Days were beautiful but nights were cold. I was not used to this. I was wearing socks, jeans, a polo shirt, a sweater, and a wind breaker.

And I was getting really tired. I had to cut my naps down to ten minutes, and later to nothing because of the shipping traffic. To stay awake I took Sudafed, No Doz, and coffee. The worst is always when trying to stay awake just before dawn. I was impressed that the large ships, recognizing from my navigation lights that I was under sail (meaning with no motor) kindly altered their course for me.

In the morning I docked at the Puerto Calero Marina office and checked in. They assigned me a berth. I was moored in my slip by noon, had a beer, and went to bed.

This became another of my favorite marinas. In the Canaries there is a five foot tide, but that was no problem with the marina's floating piers. Here facing the docks was an array of markets, a marine store, Internet, a laundromat, restaurants, and pubs, a sailmaker, two engine mechanics, and a boatyard.

I had lots of time until late December, which is the beginning of the best time to cross the Atlantic.

Visiting Patricia

I flew to Madrid, stayed a night in London, then on to Tampa Airport where Patricia met me. After a few days in her condo, we spent two nights in the quaint, old Casablanca Inn in St. Augustine overlooking the harbor. Perhaps Humphrey Bogart stayed here!

From Patricia's place we drove to Sarasota to visit my daughter Susan, her husband, Kelle, and their kids, so they could all meet Patricia.

I needed to buy a few special parts for *Chyka* at Island Packet Yachts in nearby Largo. While there, Patricia met their people. They gave us a plant tour. For years they had been publishing articles by me in *The Island Packet Newsletter*.

We spent three days at the Disney parks in Orlando. While having lunch at Epcot, we spoke with a lady at the next table. She lived on

Lanzarote, where *Chyka* was! And so here at Disney we had more proof that, "It's a small world after all."

Lanzarote Again

I returned to *Chyka* in Lanzarote arriving November 16, 2007. First thing, I arranged for a haul out at the boat yard to have the bottom cleaned and painted.

Jack Oldenburg and his wife Kerstin came to visit the last week of November. I had not been with them since Thailand. They stayed at the nearby luxury Hotel Hesperia. We rented a car to tour the island for a few days.

The interior of Lanzarote is highly elevated and a bone dry volcanic landscape as you could imagine being on the moon. From my journal, "We drove to the north end of Lanzarote. We looked down from the observation balcony to the island, La Graciosa, where Jack had once anchored." At that time Jack stayed in Lanzarote one year before crossing the Atlantic and on to the Pacific where we first met.

Patricia Will Marry Me!

On November 29, 2007 I emailed Patricia and asked her if she would please marry me. She accepted! How wonderful!

After *Chyka* was finished in the boatyard, I brought her to her slip. The wind was blowing hard from the wrong direction. To dock bow first I had to back up almost touching the bow of a sailboat on the opposite side. A pretty lady stood there watching. Instead of panicking about my probably destroying her boat, she smiled at me. After more maneuvering I got *Chyka* into her slip. Then I walked around to the lady's boat to meet her.

She was Sylvia Brownlee. Her husband was Lawrie. Their boat was *Saltire*, the name of the flag of Scotland. We all became good friends.

A week before Christmas, Sylvia and Lawrie were about to depart. I ran over to tell them that they first needed to climb up to look over the seawall at the state of the sea. They came with me and saw the turbulent waters they would have gone into. They stayed another week. We had Christmas Eve dinner on *Chyka*.

Christmas morning we had breakfast sitting with their friend Hillary in front of her bakery. We exchanged gifts. Our Christmas Dinner was at a marina restaurant with many courses that lasted over three hours. After coffee we went to *Chyka* for drinks, snacks, and Scrabble. The next day they departed. I did not see them again until St. Thomas, Virgin Islands.

Believe it from the Beatles or me, there actually is a yellow submarine. From here I took it with 41 others. We descended 132 feet into clear water to observe huge schools of reef fish, barracudas, enormous sting rays, and two sunken ships, one wooden and the other of metal.

Rachel

In all the days I was in Puerto Calero Marina, my favorite hangout was McSorley's Irish Pub. There were always interesting, friendly people at the bar and Guinness Stout on tap.

They had common British Isles meals served at the bar or at the few tables inside and also on their small terrace overlooking the marina. The waitress was Rachel.

As waitresses do with male customers in British pubs, Rachel always asked, "What'll ya have, love?" In time I also called her that. We called each other, "love," and, "my love," and by our names. (She was about one-third my age.)

One morning before departure I went there for brunch and took a table at the end of the terrace. Rachel came out, saw me, and called over, "Henry, how are you?"

The devil got into me. I shouted at her, "Miserable!"

"Henry, whatever is wrong?"

"Rachel, you've been cheating on me!"

Now, everyone suddenly stopped talking, even stopped chewing, just watching us, thinking, *What the....?*

"No, Henry, never. I would never do that to you."

I stood up and said, "Yes, Rachel. I know it."

"It is not true, Henry. What has made you think so?"

I said to her, "Last night I heard you call another man, 'love'."

"But, Henry - "

"Never mind Rachel, I can't stand it. We are done! Finished!" Then I said slowly and with a deeper voice:

"And if I ever find out who the man is, I shall, (dramatic pause then louder) I shall…"

A lady at another table said loudly, "You will kill him." I looked over to her and said,

"Thank you for understanding," then over to Rachel,

"Yes, I will kill him! He deserves nothing better."

Rachel couldn't keep it up anymore and burst into laughter, as then everyone did.

Planning the Atlantic Crossing

Some 200 sailboats in the annual ARC, Atlantic Rally for Cruisers, crossed over starting, as they always do, in late November. The seas were violent. Boats were damaged, sails wrecked, rigging lost. Some crews were rescued by other boats. Some boats were abandoned.

January is generally a safer, better month for the crossing. But the ARC always leaves in late November because the people want to get to the Caribbean in time for Christmas. I think their priorities are a little out of order.

Columbus

In 1492 very few people had any idea how large the earth is. And Columbus , intending to sail from Spain west to Asia, did not know that the Western Hemisphere was in his way. It was good for him it was, because without being forced to stop there, he would never have been able to make it all the way from there across the Pacific to Asia; no ships at that time could carry enough food and water to sail so far.

Alexandria

Earlier in this book I mentioned that Alexandria was once the recognized center of knowledge, mathematics, and research of the world. This was born of the guidance Aristotle gave Alexander and Ptolemy. In about 240 BC, so 1,700 years before Columbus, the Chief Librarian at the Library of Alexandria, Eratosthenes, calculated the circumference of the earth very accurately. How did he do it?

Eratosthenes planned how to do it by using what he learned from the then recently written *Elements,* the classic geometry of Euclid of Alexandria, who is called, "The Father of Geometry."

There was (and still is today) near Aswan in the south of Egypt, a wide well with spiral stairs to its bottom to where the sunlight shines down from directly overhead at noon of the day of the summer solstice. This event Eratosthenes observed. In Alexandria on the same day of the following year, he calculated the angle of the sun there at noon. Having had walkers pace off the distance between the two places, about six hundred miles, Eratosthenes could then calculate the radius of the Earth and the resulting circumference of it. But knowledge still in those ages moved slowly or not at all. If Columbus or his sponsors had known how large the Earth is, his voyage would never have been attempted.

Then probably the discovery of the Americas would have much later proceeded gradually down the coast of North America from Nova Scotia to South America.

Alexandria is called, "The Birthplace of the Modern World." Sadly, the gathering of knowledge from all sources by scholars was gradually closed down in Alexandria and elsewhere by the early Christians, who thought that they knew all that mattered, and that their doctrines had to be believed and obeyed without question.

Crossing the Atlantic

The Portuguese and the Spanish knew a lot about the winds off the Atlantic Islands. Columbus's four voyages to the Caribbean all went by way of the Canary Islands. From his third crossing on, Spanish ships continued southwest from the Canaries 800 miles before turning west. There they caught the trade winds at about 20 degrees north latitude. Most sailors have followed that route ever since, and of course, so did I.

I was prepared for the long passage. From Lanzarote it was to be a total of 2,900 miles. My longest passage, as you may remember, had been 4,200 miles from Ecuador to Tahiti, much longer but in general less difficult than the Atlantic.

I departed on December 29, 2007. I will call it Day One. The winds through these islands can be tricky, and there was quite a bit of shipping traffic to dodge especially the first night. I sailed along well with a single-reef in the main, a single-reefed genoa, and the staysail.

On Day Seven the mount to the trolling generator broke off and the whole assembly went overboard. I had never thought of attaching a safety line to it: It had seemed so solidly secure. It was a fatigue fracture. They give no warning of something going wrong until the thing breaks. Now my sources of electricity were down to running the engine two hours a day under no load, to save fuel, and the solar panel, which I soon moved to what was to be the more sunny, port side of the boat.

In the oceans at night there are no shore city lights to dim the view of the stars. There, especially with no moon, you see a vast, thick array of them. As you have read from my times in the Pacific, I had learned the names of many stars, planets, and constellations. Now I learned to recognize the progress of the planets as they, over weeks, moved over the zodiac. Shooting stars were not unusual. A really bright one of them shot across most of the sky over me. I doubt I will ever see something like that again.

It was gradually getting warmer. The skies looked friendly, and soon I would be in the trade winds northwest of the Cape Verde Islands. There I was to turn almost due west with a slight angle to the south to go directly to St. Lucia in the Caribbean.

For some days the wind had been ENE 20-25. Patricia told me that in a few days the wind would go due east. So I continued south of the intended course while I could easily do so and wait for the change. When the wind went due east, as Patricia said it would, I jibed onto a fine starboard tack and stayed there, gradually getting back to the course.

All was going so well. I was reading my books. One of them was a reread of the extraordinary book *Sailing Alone Around the World* by Joshua Slocum, who in 1895 to 1898 was the first one to do so.

On Day 12 I passed close by a huge wooden cable spool. If I had sailed into it, there could have been serious damage. Stowed deeply below was my collision mat, which was designed to deploy under the bow and cover a stove-in hole giving a sailor time to patch up the hole from the inside.

I brought the collision mat up to the forecabin to be more handy in case I hit another spool or something else serious. The time saved by this could have been critical. Always learning. I often said to people that by the time I finish this circumnavigation I will know enough to do a circumnavigation.

The sea was beautiful. There were dolphins, flying fish, and storm petrels.

For most of the remaining distance I jibed back and forth across the course line to avoid the rolling of going directly downwind. And as I previously explained when sailing to Tahiti, the progress to the destination that way is improved by greater speed through the water even though the distance sailed is longer.

In unsettled weather there is no predicting squalls. They don't last long in the Atlantic, but they hit without warning. One did at midnight of Day 18 blowing suddenly from ahead SW 30-35. It was pitch dark and I didn't know what was going on. The coffee pot was screaming. My first move was to go below and shut off the stove. With whatever might happen, I wanted to avoid having a fire on board.

Then, the boat being out of control, I hove-to. I turned on the foredeck light and went forward, of course harnessed to a jackline. The staysail's clew (the aft corner of a sail) had ripped away. I furled the sail and tied it up with a rope, and so it stayed that way for the rest of the crossing. My foredeck light shined down from half way up the mast brightly illuminating everything on the foredeck and the sails over it. With it on, working there at night was always made so much easier.

From my notes, "As usual in heavy weather, *Chyka* rode the following waves easily, rising to them nicely as they approached, happier about it all than I was."

The next day was difficult with a lot of rain. Again, the wind turned against me, and I knew it meant another squall. I was prepared for it. It took another day of bad weather until the normal trade winds took over for most of the final five days, except one:

On Day 23 there was a lot of rain and increasing wind. Squalls came all night. Often I had to be at the helm and got drenched in spite of the dodger and the Bimini. I changed clothes three times.

The next morning after I called Patricia, a boarding wave hit hard. It tore away the solar panel, ripping the bolts right out of its aluminum mounting bars, and took it overboard.

I was amazed to see that its thick electric cord to the boat held on, dragging the panel along through the water. I hauled it out, washed it carefully with fresh water, and stowed it. Later in St. Lucia after drilling new holes in the bars, I remounted the panel with new bolts. It then worked perfectly, and from then on it always did.

Now my only source of electricity was Big Rudy, which I then had to run four hours a day. There were only 334 miles to go and I still had a lot of fuel. If Big Rudy were to die, I was prepared to cut way back on electricity usage. I could have gone to my battery powered navigation lights and battery handheld VHF radio. Nothing else was using much electricity except for the autopilot. The four large boat batteries, then fully charged, would have powered it for the rest of the trip.

After clearing up the mess from the boarding wave, I rested a lot. My body was worn out with many muscles complaining. There was another squall.

Back to the Caribbean

I came close to Martinique, where I had been several times with family and friends, mostly on *Chyka*. As I jibed to then go south, I was very close to Diamond Rock, a high rock island. It is just offshore Martinique.

When Napoleon controlled most of Europe, the British Navy was strong in the Caribbean. They fortified Diamond Rock as if it were a battleship. It long plagued French shipping to and from Martinique. This annoyed Napoleon. His Josephine was born and raised in Martinique, which is still an overseas region of France.

Saint Lucia

I sailed the last fifteen miles south to St. Lucia, rounded Pigeon Island and motored into the bay of Rodney Bay Marina.

Ron Peterson and I had one time anchored at Pigeon Island and from there climbed up to the top and its old English fort. Rodney Bay was the major English naval base in the area.

Chyka had been twice before in St. Lucia. So this actually was the end of an eight year circumnavigation. But in 2000 to 2002 I cruised from St. Lucia back to the East Coast, north to New England, and later back down to the Bahamas, adding two years to that circumnavigation. So for this story I consider the Bahamas as the start and the finish, not St. Lucia.

The Atlantic crossing had taken 26 days. From my journal:

> *I am amazed how much energy the crossing took. I had provisioned for two months, in case of troubles, only sadly ran out of beer five days before arrival. I had been eating like a*

horse but ended up having lost nine pounds. I am exhausted, relieved, and grateful.

Patricia was to arrive soon to sail further with me in the Windward Islands. We were engaged. What a wonderful life!

At the marina many of the ARC (Atlantic Rally for Cruisers) boats were still here. All had interesting stories of what they had endured during their crossing, some still licking their wounds. Next to me were Cedrik and Janet. I knew them in Finike, Turkey. We traded hosting dinners on board our boats and ashore.

Most boats crossing the Atlantic from east to west finish here at Rodney Bay. The manager of the marina told me that every year some of them arrive having circumnavigated, but that very few of those are single-handers. He wanted to arrange an interview with some publication, but I was getting busy and had no time.

The only other Island Packet that has circumnavigated single-handed was an IP-35, the forerunner to my IP-350. The skipper was a man from Brazil, Andre Homen de Mello. He did it in 2001 and 2002 in 193 days allegedly nonstop, which it must have been, or nearly so, to do it so quickly. But just think of what a shame it is; he missed so much by not stopping in the wonderful places that any route around the world offers a sailor!

There were repairs to be made, such as the torn staysail. I hired a local man, Elvis, to help me with varnishing, and polishing the stainless steel. In a few days we made *Chyka* look so much better, which was important to me because a VIP was to soon arrive.

Patricia Arrives

On February 5, 2007 I met her at the little St. Lucia airport. What a joy to see her, to be with her again! We went directly to the lovely Bay Gardens Hotel in Rodney Bay. There we stayed four nights before departing south on *Chyka*. The terrace of our first floor room was surrounded by bushes and trees giving us privacy. On our terrace we danced to the soft music of the calypso band.

We visited *Chyka* several times to determine what we needed to buy for the next travels. Patricia, who has diabetes, told me, "While shopping I could not find any sugar-free products. They must not have diabetes here."

We enjoyed the local restaurants. There was even a Chart House. We both knew their restaurant in Avon, Connecticut.

One afternoon when I was away somewhere, Patricia lay in bed reading. Suddenly, she felt the bed and the wall next to her shaking. We were told it was a minor earthquake. They are common in the Caribbean.

Saturday February 9, 2008. In the early morning we moved out of our hotel and onto *Chyka* to sail south to Marigot Bay. The wind those days was unfortunately strong. I did not want Patricia to be seasick. So a half hour before departure I gave her two Bonine tablets. We departed into windy conditions. She steered as we made our way out and beyond. Remember, steering is a prevention for seasickness. And we were sailing in the lee of the island. She felt fine the whole way.

Marigot Bay

It was only nine miles down the west coast of St. Lucia and into this spectacular bay anchorage. On our mooring we were surrounded by lovely high green hills. Patricia cooked clam sauce pasta.

I had sailed to this bay many times with friends and family over the years. This was the site of the film *Doctor Dolittle*. At its entrance is a sand spit on which is the terrace restaurant, Dolittle's.

Many years before, I was taking a week long cruising course. Our boat was returning to the Moorings base here at Marigot Bay. I was at the helm. As we entered the bay I saw Sonja and Susan at Dolittle's waiting for me. We waved to each other. Being distracted, I ran our boat onto a sand bar! It was embarrassing.

The next evening Patricia and I had dinner at Dolittle's. Later, we watched the stars from *Chyka's* foredeck.

After Patricia made a gourmet lunch for us, we sailed a little over two hours down the coast to Soufriere where we took a mooring. This small town lies at the foot of the amazing Pitons, two conical mountains rising vertically out of the sea to a height of 2,500 feet.

Patricia wrote, "The town was full of tin roofed houses, pigs, dogs, chickens, and laundry hanging out day and night."

We departed early. In the lee of St. Lucia the sea was smooth.

But then, during the 25 miles of the passage between St. Lucia and St. Vincent, we had an east wind of 20 knots making rough seas.

Over years of cruising in these islands I always had easier winds than now. Poor Patricia lay on the cockpit cushions during most of the seven hours across until we came into the lee of St. Vincent. Then the sea calmed and she felt much better.

Saint Vincent

We sailed into the bay of the tiny town of Wallilabou. I had been here twice before to visit another of our exchange students, Suzette, who lives nearby and whom we soon met.

Here, you drop anchor offshore, back up towards the beach, and then a local boat takes your 300 foot rope to attach your stern to a dock or a tree.

It was a fun evening. We took *Li'l Chyka* ashore to clear customs. Then we viewed the sets that were constructed there to film *Pirates of the Caribbean*.

There was still the same and only restaurant, mostly open-air, on the beach. A steel drum band was playing. They are always so delightful. And they don't spoil their music with amplification. Our waitress was the one who had served Suzette, the Groves, Ron, and me eight years before.

At 2:00 AM we awoke. The boat next to us had dragged anchor and drifted onto *Chyka*. They were pleasant Hungarian people. I told them what they should do to fix the problem, which they gladly did. Then Patricia and I watched the stars.

In the morning it was a repeat - easy sailing along in the lee of the island, then south of it heavy wind as we rounded the southwest corner of St. Vincent and headed to the Blue Lagoon on its south coast. On the way *Li'l Chyka,* being towed behind *Chyka,* flipped and had to be pulled up and tied to the stern.

Then there was the wonderful quiet of the Blue Lagoon. We went ashore and had a drink at the Green Flash Bar. I had forgotten that here in the tropics it becomes completely dark 30 minutes after sundown. While there was still some daylight, I took *Li'l Chyka* back to *Big Chyka* to turn on her anchor light and to get a flashlight to help us find our way back home in the dark after dinner.

I awoke early as usual. It was February 14. There in the loo was a Valentine's Day card from Patricia. Then, one by one, I found five more of them around the boat with messages from humorous, to sweet and to thanksgiving for our love. I had only one card for her. She also gave me an Oh Henry candy bar. I would have shared it with her, but remember, she has diabetes. In the afternoon we moved ashore to the Lagoon Marina Hotel.

That evening we had dinner with Suzette at the Lime-n Pub. She was due to have a baby in October. When she did she named her Arianne. Occasionally, we receive photos of her. She is beautiful.

A taxi driver, Vernon, took us on a tour up a narrow winding road to the Montreal Gardens, a tropical park in a rain forest. We enjoyed Vernon's stories of the island.

A Grand Reunion

Flying in to join us were Cyndie and her children, Zak and Molly. She had chartered a boat in Blue Lagoon to sail along with *Chyka*. Mutual friends, Wayne and Bobbi, whom I knew from the Caribbean and Annapolis, came also to sail on Cyndie's boat.

Cyndie's flight was delayed until late. We did not see them until morning. Patricia and I had dinner with Wayne and Bobbi. We four talked about our love stories.

In the morning we all attended a chart briefing of the Grenadines to where we were going. It was given by TMM, Cyndie's charter company.

The Grenadines are a chain of 600 small islands stretching about 90 miles from St. Vincent to Grenada. They are part of the country called Saint Vincent and the Grenadines. The first of the Grenadines south of St. Vincent is Bequia.

Bequia

(Pronounced BECK-way)

Both our boats departed at 1:15 PM to sail an eight mile easy broad reach across to Admiralty Bay on the west coast of Bequia. Zak was the captain of Cyndie's boat. We anchored off Princess Margaret Beach within an easy half mile dinghy ride to Port Elizabeth, the main town on Bequia. Cyndie, Molly, and Zak swam over to *Chyka*.

With our dinghies we all then went to town to have dinner at the Gingerbread. There we celebrated our reunion, now including Patricia.

Hurricane Lenny - November 1999

As you may remember, Barry Grove had crewed for me at the start of this voyage. Nine years before, he, Cyndie, and their kids, Zak and Molly, on *Breakaway* as well as *Chyka* were anchored off this same Princess Margaret Beach. Ron Peterson was cruising with me then. Before dinner we all spent time at the bar of the Frangipani. We talked with locals and cruisers. No one said anything about an approaching hurricane. After dinner and cards on *Breakaway*, Zak came with Ron and me to sleep over on *Chyka*.

We had no warning at all. Caribbean hurricanes had always developed in the eastern Atlantic and from there moved west giving at least several days warning. "Wrong Way Lenny" was the only known hurricane to ever originate in the middle of the Caribbean and from there move east.

In the early morning, waves were building coming into our anchorage from the open sea to the west. Barry came over to get Zak to help him raise anchor. Both our boats moved to moorings off better protected Port Elizabeth. From there we looked back with binoculars to where we had been anchored and were amazed to watch the incoming waves, huge and breaking.

The harbor around us became increasingly rough. From radio weather reports over time I tracked the path of Lenny. I could see that Lenny would pass 320 miles northwest of us. Here for the next six hours, the wind would not be so bad, but the waves would continue to build higher where we were moored. *Breakaway* had already moved out, and I decided we should leave also.

We motored out of the bay and around to the south and lee side of Bequia to the well protected anchorage of Friendship Bay. *Breakaway* was already there.

Lenny was a Category 4 (Extreme) hurricane with 155 mph winds. Many boats were washed up on the beaches. Most towns are on the west sides of these islands, and so are protected from the normal east trade winds. But Lenny hit them from the west. There was enormous destruction to shore buildings in Bequia and in other places. Seventeen people lost their lives, six of them at sea.

Within only eight years of cruising I had experienced five extraordinary weather events, a major hurricane going in the wrong direction, a rogue wave, a Sumatra southwest squall, a tsunami, and a levanter gale.

Back to the Present - February 2008

For two days we enjoyed Port Elizabeth including, of course, our favorite bar at the Frangipani. Near it was the Gingerbread where we all had met for dinner. There I reserved a room for Patricia and me for our last night together before she was to fly home from St. Vincent two weeks later.

Watching the stars from the foredeck one night, Patricia was excited to see the distinctive constellation, Southern Cross, for her first time. She had never before been south enough to be able to see it.

From the cockpit one morning we saw our second double rainbow. The first had been from her condo balcony.

In the morning I found the wind had flipped *Li'l Chyka* over with Li'l Rudy drowned (for the second time!) I hauled the outboard on board and worked on it for two hours. It would not start, until I realized I had forgotten to put back the spark plug. After I did, Li'l Rudy started with one pull on the starter rope. (The previous time was in Niue, when I had forgotten to open the fuel valve.)

Right away we set off for the Tobago Cays 25 miles south, not to be confused with Tobago, which lies another 100 miles further south near Trinidad.

Tobago Cays

We passed the islands of Canouan and Mayreau then east and into the Tobago Cays. They are four tiny, high islands protected from the Atlantic Ocean by Horseshoe Reef.

I had been here three times before and knew where to anchor which was just past the island, Petit Bateau (Little Boat) and inside the reef. It was similar to my time anchored at Beverage Reef in the Pacific near Tonga, where Deb, Al, and I could see out there only the ocean but being pleasantly at ease well protected from the waves by the underwater reef.

Burial at Sea

Barry Grove had died at home in Canada. Everyone came over to *Chyka* for his burial at sea. We looked at my album of pictures of our cruising days in the Caribbean. Barry had loved these islands. Wayne and Bobbi spoke well of their memories of him. I played a CD of Barry's favorite songs Zak had brought. Cyndie read from Barry's writings. After some tears they scattered Barry's ashes into the sea. Patricia and I were glad to be a part of the ceremony.

Snorkeling here is excellent. What you do is motor your dinghy right up to the reef. The Tobago Cays is a national park. To protect the reef from anchor damage they provide dinghy moorings. Then it's a short swim in beautiful clear water over coral sand to the reef.

You need flippers because there is a current. With your mask you can explore the reef with its coral underwater hills, the sea plants, turtles, and the coral fish of wonderful colors and shapes, all designed, I think, by Walt Disney.

A Day Patricia and I so well Remember

Cyndie and her people departed to go on to Union Island. Patricia and I stayed. We dinghied to the beach on Petit Bateau. There we snorkeled.

On the beach a local lady, Mary, had a display of wrap-arounds. Patricia bought one. Petit Bateau rises up to 140 feet. We climbed most of the way to the top and had a fine view of the other islands, the brightly colored reef in clear water, *Chyka,* other sailboats at anchor, and the sea. We walked the beach around the corner of the island. At the channel between the cays were several beach vendors. Patricia bought another wrap.

There was Romeo, who operated a beach BBQ with a few tables under cover. He caught, cooked, and served fish and lobsters. After some discussion we arranged that he would cook and bring out to *Chyka* a four pound lobster at five PM.

After we snorkeled more off *Chyka,* exactly at five, Romeo came in his boat and delivered the lobster. Patricia expanded on it to make the meal a feast.

After a fine sunset we waited for the lunar eclipse. The sky was clear. The eclipse started at 9:43 PM and became total at 11:01 PM.

Back North to Canouan

On the way, Cyndie's boat returning from Union Island, being larger and faster than *Chyka,* caught up with us. Our boats anchored in Charlestown Bay. In the normal trade winds the hill behind the town protects it, but with the strong winds of these days we were rolled some. The biggest place in town was the Tamarind Hotel. We went there to do email and have dinner.

In the morning the wind had again flipped *Li'l Chyka* over. Zak and Molly helped me get control of it and administer CPR to Li'l Rudy. Wayne and Bobbi scuba dived while Cyndie and kids played games with us on *Chyka,* rummy 500, and chess.

We all wanted to get back north to Bequia. The wind was blowing NE-25. Not good. Patricia seemed to have her sea legs now and was confident. This rolly anchorage helped us decide to go. We departed at noon and in six hours were safely at anchor just off Port Elizabeth.

The next day Cyndie and her crew returned to Blue Lagoon to fly back to their homes. Patricia and I stayed anchored in Bequia another four quiet, pleasant days.

One morning a local man, John, came alongside on his paddleboard. In front of him was a display of his catch of the morning. We bought two groupers and two snappers after discussing the price some.

He agreed to filet the fish for us, because when I filet such fish I end up with fishburger. Instead of the agreed money, John asked for pasta. Patricia remembered, "I gave him a bag of macaroni and another of spaghetti, which got a big smile from him."

One nice benefit of this place I have always liked is Daffodil Marine Services. Their bright yellow boat comes alongside to bring fresh water and fuel, take away trash, and pick up laundry to be washed and delivered the next day.

On a tour of the island with Doc's Taxi we viewed the sights of the island including Friendship Bay, where the Groves, Ron, and I hid out from Hurricane Lenny in 1999.

We toured the Turtle Sanctuary. There they raise new born turtles, feeding them sardines and tuna. When they have grown enough to do well on their own they are released. Turtles are endangered in this area; the survival rate of newly hatched babies is about five percent.

When snorkeling just off Jack's Place, a shore restaurant, Patricia had a problem with her mask. Working on it, I backed onto a rock with a sea urchin perched on the top of it. The urchin stung me painfully in the rear. We immediately went to Jack's Place for serious treatment of my wound, vodka drinks and lunch.

We moved from *Chyka* to the Gingerbread for the night so that we could take the ferry to The Blue Lagoon, St. Vincent, the next day.

We were glad we did not have to try it with *Chyka*. The weather was not good. Even riding over on the ferry was a rough ride. We stayed again at the Lagoon Marina Hotel. Patricia departed the next morning.

From my journal:

> *It has been 24 wonderful days with Patricia. Sometimes she was seasick. Still, she was always such a good sport about it, never complaining, cooking delicious meals on board, helping wherever she could, so much fun, charming, interested in everything, gentle, and loving. She is the perfect woman for me.*

450 Miles North to the Virgin Islands

In sailing directly there I bypassed so many of the wonderful Windward and Leeward Islands. But I had cruised them thoroughly twice before and wanted to get back to Florida and Patricia.

After four days of mostly pleasant sailing with winds E 15-25, a nice broad reach, I arrived. I had made a reservation for a slip at American Yacht Harbor in Red Hook on the east end of St. Thomas. But I had sailed too fast and was there a day too early.

Just across from Red Hook is Caneel Bay on St. John Island. There I moored *Chyka* for the night until my slip would be available for me the next afternoon.

Then, American Yacht Harbor radioed my slip was ready for me. I was glad to find there my friends from the Canary Islands, Sylvia and Lawrie on *Saltire*.

The Last Home Leave

While staying with Patricia, we discussed our many plans, our families, and the wedding. All her life Patricia had hoped to someday go to Egypt. When *Chyka* was in that area the weather was way too hot. We arranged a tour for us in Egypt and Jordan in the coming December and January when the weather there would be pleasant.

I had a very early flight from Tampa to return to St. Thomas. So we stayed the night before at La Quinta near Tampa Airport. This was to be our last long separation as I brought *Chyka* 1,300 miles from the Virgin Islands to Florida.

From St. Thomas Sylvia had gone back home. Lawrie's friend Jerry had joined *Saltire*. They wanted to sail along with *Chyka*. And so it happened that our two boats, later joined by two others, as you will read, cruised all the way back to the Bahamas and on to Florida.

Puerto Rico

First was Culebra, a small island east of Puerto Rico. Culebra is a favorite of mine.

Along the south coast of Puerto Rico we stopped at Isla Pineros, Puerto Patillas, Salinas, Guanica, and Boqueron on the southwest coast.

Except for in its capitol, San Juan, there is little English spoken in Puerto Rico, as well as in the Dominican Republic. Fortunately, I had again worked to revive the Spanglish I had learned during my earlier years in the Caribbean.

Between Puerto Rico and the Dominican Republic is the 75 mile wide Mona Passage. It is always difficult due to the equatorial current moving suddenly from the deepest part of the Atlantic Ocean to the shallow depth of the Mona Passage. The results are strong currents and sea turbulence.

Obviously, you want to do this in the most favorable sailing conditions. We waited two days for thunderstorms to get out of the way, then we went. During the overnight passage we had lots of rain but no real trouble.

Dominican Republic

We anchored off Samana, from where Columbus returned to Spain at the end of his first voyage to the Caribbean. The next day we brought Jerry and his luggage to shore. He took a bus to Santo Domingo to fly home.

Lawrie and I talked about it being so hot. He told me he had no fans on *Saltire. Terrible! A sailboat in the Caribbean! Chyka* had four fans mounted high up on the walls, one in the forward cabin, two in the main, and one in the aft cabin. All of them were on one circuit of the control panel. They take very little electricity and make a world of difference. Even the rare mosquitoes are driven away by them. I always had two spare fans on board. I brought one over to *Saltire* and helped Lawrie install it. (Air conditioners take way too much electricity, unless the boat is at a marina with shore power.)

We were ready to go on, but Patricia told me to wait two more days, as there was another cold front just arriving. Of course, we waited.

We sailed along the north coast of the Dominican Republic anchoring each night at Escondito, Rio San Juan, Sosua, and to Ocean World Marina, which was a new modern resort and marina, a welcome addition to the places to stop between the Bahamas and Puerto Rico. Before Ocean World, we cruisers sailing along this coast had only the pleasant anchorage of Luperon town to rest and shop in town for groceries, but there were no marine facilities at all.

We stayed nine days preparing and waiting for good weather to cross over to the Turks and Caicos Islands on the way to the Bahamas.

One day I was at a marina computer. Next to me was a man who had just sailed here from South Africa. He told me he and his wife would sail the next day to the nearest of the Turks and Caicos Islands. He was new to these waters.

I advised him to not sail anywhere the next day due to weather, and that his intended destination was easy to get to but difficult to make safe passage from it onward.

He was John Morley, and his wife was Diana. We became friends. They decided to join me and Lawrie sailing north. We all took the aerial tramway to the mountain top, Pico Isabel de Torres, overlooking the city of Puerto Plata. There we walked through the botanical garden and around the ancient crater. John and Diana made dinner for us on their catamaran, *Dream*.

The next day was Lawrie's birthday. We all celebrated it with a dinner on *Chyka*. Chef Extraordinaire Henri, produced his World Famous Cream of Mushroom Crab Meat Pasta. Diana remarked that it was good, but that it tasted a little sweet. *Damn*! I realized I had loaded the salt shakers with sugar. I demoted myself to Chef - Not so - Extraordinaire.

We decided to leave on Thursday May 15, 2008 and sail overnight to French Cay in the Turks and Caicos Islands. We departed in no wind and had to motor three hours until we caught a pleasant close reach wind NE-15.

The Bahamas Again

From French Cay another overnight sail brought us to Mayaguana, the most remote of the Bahamas Out Islands.

Why did the other boats sail so fast? They arrived way too soon at the entrance and had to wait for me. I had told them we must not enter the bay until 1:00 PM to catch a rising tide. (If you do go aground, it is good to have the water depth increasing, not decreasing.)

I led them into the bay, through six miles of dodging coral heads, and to the anchorage off the town. There we anchored in seven feet of crystal clear water over bright green coral sand. We swam and had snacks and drinks on *Dream*.

The next morning we dinghied into town. It was a sad, dusty, half-deserted place. To clear in, the supervisor said we needed to pay $300 per boat! No credit cards. Cash only. *What the hell? Ridiculous!* He apologized and said it would be OK for us to clear in later when we arrived in Georgetown.

From my journal:

> *I think it is worse in this miserable town than when I was here the times before. No one does anything. All food is brought in mostly by boat, even eggs and vegetables. Why are there no chickens, no gardens? There is one miserable windowless shop with only canned goods, frozen bread, and refrigerated eggs. Lawrie bought some of them and later found they were rotten.*

But the swimming around our boats was wonderful. In the morning I dove down and found a sand dollar. Back on *Chyka* I called Patricia about a few things. She was so happy about the sand dollar and wondered if I could perhaps find more.

Back down I went. And not only did I find more of them, but also a sea biscuit, a much larger cousin of the sand dollar. They are all now on display in our living room, along with my other treasures of the journey.

We all raised our anchors at the same time to go on to Rum Cay 120 miles away and so an overnight sail. On the six mile way out of the bay, the others thought they now knew how to read the waters and went ahead of me. I saw *Saltire* go way off to the north. I radioed Lawrie that he was getting into big trouble. *Saltire* and *Dream* then came quickly back to follow *Chyka* the rest of the way out. From then on Patricia called them my 'ducklings'.

Rum Cay Again - End of the Circumnavigation - May 21, 2008

The Canadians and I had sailed south from here to Great Inagua on the way to Panama. I was now returning here from the southeast completing the six year circumnavigation.

We all docked at the marina and had drinks at the bar with Bobby Little, the manager. He had a new wife. With all he does, running the place and making huge improvements, he still had time to make intricate limestone sculptures which were displayed on the lawn.

We walked to town and Kaye's Bar. It was so good to again see Delores Wilson. She had written a book about her memories over her lifetime on Rum Cay. I went to Kaye's Last Chance Market. I bought supplies and a copy of Delores's book. Everyone came to *Chyka* for beers and nuts followed by grouper dinners at the marina.

Hurricane Irene of 2011 ruined much of the town including Kaye's Bar. It damaged the marina closing off its entrance with sand. In 2013, I wrote to Delores asking her to send me more copies of her book. After I sent her a check to pay for the books, she wrote me a sweet letter mentioning that the town was rebuilt including Kaye's Bar.

Finally - A Few More Stories

An easy light wind motorsail brought us to Conception Island and my usual well protected inlet on its west side. It was so pleasant there; the others did not want to leave.

I was now getting National Weather Service forecasts on VHF. They predicted that a cold front with high winds would arrive in two days. I told the others I wanted to leave at 4:00 AM to get to Georgetown before the trouble would arrive. They joined me.

We were lucky to have a fast close reach sail. By noon we entered the southeast entrance to Georgetown Harbor and anchored off the town.

We had lunch at Sam's Club and later drinks at The Peace and Plenty. The Two Turtles, a favorite of mine, was closed for repairs. I was sorry to learn that Jean had sold the Dog House, which had been her food truck serving mostly hot dogs. She had health problems and was now in Nassau.

John and Di had planned a BBQ on board *Dream*, but the cold front was already brewing with heavy rain, so the BBQ was canceled.

At 2:00 AM it hit hard blowing NE 25-30. John and Di slept and did not realize that their *Dream* was dragging anchor. At 5:45 AM they were being slammed by the wind and waves against a dock. They called us for help. Lawrie and I took our dinghies to town and scrambled over to help them get away from the dock. We stayed on *Dream* to move her about a mile across to the other side of the harbor. There in the protection of Stocking Island we anchored *Dream*. Later, Lawrie and I also moved our boats over there.

At a breakfast in town we met a most interesting Englishman, Red, a career military man. We later met his wife, Liz, and their son, Freddy. Their sailboat was *Shiver*. In the evening we discussed the John Masters' books about early India, both world wars, Napoleon, and more. Red and Liz decided they would like to join our three boats going north.

Shiver was a larger boat. Her keel drew a deep 6 ½ feet. I led the group going out the north entrance of Georgetown Harbor. I was glued to the charts and knew from the tides how we should do it. I read out to the others the depths that I was seeing. *Shiver* just made it.

North to Florida

Our four boats moved north 11 days through the Bahamas to Florida. I learned Red was solidly competent. Lawrie and John were still getting confused by their electronic charts, which too often had been dangerously wrong. My paper charts were usually accurate, and being many times larger than a screen, much easier to read giving a better overall view of a situation. Plus, I could make calculations and notes on them. And on them I plotted Chyka's positions with the times they were determined.

The cruisers I had known who used electronic charts all said they had paper charts in case. But I always wondered if they really completely did. I was usually sure to have all the charts covering my intended areas and had continuously organized them to be ready for use as needed. (I am thinking of the German, Dieter, who arrived in Fiji with no detailed charts of the area.)

John, Di, and I enjoyed snorkeling in Thunderball Grotto of Staniel Cay. It was a location for the James Bond movie *Thunderball*. It reminded me of the caves in Tonga.

My friends especially enjoyed our stop at Exuma Cays Land and Sea Park. I had usually stopped here when cruising through the Exuma Islands. The only building on the island was Park Headquarters. They maintain the island in pristine condition. There are hiking trails going up hills with spectacular views of the seashore and the terrain.

In Fort Pierce, Florida, we all wished each other "Fair Winds and Following Seas."

Now, Patricia and Henry

After visiting Patricia for two weeks on Treasure Island, I sailed *Chyka* north on the Intracoastal Waterway to Annapolis. Patricia joined me there where her daughter, Jennifer, lived. From there Patricia and I sailed *Chyka* up to New York, New England, and out to Nantucket, visiting relatives and friends along the way.

After the winter together on Treasure Island, we sailed *Chyka* from Connecticut back south. In Beaufort NC we docked in front of Sinbad's pirate ship *Meka II*.

Sinbad

I had met up with Sinbad and his mate, Terry, over the years in many places along the East Coast and in the Bahamas. Forty years before, Sinbad built his *Meka II*, a 54 foot 2/3 scale replica of a 17th century pirate brigantine. Beaufort is her home port.

From here Sinbad on *Meka II* with other pirate ships invade boat shows and towns along the East Coast to "pillage and plunder", which they are still doing.

In 2006 the Governor of North Carolina gave Captain Sinbad a Privateer's Commission (long ago, a license granted to a private ship to attack and capture enemy vessels, combining patriotism and profit).

We four socialized on each others' boats and ashore. Patricia and I loved *Meka II*. Its cozy intricate interior was a nautical museum.

Patricia and I were soon to fly back to Treasure Island to be married.

Sinbad found a perfect, nearby hurricane hole for us to hide *Chyka*, in case a tropical storm might arrive during our absence.

Terry drove us to the airport.

Our Wedding

The wedding was on August 8, 2009. Nearly all of our families had flown in well ahead of time for an active fun week. Many of our friends came. The ceremony and dinner party were on a river boat we had hired. Professional musician son-in-law, Willy Porter, played his guitar for the ceremony. After dinner, toasts, and some talks, Willy joined the band. It was so much fun with everyone including our little and older grandchildren dancing to their lively music.

Our Wedding

We flew back to *Chyka* and spent more time with Sinbad and Terry. She took us shopping.

Captain Sinbad's Code: *To rule the waves, you wave the rules.*

For three weeks we sailed south, mostly motorsailing, along the Intracoastal Waterway. One night at anchor after dinner, Patricia was reading my cruising guide of Florida. She said, "Henry, we don't have to sail all the way around Florida. We can sail across it on the Okeechobee Waterway."

"No Patricia, I know all about it. There is a railroad bridge across the waterway that is four feet lower than *Chyka's* mast. We can't go under it."

"But Henry, they can barrel us under it."

"Patricia, what does that mean?"

She said, "I don't know, but they can do it."

And they did. We motored up to the railroad bridge. A small boat came alongside with seven empty 50 gallon drums. They attached them to our port side. Into them they pumped seawater until *Chyka* heeled over enough so that the mast could clear under the bridge.

We cruised across Lake Okeechobee, further on the waterway to Fort Meyers, north to Sarasota to visit my daughter, Susan, and family, then on to our home on Treasure Island.

Chyka at Home

For three years we could see *Chyka* docked at her slip from our balcony. Patricia and I took wonderful cruises on *Chyka* along the West Coast of Florida. We sailed short trips with our children, grandchildren, and friends. As time went on, we were not sailing *Chyka* enough. Sailboats take money and time to maintain whether they are sailed or not. Other priorities became more important. I sold *Chyka* in 2012. I think of her often and will always miss her.

Reflections

From the start, I had known there would be difficult situations. Well, this adventure was more challenging than I had anticipated. Probably most serious adventures are like that.

But in my memories of those years, the troubles I had fade in comparison to those wonderful sailing days; the exciting feel of the vast oceans; the beauty of soaring birds, sunsets, stars, whales, quiet island anchorages, and colorful reef fish; mountains soaring nearly straight up out of the sea; getting to know so many interesting, kind local people along the way; places of history; my exchange student daughters; and the joy of good times and adventures I had with my many friends, and with Patricia.

This chapter in my life closed as the next one opened. In our wedding invitation Patricia and I included, "We begin the adventure of a lifetime."

THE END

Murphy's Laws

Every cruising blue water sailor knows things will go wrong.

If well prepared, a sailor should be able to relax most of the time. Avoiding constant worries about whatever might happen requires an appreciation of Murphy's Laws.

Then in serenity one waits patiently for something to go wrong. Most of the time nothing does. You then wonder why not and snoop around a little to try to find it. Sometimes you do.

"Aha! There you are!" you exclaim with satisfaction, knowing that because of Murphy you can fix it now while you have time to do so before it becomes a serious problem. And if you find nothing, it is easy to accept.

Murphy's Law #3 prepares you for worst case scenarios. You cannot say that such and such is unlikely to happen and leave it at that. If you do, eventually Murphy will pounce on you and punish you for your audacity.

It seems to me Murphy must have been a sailor. Well, perhaps not. His laws also apply to you landlubbers as well. So, for the benefit of you all, I remind you of Murphy's helpful laws:

Number One – Everything will be more difficult than you think.

Number Two – Everything will take longer than you plan.

Number Three – If something can go wrong, it will go wrong, and at the worst possible time.

Number Four (This one is of dubious authenticity.) – The other line always moves faster.

Preparing for Offshore and Blue Water

Both my editor and my author account manager at FriesenPress suggested I write this additional section about, what they called, 'practical tips and suggestions'. It will be of interest particularly to people considering buying a sailboat and those wanting to improve their ability to cruise safely and comfortably.

This is a summary of the bits and pieces of knowledge and opinions I acquired during my ten years of cruising as well as the years of my sailing history before. It covers only what I think you will not find in the usual books you will need anyway, such as *Chapman Piloting and Seamanship*, *The Annapolis Book of Seamanship* by John Rousmaniere, *The Boatowner's Mechanical and Electrical Manual* by Nigel Calder, the *Onboard Medical Handbook,* magazine articles, as well as what I have already written in this book.

I hope none of you will be intimidated by the long descriptions of all you will need to have and to do. Think of it as taking a new job in another state and there buying a house for you and your family. I did not know a lot of what I recommend here when I started. There are many successful ocean cruisers who do not know about all of this. And many of them will not agree with all I write. Ask questions, read, learn as you go, and decide for yourself.

Selecting and Equipping Your Boat

There are advantages to buying new boats, and also to buying used boats, as long as the used ones are found to be in good condition by a marine surveyor.

When I bought my new Island Packet I was glad to know there was no wear and tear. But there was so much more that needed to be added. After doing research on each item, I chose what I wanted of electronics, radios, a bimini, a dodger, anchoring equipment, a self-steering system, etc. And I had the opportunity to decide where all the instrument displays would be placed in the cockpit and at the nav station.

Of course, a used boat will already have much of what you want and need to have. But in time you will want to improve and add better equipment.

Confusing the selection process of new equipment, there always seemed to be two or more schools of thought by the experts as to what is the best a cruising sailor should go with. And there was never any doubt in any of their minds that they were absolutely right and the others dead wrong. Here is an example:

I had to choose which mainsail reefing system I wanted on my new Island Packet 350, the standard slab reefing or the newer type, in-mast roller furling. I read all I could about the subject, discussed it with experienced sailors, and at boat shows talked to the authors of sailing books I had read. Just about half of the experts were for one option and the others were convinced the other choice was much better. And again, as I have written, after considering all inputs I had to decide on my own. The result was good. During the years of owning my boat, I was so glad I had chosen in-mast roller furling. With it, all control lines lead aft to the cockpit, a great advantage for a single-hander, especially in heavy weather.

I strongly recommend buying a boat with geared steering, meaning that from the wheel to the rudder the steering motion is transmitted by solid gears, shafts, and levers. I had learned to distrust cable steering, which moves the rudder by way of cables and pulleys. As you have read, cable steering caused serious trouble for a boat I was on in the Atlantic by failing twice.

When buying my boat, I asked the dealer to remove the microwave from the galley. I did not want to pay for it; it could only be used with shore power; I wanted the space it took for other kitchen things; I knew I would cook by frying, baking, grilling, or roasting. And I did not want a toaster, preferring to fry my bread in bacon fat as the English do, or over olive oil.

I was glad to not need a watermaker. They require a lot of electricity and maintenance. My 100 gallons in the water tank and the extra five gallon water containers held way more water than ever needed, since my ocean sailing was mostly solo.

I chose anchors and anchor chain one grade heavier and stronger then recommended for a boat the size of *Chyka*, but still not too heavy for me to haul the chain and anchor up by hand in case the windlass would fail. Only one time, with a soft mud bottom my 45 pound CQR anchor did not hold. I retrieved it and then used my other bow anchor, the 25 pound Danforth, far better in mud. The other times the Danforth was used was when I needed to deploy a second strong anchor for heavy wind or reversing tidal current situations.

You will also need a smaller anchor as a lunch stop stern anchor.

Do not go anywhere in your dinghy without its little anchor and the attached rope rode. You will find that the required weight and space for both of them are almost nothing. They can prevent serious danger if your outboard fails with an offshore current, possibly being too strong for you to paddle or row against.

While recommending oversize anchors and chain, I do the opposite as to dinghies and outboard engines. Large dinghies with big outboards may impress others as you zip around in the harbor proudly standing up holding onto a rope to the bow of the dinghy for balance. My little eight foot dinghy could haul four of us to town and back with our groceries. It was light and easily hauled up on deck.

My 3½ HP outboard, Li'l Rudy, gave *Li'l Chyka* all the speed I wanted. It weighed only 25 pounds. So from the swim platform I could easily lift it up with one hand to its mount on the stern rail.

In this book I already wrote a lot about the life raft.

At the time I bought the boat, someone suggested I install a third halyard. The first one is to haul up the mainsail. The second hoists the genoa. The third one, called the spare, is rigged forward of the mast and then can serve to lift things out of the water such as the dinghy when you want to store it on deck. And it also provides safety by clipping it onto whomever is going up the mast. (The slack is then repeatedly taken up by someone at a winch in the cockpit or the person himself going aloft.)

In the beginning, while *Chyka* was in winter storage in Milwaukee and her mast was laid out on horses, I installed mast steps. At home I had built out of boards a mock of the spreader area of the mast so as to determine where to place the steps and be able to easily climb past the spreader and on to the top.

Some young monkey sailors scramble up a bare mast with only a halyard. I was old and could not do that. I placed the steps closer together than recommended. In the following years the mast steps helped very much. I did not have to use them often, but when I did, they provided an easy and safe way of going aloft.

Soon after buying the boat I replaced the standard propeller with a three blade Max-prop. They feather to zero angle when sailing and so almost eliminate prop drag. (To reduce drag by allowing a standard prop to spin when under sail with the transmission in neutral is not good for long distance ocean sailors: There will be too much wear on the prop shaft bearings and parts of the transmission.) With the engine in reverse, the blades switch angle sides and provide the same amount of propulsion as in forward. And the angle of the blades can be adjusted to the weight of your boat, which over time will increase as your range of sailing increases and you pack into the boat ever more fuel and water containers, clothing, bedding, food supplies, spare parts, equipment, books, charts, on and on.

You will need to rig another very small halyard from the spreader to fly courtesy flags of the host countries you are visiting.

I seem to have been one of only a few who knew about flower pot heaters. You are not always in the tropics. When the cabin gets cold, you put a clay flower pot upside down over a low flame on a burner of your propane stove and place the fan on the mount you have prepared for this just to one side of the stove. It blows the warm air from the pot into the cabin. It's marvelous. The cabin gets as warm as you want. Leave a hatch partly open to provide oxygen. And remember to turn the stove off before going to bed.

You will read about dock and shore lines. Buy them five feet longer than recommended. You will be glad you did. You will need a 300 foot shore line. But don't buy one. You won't need it often. When you do, just tie two 150 footers together or three one hundreds.

Clear Plastic Storage Boxes

Returning to your boat from shopping, you need to immediately check the food you bought in cardboard boxes for crawling things. If OK, it then must be immediately put into your small, closed, plastic food containers, or you could acquire the crawling things anyway.

My plastic storage containers were from small to two feet long. They are essential. Rain or seawater will eventually find its way to the bottom of most storage areas and will corrode or damage whatever is there, cans of food, clothing, bedding, office supplies, files, tools, spare parts, special equipment, and so on.

When *Chyka* was at a marina in Ft. Lauderdale, a sailboat at the next slip had just returned from the Caribbean. The owner was clearing out his boat to be trucked north somewhere. He was giving away all he could, but most people did not want any of it. He had stored so much in his bilges with no protection. It was mostly a vast watery rotten pile of debris and rusty cans.

Chyka was already then equipped to prevent that. When I was first outfitting *Chyka,* I made many trips to buy plastic storage boxes of various sizes until they filled up almost all of my innumerable lockers, bins, closets, storage areas behind and under the settees, my huge refrigerator, even most of the two lazarettes. The containers all come with separate lids, which I usually did not use.

Maintenance

Diligent maintenance is essential. You will put on book shelves and in files, instructions from the manufacturers of your main engine, the outboard, autopilot, windlass, winches, rigging, radios, electronics, GPS units, safety equipment, the propane stove, etc.

A prime part of maintenance is checking the boat over each time before departure. This will include engine oil level, transmission fluid, and coolant. I was especially careful about the daily engine oil levels and recorded how much oil I added and when. This would have told me if I ever had a developing oil leak, which I never did. Remember, without enough oil your engine will fail, and it will not be at a convenient marina.

For everything on board requiring regular maintenance, I scheduled them for inspection or adjustment by date and engine hours as well as when each one was accomplished. That way they all got done, and the resulting proof of careful maintenance was an asset when eventually selling *Chyka*.

Like probably all fuel gages, mine was not at all accurate. Sometimes I opened the fuel tank and measured the fuel level to see how it compared with the gage. I recorded how much fuel I took on, when it was I did, the distance traveled since the last fill, and the gage levels before and after. With all this, I developed a graph to convert gage levels to actual fuel levels. Being sure of the correct fuel levels helped determine how much diesel I should take on when refueling. At those times I wanted to take on an almost full load but not risk having excess fuel dump out the tank vent overboard, which makes a dirty mess on the water for all the boats in the area. And by doing this, I learned how many miles per gallon I was getting under power with various wind conditions.

At the beginning I consulted and learned from diesel engine mechanics. After a short time I only needed them for special infrequent problems. Of course, the manual you get with the diesel engine is essential. Also useful is *Troubleshooting Marine Diesel Engines* by Peter Compton.

Before buying *Chyka* I attended a day long seminar on diesel engines and a night course on outboard engine repair. Each week we practiced at home disassembling and repairing small, old outboards all of us had borrowed from friends or somewhere. In marinas you can find various levels of mechanical help. In remote coastal and island locations you will not find any mechanics.

In my three ring maintenance notebook I had a section of notes of all I was learning about the many lubricants, glues, and sealants often used on a sailboat and for what I was using them.

I maintained a huge supply of paper towel rolls, so much better than messing with rags. Paper towels are essential when checking the engine oil level, changing oil and fuel filters, and cleaning leaked oil and fuel from under the engine. They help when removing spots on deck and below, when painting, varnishing, lubricating, washing windows, and cleaning up blood after an injury, even the wound itself; they are not perfectly sterile, but it will be followed by washing with water, iodine or an antibiotic ointment, and a bandage.

As at home you will want a roll always in the galley. The Select-A-Size type is the best. And they make practical napkins when folded over once.

Electricity

When away from shore power, it is so often a problem how to produce enough electricity to supply all the electrical systems, lights, autopilot, instruments, etc., and keep the batteries charged.

I did not want a wind generator. Often at anchor there is no wind. When there is some, they don't produce many amps and so they have to run often and long, and they make an annoying buzzing noise. Instead, I installed a trolling generator for when I was under sail, and a large Siemens solar panel. They work well whether you are sailing or at anchor.

In case of being underway and your batteries fail or a lightning strike knocks out your circuits, you should have battery powered navigation lights which can be attached to rails or hoisted up to position. In such a situation a miner's headlamp would be useful, as it often is anyway when working in dark corners of the boat. And as always, you must have various sizes of flashlights. Just avoid buying the common fully round ones that, when at sea, roll easily off work areas and deep into the bilge of where you are or off the deck to join Davy Jones.

Your boat's electrical systems are DC. Shore power brought aboard to the boat's battery charger and to the standard outlets is AC. There will be times when away from shore power, you will need to convert from DC to AC for your electric hand tools. So you should have an inverter. Your shore power cord should be lots longer than what is required to get to most shore outlets because many will be further away. My power cord was 50 feet long. And by the time you get to Australia it will be time to get a serious transformer 230 volts AC to 110 AC for input to the boat.

There often is need to rewire a circuit, improve one, or add another for new lamps, fans, instruments, loudspeakers, a solar panel, etc. Therefore there must be a supply of wire of basic sizes as well as a box of different sizes of connectors.

There are a number of DC electrical systems on boats. Be sure that with yours you can start the engine with the house batteries, in case the engine start battery fails; and that you can get a few critical lights to work with the engine start battery, in case the house batteries fail.

Tools

I had two tool boxes. Just one would have been too heavy to carry around the boat. The first one was for the standard simple hardware tools. Tool kit number two was for special purpose tools. A third was a complete socket wrench kit for inch and metric sizes.

In bins I stored the larger heavier tools such as a vice, which when I used it, I clamped onto the companionway ladder; wood clamps, an electric drill, and my Loos rigging tension gages.

Do not go off to repair anything with only the tools you think you will need, especially up on deck, which is a climb and a walk, or into the under deck and floor areas. Nine out of ten times you will have to go back and get another tool. Always take along tool kit number one. It's not that heavy.

Sometimes you will want a piece of wood of a certain size. In time I built up a small lumber supply. I had on board several sizes of saws.

You will need an oil filter wrench, and another wrench to back off the drive shaft packing nut. You will seldom have to use snap ring pliers, but when you do, they are almost indispensable. And I had a special wrench to remove the bolts of the engine water pump cover to replace the rubber impellor to it when it was due for replacement.

I had a huge plastic tray with a hinged cover and small compartments where over time I built up a ton of various sized inch and metric nuts, bolts, screws, washers, lock washers, and lock nuts.

Spare Parts

You will need extra fuses for all the electric circuits on board, of which there are many. And you will be surprised at how many different sizes of lamp bulbs you have, for which you must have spares. Before installing a new bulb, lubricate its base with WD-40, also a good idea at home, but especially important when at sea with its corrosive salt air.

You should have on board a *West Marine Catalog*. It will help you research options for new equipment and parts. West Marine will send you what you need anywhere in the world that has an address.

When it is time to service the engine, you will probably be in some remote anchorage or small town. The spares you will need are quite special. So I had on board, probably averaging five or six each of engine oil filters, primary fuel filters such as Racor, engine secondary fuel filters, several engine belts, a spare diesel injector, which I never used, etc. Each time I used a spare I added another to my shopping list for the next time I was in civilization. And don't forget to maintain a generous supply of the correct engine oil, transmission fluid, and coolant.

I had a spare water pump, several water filters, and spares of many critical parts for servicing complex mechanisms like that of the autopilots. And don't neglect your outboard motor. You need spares for it also.

Charts

At one time I tried using electronic charts. I have already written in this book why I consider paper charts to be better. I have completely lost track of how many I used. Bluewater Books and Charts, Fort Lauderdale

FL, cannot tell me how many I bought from them over the years. And I don't know how many I gave away as I went along. Plus I bought many charts also from British sources. The chartbooks you will use along the coasts of the USA and the Bahamas are conveniently put together and economical. You will need to have the NOAA chart catalogs of the world. They are free and you can order out of them charts you select.

I usually kept options open as to where I would sail, as most of us did. You must be free to change your destinations as you go. Bluewater was always sending me more charts along the way for the plans I was then hatching.

When buying charts, consider Xerox copies. They are less than half the price. I used them often. But be careful. They are only in black and white, lacking the highlights that tell you what the lines are separating. I reviewed them as I received them and often added shading of my own to show what the lines meant.

I folded and kept my charts in stacks of one or two inches packed in large plastic envelopes. On top of each pile, and showing through its plastic cover, was a listing of the chart numbers, of course arranged numerically, and the areas they covered.

When using my charts, I laid them out on the dining table; my nav station desk was usually too small for the chart I needed.

There are covers you can buy to protect a chart in the cockpit especially to be used when sailing close to a coast or entering a harbor. Wind, rain, and spray will still get into them. And having your chart suddenly blow overboard could really spoil your day. I kept the chart I was using below, and made notes on a card to take to the helm as to what to watch for and do.

Medicine Cabinet

My first aid kit was huge and ready for almost anything. In addition, I had on board the following:

Imodium for diarrhea

Cipro, an excellent antibiotic; your doctor will give you a prescription for it or another antibiotic.

Alprazolam (Xanax) to treat anxiety and panic

Bonine for seasickness

No Doz

Sudafed, a decongestant, but also good to help stay awake.

Of course, aspirin or another for pain.

Your doctor will recommend shots against diseases such as malaria and yellow fever depending on the countries you will be visiting.

Food on *Chyka*

I used my enormous refrigerator mostly for storage and extra gallon plastic bottles of water. I only turned it on when at a marina with a shore electric cord connection to the boat. So fresh food was usually exposed to warm, humid tropical air.

Most of *Chyka's* time was spent within a few days of some place where I could buy groceries. About every island with any people at all had at least some kind of little store. I liked cucumbers, tomatoes, carrots, and apples. They all last a week or more. With tomatoes I was careful to buy only the smaller, slightly yellow ones.

I didn't bother with lettuce, which does not last at all, or potatoes. They both are nutritionally of no value.

Hard cheese, and packaged meats such as hot dogs, turkey dogs, turkey and ham slices, salami, bologna, and summer sausage all last a very long time; I don't know how long, because none of them ever had enough time to go bad on me. You test eggs by putting them into a glass of water. If they float, they are bad.

Olive oil is a wonder for cooking at sea, or really anywhere. I used it in salad dressing, pasta, and fried with it unless I was frying bacon. Olive oil will last two years or more. I always used it up way before then. It is always better for sailors than butter, which takes way too much water and detergent to clean off plates, pans, containers, and silverware. And olive oil doesn't burn to the frying pan.

Perhaps you already know – after cooking, your cast iron frying pan should be lightly cleaned with detergent, wiped dry with a paper towel, allowed to completely dry over a high heat followed immediately by a light coat of olive oil while the pan is still hot.

Restaurants have caught onto olive oil. See what they now serve with bread before dinner.

Fresh bread lasts barely one day. But a stale baguette can be brought back to life by frying in olive oil. Otherwise, buy bread with lots of those preservatives you do not approve of, and it will last at least ten days.

English muffins last three weeks. I stored bread products, fruits, and vegetables in a deep-sea fish net suspended over the dining table. (It was the net that fouled my propeller off Montserrat.) In that net, circulating fresh air kept them all dry.

When on the longest passages all that was gone, there was my huge supply of canned goods, hard cheeses, crackers, peanut butter and jelly, all of which last forever. With jelly in jars opened for two weeks or more, you have to scrape off the mold at the top and it's good for another two weeks. Mold on hard cheese you simply trim away.

Now, canned goods. Chef Boyardee and Dinty Moore make great stews, ravioli, spaghetti with meatballs, and lasagna. When conditions are keeping a single-hander too busy to have time to cook, he can eat them cold right out of the can.

Other canned goods included clams, clam chowder, cream of mushroom soup, cream of everything else soups, sardines, salmon, shrimp, tuna, ham, spam, beans, mixed vegetables, and mixed fruits. I kept a good supply of nuts of all kinds and candy bars for snacks.

I cooked a lot of pasta as you have read. A little dried elbow macaroni makes a lot of good food when cooked. I added olive oil, concentrated cream of mushroom soup or one of the others, then a combination of canned shrimp, maybe a chopped up hot dog, fresh tomato pieces, olives, leftovers, and finally lots of ground Parmesan cheese. It will certainly be in my book, *The Cruising Mechanical Engineer's Cookbook*.

How many books have I told you I will write? I don't know. I neglected to keep a list of them. Anyway, Patricia and I agree, I need to take a break.

Henry Holt

Nautical Terms and Some of my Own

Accidental jibe	When sailing downwind, the wind gets in front of the main flipping the boom suddenly from one side to the other.
African Queen	An old broken-down mess of a boat
Anchor light	A bright white light at the top of the mast. It warns other boats moving in the area at night that you are there.
Barometer	It measures air pressure. High pressure is an indication of improving weather; low pressure the opposite.
Beam Reach	The wind coming from a right angle to the boat's motion
Big Rudy	My inboard diesel engine named after Prof. Rudolf Diesel
Bimini	A cover, usually canvas, rigged on a frame over the helm
Blue water	Blue water cruising is out of sight of land.
Bottom paint	Special antifouling paint to discourage the growth of sea organisms

Broach	The wind overpowers the boat. The rudder cannot keep the boat on course. Then a wave pushes the stern broadside to wind and waves, and the boat stops.
Broad reach	Sailing with the wind coming from somewhere between one side and behind.
Chyka	The name of my boat. It is the Russian word for seagull (pronounced CHIGH *sounds like eye* - ka).
Clear in	To get permission from officials to enter a country
Clear out	To get permission from officials to leave a country
Close reach	Sailing directly into the wind is impossible. Here, the boat sails upwind as close to the wind as it can with sails trimmed in tightly.
Dinghy	A small boat used when at anchor to get to shore or to other boats. On sailboats they are usually inflatable to be deflated and easily stored on deck.
Dodger	A canvas hood with plastic windows supported by a tube frame and located forward of the cockpit
Draw	Drawing five feet, the bottom of a boat's keel is five feet below the surface.
EPIRB	Emergency Position Indicating Radio Beacon
Fenders	Air-filled heavy duty plastic containers hung vertically over the side to keep the boat off a dock or another boat.
Fender board	Mine was a 2x6 five foot long weather treated board. When docked up against a post, I suspended it horizontally over the side against the post and with two normal fenders suspended between the board and the boat.
Genoa	A large jib, often larger than the mainsail
Haul out	To take the boat out of the water and place it on stands

Heave-to	To park the boat at sea facing upwind to rest or sleep
Jacklines	Strong cloth straps rigged along the side decks. When going forward at night or in rough weather, a person can clip onto one of them to prevent getting dumped into the sea.
Jerry can	Fuel or water container usually holding five gallons
Jib	The most forward sail on the boat.
Jibe	To alter course so that the sails switch over to the other side when going downwind
Lateen rigged	Having a triangular sail set on a long yard mounted in the middle of the mast and at an angle to it.
Latitude	Where a position is north or south of the equator
Lazarette	A large storage area under a cockpit seat.
Lee side	Where land or another vessel shields you from the wind
Li'l Chyka	*Chyka's* dinghy
Li'l Rudy	*Li'l Chyka's* outboard motor.
Line	A length of rope having a specific purpose
Longitude	Position east or west of the zero prime meridian at Greenwich, England.
Med moor	Anchor off the bow with stern lines to the dock - common in the Mediterranean
Motorsailing	Sailing with the aid of the motor
Motu	A barrier reef island with vegetation, usually trees
Nav station	The navigation station has a desk, and above it are panels of switches and meters to control electrical circuits, instruments, the main GPS, and radios.
Offshore	Distant from land but in sight of it

Port side	Facing forward, port is to the left.
Port tack	The wind coming from the port side
Preventer	A line to the boom to prevent it from slamming to the other side in case of an accidental jibe
Prenavigation	Plotting the route on charts and entering its waypoints in the GPS
Radar reflector	A round assembly of aluminum plates about one foot in diameter to be hoisted up before sailing into areas with commercial traffic to show the other vessels you are there.
Reefing	Reducing a sail's area. A single reef reduces the sail area 25%, a second reef by 50%.
Rolling	When waves come broadside and tip the boat from side to side.
Sheet	Sheets are lines from both sides to a sail or its boom to control the sail's angle to the wind
Sloop	A one-masted sailboat with a fore-and-aft mainsail and a jib.
Snubber line	A strong nylon line attached part way along the anchor chain, which is then relaxed. Nylon rope stretches and acts as a shock absorber.
Spanglish	Basic primitive Spanish
Spreader	A horizontal spar part way up the mast to deflect the side stays so they can better support the top of the mast
Starboard side	The right side when facing forward
Starboard tack	The wind coming from the starboard side
Staysail	A small sail between the main and the genoa
Tack	When sailing into the wind, the sailboat turns so the direction from where the wind blows changes from one side to the other.

Trolling generator	Mounted on the stern rail, it is powered by a small propeller trailed aft of the boat on a long line.
VHF	A very high frequency radio, used to communicate to shore and with other vessels
Waypoint	The latitude and longitude of a location on a route or of a destination
Winch	A small vertical drum around which a rope is wound in order to crank in that rope
Windlass	It pulls in the anchor chain, stores the chain under deck and raises the anchor.
Wide berth	To give something a wide berth is to keep far from it.
Wing and wing	Sailing downwind with the main and the genoa out on opposite sides
Yawl	A sailboat with a second, smaller sail, called a mizzenmast, behind the main and aft of the steering gear.

Lightning Source UK Ltd.
Milton Keynes UK
UKOW02f0910141215

264684UK00002B/365/P